Bt $3.67

TWO TUDOR PORTRAITS

HESTER W. CHAPMAN

★

TWO
TUDOR PORTRAITS

Henry Howard, Earl of Surrey

and

Lady Katherine Grey

WITH ILLUSTRATIONS

LITTLE, BROWN AND COMPANY

Boston   *Toronto*

CONTENTS

ILLUSTRATIONS

FOREWORD

IT has long been an accepted fact that the inhabitants of Tudor England set so low a price on human life that they were ready to gamble away their own or that of anyone they loved for a caprice. To assess or even to hold in the mind the implications of such an attitude is hard; yet without this awareness of the principal difference between our sixteenth-century ancestors and ourselves the most superficial appreciation of their point of view becomes impossible. They did not expect to live long — or peacefully; the majority seem not to have wished to do so. In this respect the careers of Henry Howard Earl of Surrey and Katherine Grey, princess of the blood, followed the pattern of the time.

As relatives of and dependants on the Tudors, Surrey and Katherine found themselves in circumstances that required tact, subservience, cunning and foresight; neither of them possessed these characteristics. In his thirtieth year Surrey was executed by Henry VIII partly because he had never been able to grasp the nature of a modern state. Although his poetry was half a century in advance of his age, his political outlook was two hundred years out of date. Katherine, rising into prominence a generation later, presumed on the tolerance of Queen Elizabeth and escaped the block, but destroyed her own happiness; so she may have precipitated the malady of which she died at the age of twenty-eight. Her arrogance and audacity faintly reflect Surrey's worst traits and might be ascribed to the curious and destructive blend of financial insecurity, semi-royal state and family feuds that helped to create the background of their early years; in all else they were temperamentally dissimilar. Surrey was a soldier and an intellectual — brave, impious, versatile and violent. Katherine was foolish, romantic and respectable; if she had not been the great-niece of Henry VIII she might have achieved contentment and prosperity. Both were the victims of a Tudor. Surrey's story shows him trying to break through their system of dictatorship and so falling upon his fate. Katherine's exemplifies a silliness that would be ludicrous if it were not pitiable.

ACKNOWLEDGMENTS

For leave to reproduce the portraits of the Earl of Surrey and Lady Katherine Grey, the author has pleasure in thanking, respectively, Museu de Arte, São Paulo, and Messrs Christie. For help and advice, special thanks are due to Miss Helen Lehmann, Mlle Jane Bussy and Mr George Rylands.

To
ADRIANNE ALLEN

HENRY HOWARD, EARL OF SURREY
(1517-47)

My tale was heard and yet it was not told,
My fruit is fallen and yet my leaves are green,
My youth is spent and yet I am not old,
I saw the world and yet I was not seen;
My thread is cut and yet it was not spun ...

CHIDIOCK TICHBORNE

HENRY HOWARD, EARL OF SURREY

by Holbein

CHAPTER ONE

THE name of Howard, so long an accompaniment to English history, has been festooned with genealogical legends by seventeenth- and eighteenth-century antiquarians. These writers, not content with the real splendours, tragedies, triumphs and disasters that crowd the records of the Dukes of Norfolk, chose to remove their origins to an apocryphal region where Norman knights, Saxon thanes and Celtic chieftains struggled for predominance in a romantic mist that for many years obscured the figure of the able and hard-working country lawyer who established the family fortunes during the reign of Edward I.

This gentleman was William Howard, Counsel to the Corporation of King's Lynn. In the middle of the thirteenth century he bought the manor and lands of East Wynch, taking possession in 1298. By this time he was Mr Justice Howard and had been summoned to attend Parliament in that capacity; he married twice and prosperously, and was knighted a few years before his death in 1308. For the next four generations his descendants rose steadily in the social scale; in 1385 Sir Robert Howard married the Lady Margaret Mowbray, elder daughter of Thomas Mowbray, Duke of Norfolk and Earl Marshal of England; their children could therefore count Plantagenets, Capets, Bigods, Warrennes, Percys and FitzAlans among their ancestors. In 1454 their eldest son John took the Yorkist side in the Wars of the Roses; twenty-nine years later he was created Duke of Norfolk, Lord High Admiral and Earl Marshal by Richard III, for whom he fought and died on Bosworth Field. His fate was foretold in the rhyme that Shakespeare adapted –

Jack of Norfolk, be not too bold,
For Dickon thy master is bought and sold.

Jack, or the Jockey's, eldest son Thomas, wounded and captured at Bosworth, was attainted by Henry VII; in 1514, as a result of his victory over the Scots at Flodden, Henry VIII removed the attainder and granted him his father's dukedom and honours, adding to them the post of Lord High Treasurer. This nobleman, a high-minded and incorruptible patriot, was the father of Thomas, third Duke of Norfolk (of the second creation) and the grandfather of Henry Howard, Earl of Surrey.

Until the accession and rise to power of the third Duke in 1524, his family history, for centuries interlaced with that of the English kings, shows no stain of treachery, cowardice or time-serving. The glory and power of the Howards sank with the death of Richard III, when the first Tudor monarch confiscated their lands and imprisoned the head of the house; yet none of them had betrayed a trust or failed in his adherence to the state; and for some time after he succeeded to the title, Surrey's father sustained that tradition. With his acquisition of greater fame, more pervasive influence and vaster wealth, the picture changes. During the 1530s and '40s the Duke of Norfolk emerges as a brutal, unscrupulous and brilliant scoundrel: ready to barter dignity, faith and honour for his position: offering himself as the procurer, and then the executioner, of his nieces for Henry VIII: willing, in the last, hideous extremity, to sacrifice his son's life for his own. The gradual degradation of this remarkable man stands out, a black zig-zag, cutting across all the other intrigues and corruptions of his day. He was, finally, successful in his ruthless efforts to retain place and riches; and the ebb and flow of that struggle, lasting more than thirty years, is the background of Surrey's story. The father's attitude set the son's standards and twisted his purposes, as it flouted the moral values of his education. If Norfolk's house had perished with him, its proud motto, *Sola Virtus Invicta*, might well have been exchanged for the 'bought and sold' of the old rhyme. For indeed it was Norfolk, ever substituting one loyalty for another in the political market of the Reformation, who helped to send

Surrey to the block; and so his career, perhaps the most sinister in the records of the age, complements that of his son.

Norfolk was born at Ashwell Thorpe in 1473, and brought up there with his brothers and his half-brother Lord Berners, later the translator of Froissart's *Chronicles*, *Huon of Bordeux* and other French romances.* Nothing is known of his early education but that he learnt to speak and write Spanish, French and Italian fluently. In 1494 he married the Lady Anne Plantagenet, daughter of Edward IV and sister-in-law of Henry VII, to whom he had been betrothed some years before. The match was magnificent but unprofitable, for the bride received no dowry from the King. During the eighteen years of their marriage Lady Anne bore four sons who all died of consumption. When she died in 1512, Norfolk, now in his fortieth year, made an alliance with a great heiress — Elizabeth Stafford, daughter of the Duke of Buckingham beheaded nine years afterwards by Henry VIII. By this time Norfolk had fought, commanded and administered by sea and land in Spain, Scotland, Ireland and France and was high in the favour of Henry, who looked on him as one of the ablest and most reliable men in the state. Of his many enemies and rivals the most powerful was Cardinal Wolsey, whose downfall the Howard faction had been planning for more than a decade.

The need to appear on the best possible terms with Henry's favourite minister throughout the variations of a contest lasting some fifteen years suited Norfolk's temperament (although he once so far forgot himself as to draw his dagger on Wolsey in the Privy Chamber)[1] and helped to develop his instinctive genius for deception. As he reached middle life his physique settled into lines that did not alter with old age and that might have been purposely designed to reassure and please anyone likely to mistrust him. He was small and spare; sallow, clean-shaven, aquiline, his narrow face was thrown into relief by the bands of fine dark hair, just beginning to turn grey, that fell over his ears, a long abandoned fashion that gave him a curious and subtle distinction, as of one belonging to a more elegant

* He was then Lord Thomas Howard, becoming Earl of Surrey on his father's accession as second Duke of Norfolk. For the purposes of clarity he is referred to as the third Duke throughout this narrative.

period; this emphasized the delicacy of his pointed chin, compressed lips and thin, arched eyebrows. The impression he made, judging by the reports of those who met him for the first time, was that of a highly intelligent, kindly man, not easily known, but approachable and unpretentious – one to confide in and quick to grasp another's point of view. Norfolk became famous for the informality of his manners and what would now be described as his democratic way with all classes. His attitude towards his humbler dependants was quite fatherly: his tenants adored him. (He was of course far too astute to fall into the errors of absenteeism or false economy.) He was seldom ruffled and always ready for a joke; his quick decisions and thoroughness over detail were not always appreciated by those who saw him simply as a great nobleman and an accomplished courtier, rather than as an experienced commander; and so the comments of the persons he defeated and punished are rare – partly because few of them survived to make any. In an age of extreme and cold-blooded brutality, Norfolk's mercilessness was celebrated. On one occasion even Henry VIII – not the most sparing of invaders – had to apologize for the Duke's 'foul warfare' in France; and after his first raid on the Border it was jubilantly announced that there was left 'neither house, fortress, village, tree, cattle, corn, nor other succour of man'.[2] That hardly mattered: for none remained to succour. Such practices were the custom of his day; yet again and again his methods are described by his contemporaries as exceptionally, calculatingly cruel.

These judgments did not affect Norfolk's local popularity or his political influence; and the fact that his attack on the Cardinal went unpunished showed the measure of his greatness, for the penalty for striking an equal within the precincts of the palace was very severe. He escaped with a rating from the King and temporary banishment from Court. He and his wife then retired to Hunsdon in Norfolk and there, in the spring of 1517 – the exact date is not known – Henry Howard was born.

In 1520 Wolsey, alarmed by his rival's increasing power, arranged for him to be sent to Ireland as Deputy. Norfolk carried out his duties with success, and surprising leniency, for two years. He was fifty-one when he became third Duke and the most powerful nobleman in the kingdom. By this time he had a second son, Thomas, and a daughter, Mary. Henry, now in his eighth year, was given the courtesy title of Earl of Surrey. The character of this beautiful, intelligent and lively boy had already been formed and his temperament fostered in conditions that, outwardly splendid, privileged and secure, were in fact peculiarly detrimental, tempestuous and uncertain.

NOTES TO CHAPTER ONE

[1] Cavendish, *Life of Cardinal Wolsey*, p. 170.
[2] Froude, *History of England*, vol. I, p. 121.

CHAPTER TWO

UNTIL Surrey was fifteen – by which time, according to the standards of his day, he had reached manhood – he lived in the country; but never quietly or in one place. He was four when his parents came back from the mingled squalor and grandeur of vice-regal life in Ireland. Thereafter they were always moving from one estate to another in Norfolk and Suffolk, where they inhabited Stoke Nayland, Tendring Hall, Framlingham, Kenninghall and Hunsdon. Kenninghall was the Duke's favourite residence, perhaps because it was his own creation; when he succeeded he pulled down the medieval fortress of his ancestors and rebuilt it in the form of an H; from here, when he was not at Court or on foreign service, he preferred to administer his properties. These intervals of domesticity were rare; during the greater part of Surrey's childhood he seldom saw his father, and then only for a few weeks at a time. It is therefore obvious that as the heir of the greatest landowner in England, he received, from his earliest years, not only the tributes usually accorded an elder son, but the doting indulgence lavished on a child brought up among women, tutors and household officers who looked on him as their temporary lord.

There was another incentive to arrogance. Surrey's mother, the descendant of John of Gaunt, the Percys and Edward III, seems to have been obsessed by her royal blood and her Plantagenet connections – in fact, her father had been executed for his pretensions to the throne – and must have infected Surrey with a sense of privilege that in her own case finally outran discretion and broke up the solidarity of family life.

The architectural settings of Surrey's earliest memories were sombre, soaring and grimly impregnable. The huge brick castle of Framlingham with its thirteen crenellated towers, double moat and fortified bastions produced, in spite of its bulk, a high, narrow, severe effect, intensely yet primitively Gothic, as of a wicked giant's enchanted stronghold, dominating the wild and desolate country-side. The modern accretions of knot-gardens, porticoes and terraces enhanced the fantastic intricacy of a dwelling that stood apart, not only in fact but symbolically. Such a building, set against the skyline in bleak and solitary power, gave rather the impression of a walled city than of a mansion or a home; to be brought up in one and to be treated, most of the time, as the greatest person in it, would induce, in a vigorous and imaginative child, a sense of limitless authority and of segregation from the rest of mankind. Surrey's personal recollection of these days survives in one of his poems. He longed to be independent, and was frankly rebellious. 'I saw the little boy,' he wrote, 'and thought of how that he Did wish of God to 'scape the rod, a tall young man to be'; and after a passage of disillusionment and pessimism, he concludes, 'Trudge from me to every little boy, And tell them this from me; their time most happy is, If to [in] their time, they reason had to know the truth of this.' Both thought and form are commonplace enough, showing that Surrey was resentful of such punishments as even he had to endure, but no more discontented than most spoiled children, and taking the rod for granted: for no other discipline seems to have existed, save that of an extreme formality of behaviour, as described in the etiquette books of the time.

In the early years of the sixteenth century the country life of a great nobleman and his family was more elaborate than that led in his town house, where the number of servants was limited. In his father's East Anglian palaces Surrey had at his command a staff of some four hundred persons, a hierarchy headed by the marshal whom all obeyed ('even the master-cook, be he loth or lief') and ending with the scullions who slept, naked and filthy, on the kitchen floors among the refuse. Between these extremes stood tutors, chaplains, bedchamber women, nurses, ushers, singing-master, butler, grooms of the chamber, treasurer, stewards, clerks, ewerers and almoners; in the background flitted the more shadowy figures of rockers (two to each nurse), bear-wards, arras-menders, farriers, huntsmen, fools, choirboys and minstrels. With the exception of wines, spices and sugar, all these persons' meals were produced by the estate.[1]

For Surrey, as for most of the household, the day began with Mass at six o'clock, followed by breakfast, which he ate in the nursery till his fifth or sixth year; after that he had meals with his parents, who observed the medieval custom of dining and supping in the great hall on a dais, while the 'messes' for the different ranks of their staff were served at separate tables below them. In the Household Book of Framlingham Castle the order for the nursery breakfast was for a chine of beef, a joint of mutton, butter-milk, six eggs, a chicken and a pottle of beer; on Fridays they were given salt fish with melted butter poured over it. As soon as Surrey's infancy came to an end he spent the greater part of the day with his tutor, being free to amuse himself for an hour after breakfast; then came lessons till eleven and dinner at twelve. This meal consisted of three courses; the first was soup; then came a choice of roast capon, boiled beef or venison, the latter sometimes served with a 'custard', or sweet sauce; then there were rabbit and chicken pasties, roast pork, fish, almond tarts and baked apples, all appearing together. After dinner a concert of music and singing was given; this lasted some two hours. From two till three Surrey studied again (he worked at his classics and the sciences in the morning, relaxing over modern languages in the afternoon) and at three went to evening prayers; this was followed by supper, a longer and more elaborate meal preceded by 'appetizers' of plums and grapes; on Fridays eight or nine kinds of fish (including oysters from Colchester) were produced, some 'done up' with eggs, cream, butter, onions and herbs. Gingerbread and jellies made the third course on ordinary occasions; for banquets, feast-days and parties, when there might be some twenty guests and two hundred extra servants staying in the castle, the master-cook, who wore a gold chain of office and ranked next to the marshal, expressed his genius in 'devices' or 'subtleties' made of almond paste and sugar, the most popular being those of Mary and the Angel Gabriel, a young man piping on a bed of clouds, 'an angry man of war', or 'Winter, with grey locks, sitting on a stone'.

After supper there were games. In winter a masque might be presented, under the direction of the master of the revels; and in summer the bear-ward staged fights between bears and dogs. These diversions continued till about eight o'clock; then Surrey had a short music-lesson, going to bed at nine. On holy days and anniversaries his time was given up to hawking, hunting, tilting and archery; dancing and fencing lessons were also fitted in, although no special hours were allotted to these.[2]

Every event in the day had its inexorable routine. When Surrey was called by his gentleman-usher, who had the right to carry a longer staff than anyone else in the household, and who slept outside his young master's door on a pallet-bed, the fire was lit, his clothes warmed and his night-gown wrapped round him; he sat by the fire while one servant combed his hair and another helped him to put on his hose and shirt. After that he washed his hands and face in warm water sprinkled with sweet herbs. The yeoman-usher, kneeling, then asked him what suit he would wear, and this was shaken out and brought forward. Meanwhile his pew was being prepared for him in chapel and his privy freshly scrubbed and emptied ('let there be blanket, cotton or linen to wipe his nether end') and basin, jug and towel were got out for washing again. He was attended to bed with the same ceremonial. A 'bath, or stew' was a rare event and prepared with great care, for fear of taking cold. First, the roof of the bath-house was hung round with sheets, the bath itself filled with warm rose-water and herbs and a sponge placed for him to sit on; he was then washed, dried and put to bed for some hours.[3]

After Mass Surrey visited his parents, and received their blessing; taking off his cap he knelt, and must look up at them 'modestly', without staring – how was this done? At meals he was taught to sign his lips with a cross before beginning on the first mouthful; breaking a piece of bread in two, picking his teeth with a knife, scratching, belching and noisy conversation were forbidden. When the Duke was in residence, Surrey sat on his right hand; his younger brother sometimes acted as carver, waiting on them both.[4]

The panorama of an existence that comprised so many contrasting activities required equally rich and variegated interiors. These were provided by a blend of English Gothic and Italian Renaissance decoration that resulted in a phantasmagoric exuberance, a gorgeous and startling display of colours and shapes only possible in vast rooms containing little furniture and no bric-à-brac or pictures. Everything that sculptors, painters and plaster-workers could imagine and produce was spread over walls and ceilings in a dazzling pattern of glass, terracotta, marble and wood – a pattern enhanced by peculiarly involute and subtle designs of which the most typical, and a favourite one for the banqueting hall, was a series of rounded and arched hammer-beams supported by golden angels within a pointed roof; the impression created was that of co-ordinated intricacy and formal elegance. The same effect was sometimes differently achieved by inserting a triple bay-window that reached from the rush-strewn floor to a foliated barrel ceiling, so that the entire wall looked as if it had been covered with jewelled imagery; for the panes were divided into brilliantly stained sections outlined in black, in which sacred, legendary and classical figures – Godefroi de Bouillon, Paris and Helen, Lancelot of the Lake, the Blessed Virgin, Queen Esther and Charlemagne – stood transfixed in perdurable splendour. On the side walls a profusion of carved heads, flowers, fruit, animals, birds and coats of arms alternated with hanging pediments, armour and strap-work; these led into vistas of double staircases that wound round one another – or huge, wide flights up which a high-spirited young man could have put his horse – and delicate barriers of galleries and screens.

There is no evidence that Surrey was consciously affected by or responsive to the indoor background of his most impressionable years; when he composed his 'free' translations from the Italian poets which he may perhaps have attempted before his teens were over, his taste inclined towards their descriptions of nature, changes of season, wild flowers, birds and beasts; in one of his best known poems, an adaptation from Petrarch, he gives the impression of having been happiest out of doors, roaming the countryside hawk on wrist, following his hounds or practising the quintain in the great tilt-yards of his father's castles. In these lines on spring ('the sweet season') he enumerates what he may have absorbed without realizing how much he cared for it:

> The hart hath hung his old head on the pale;
> The buck in brake his winter coat he flings;
> The fishes float with new repairèd scale;
> The adder all her slough away she slings;
> The swift swallow pursueth the flies small;
> The busy bee her honey now she mings.

So a boy might observe the remembered magic of renewal, as he wandered through familiar scenes with his troupe of friends; for Surrey and his brother worked and played with a number of young relations whom the Duke received into his household as pupils and pages, and for whose careers he was partly responsible. Among these were another Henry Howard and his brothers George and Charles, sons of Lord Edmund Howard who had fought with the Duke at Flodden, Norfolk's half-brothers Lord William and another Lord Thomas (they were only a few years older than Surrey) and a more distant cousin, Richard Southwell. It was not considered necessary for the Lady Mary Howard to have the companionship of these boys' sisters; the girls remained at home, or went to less wealthy families, and had rather a dull time of it. Before he succeeded, the Duke had tried to do something for one of his nieces — Anne, who was some ten years older than Surrey, and the daughter of Norfolk's sister and a London merchant, Sir Thomas Boleyn. An intelligent and promising child, though no beauty, she had been put forward by her uncle as a suitable bride for the Earl of Ormond's eldest son: but Sir Thomas, who was doing rather well at Court (his elder daughter Mary had been the King's mistress for a short time), haggled so long over her dowry that the match fell through, and Anne was sent to finish her education at the Court of France.[5] Another, younger niece, Katherine, sister of Henry, George and Charles, was placed in the household of the Dowager-Duchess of Norfolk at Horsham, where, very much neglected (it is doubtful whether she was even taught to read or write) and inclined to bad habits, she remained in obscurity and indigence; it seemed that neither of her parents cared what happened to her, although she was remarkably pretty and attractive. At this time Norfolk had never seen her. Surrey did not meet either Anne or Katherine until they had become, in turn, very great ladies indeed and were being hurried towards a dreadful end.

Surrey's education was entrusted to John Clerke, an exceptionally brilliant scholar and the author of several books; his *De Mortuorum Resurrectione* was dedicated to his pupil and his *Treatise of Nobility* to the Duke. He had lived on the continent for many years, and began life at Kenninghall as Norfolk's secretary; he taught Surrey Spanish, Greek, Latin, Italian and French, and encouraged him to make verse translations and adaptations from modern and medieval poetry as well as from the classics. These early attempts, especially Surrey's studies of Virgil, were to have lasting effects on English literature. Another, older companion was John Leland, the famous antiquary; and Henry VIII's Poet-Laureate, John Skelton, was sometimes the Duke's guest and always the Duchess's *protégé*.[6]

So all the cultural influences of Surrey's boyhood were of the highest order; his education would seem to have been ideally planned and perfectly carried out; but there was a long, jagged tear in this rich fabric, one that could not be mended. The relationship of the Duchess and her husband deteriorated rapidly from the moment he left Ireland – how or why, will never be known, except that her temper, always haughty and unbalanced, became increasingly violent, with the result that the Duke withdrew himself from her when he was at home. By 1525 he had a mistress – Elizabeth Holland, one of the Duchess's women, who had entered her service first as laundress and then as waiting-maid some years before. (She was the daughter of a neighbour, Sir John Holland of Redenhall.) The Duchess, insatiably raging, complained, stormed, made scene after scene. The Duke ignored her diatribes, and Bess, as the other servants called Elizabeth Holland, retained her place. Gradually the whole household, including Surrey, his brother and sister – and perhaps also their cousins and step-uncles – began to take sides; the Duchess's temperament was such that the majority turned against her.[7]

Yet on the surface all was gaiety, glitter, and ordered activity, as life in the various Howard mansions, running its splendid course, sometimes entered into the outside world and what we should now call local politics, while on feast-days the country people enjoyed the religious spectacles in which the Howards had taken part for hundreds of years. On Easter morning a play of the Resurrection was acted in the churches; on the following Monday the head of the house observed the custom of creeping to the cross; on New Year's Day he made gifts to certain shrines: on Maundy Thursday he presented gowns and money to a selected number of poor men and women. Once or twice a year he and his retinue went on progress through Norfolk and Suffolk, scattering largesse in the towns and villages.[8]

The Duke showed personal care for his tenants in more practical ways than these. In 1525, when Surrey was in his ninth year, there was a revolt against the new tax, euphemistically described as the Amicable Loan. Some four thousand people rose, broke the bridges and began to destroy the properties of the smaller gentry. Another great landowner, the Duke of Suffolk, brother-in-law of Henry VIII, used brutal repression, with the result that the anger of the people intensified, and revolution on a large scale became a possibility. Norfolk managed to restrain the Duke of Suffolk, and went as far as Huntingdonshire to meet the leaders of the rebels in person. 'Who is your captain, that he may answer for you all?' he asked. An elderly man came forward. 'Poverty is our captain,' he said, 'the which, with Necessity, his cousin, hath brought us to this.' 'I am sorry for your case,' said Norfolk. 'If you will depart home to your dwellings, I will be a mean for your pardon to the King.' He then put the people's grievances before Henry VIII — the tax was that of a sixth on everyone's goods — taking care to point out that it had been evolved and enforced by Wolsey. Henry professed ignorance of the innovation. 'This touches my honour,' he said, 'that my commons should be so entreated,' and rescinded the Cardinal's order. Wolsey tried to make out that it was he and not the Duke who had pleaded for the populace; he was not believed, and in East Anglia Norfolk's reputation for clemency soared. 'I'll serve the good Duke of Norfolk' became a catch-phrase, and a rhyming game grew out of it. One player would sing, 'I am the Duke of Norfolk, newly come to Suffolk. Say, shall I be attended, or no, no, no?' The reply was 'Good Duke, be not offended, And you shall be attended, Now, now, now!' The singer then sat on a table while the rest danced round him, shouting the refrain; having drunk a jug of ale without spilling a drop, he was crowned with a cushion.[9]

The remission of such taxes as these did not of course affect Norfolk personally; if it had, he would have behaved very differently. He himself was strangely mean in little ways. He had fifty jewelled rosaries; yet he wore his dressing-gowns till their fur linings were rubbed almost bare. He was ready to receive and feed two hundred poor persons or travellers every day; but he grudged the Duchess her pleasures, and Surrey, as he grew up, was always short of money.[10] The discrepancy between public open-handedness and private economies contributed to the disturbed and disturbing atmosphere of Surrey's adolescence; the seeds of the insecurity that was the partial cause of his greatest follies were planted at this time. The quarrels of his parents, his father's long absences, the bewildering inconsistencies of a life in which indulgence, severity, power and helplessness alternated from one month to another deprived him of stability.

Yet to the outward eye Surrey was developing on lines that must have satisfied the most critical and ambitious parent. His beauty became celebrated. Pale, slender, of medium height, he had his father's long oval face and aquiline features, although his were more delicately moulded. His eyes were large and brilliant, the outline of brows and forehead and the set of his head nobly, classically pure. He delighted most people by his energy and charm, his care for and knowledge of the arts — after poetry, architecture became his principal hobby — and his skill in games, sports and such amateur soldiering as came his way at this time. He was cited as a boy of extraordinary promise, an example to his contemporaries. Yet there was a flaw, basic, permanent, splitting the whole pattern of his character. Variable, innately arrogant and quite unable to control his outbursts of temper, he could never adapt himself to untoward circumstances, or attempt to get round any difficulties that arose. He took, always, the direct route, breaking through conditions that might have yielded to manipulation. None among those responsible for his upbringing seems to have perceived this tendency; if anyone did, it was not corrected. So Surrey's wilfulness and pride, sometimes turning into a passionate and almost maniacal obstinacy, crystallized as he matured.

By the time he was fifteen the world, as the saying is, was at his feet. But in the years between his birth and his adolescence, his part of it had begun to change — and Surrey did not take in what was happening. This curious and inexplicable lack of a certain sense, this mental blindness, was to destroy him. Eager, warmhearted and gay, he carried his death with him, as a man might carry a sealed packet through a half-seen country to a hidden destination, not knowing what his mission is, nor what his fate.

NOTES TO CHAPTER TWO

[1] Furnivall, *Treatises on Manners*, pp. 3-5; *Household Book of the Earl of Northumberland*, pp. 31-54.
[2] Furnivall, pp. 85-100.
[3] Ibid.
[4] Ibid.
[5] Friedmann, *Anne Boleyn*, vol. I, p. 35.
[6] Brenan and Statham, *The House of Howard*, vol. I, p. 152.
[7] Calendar of Domestic State Papers, vol. XIV, pt. 1: p. 160.
[8] *Household Book*, p. 54.
[9] Holinshed, *Chronicle*, pp. 709-10.
[10] F. Nott, *Works of Surrey*, vol. I, Appendix, p. xix.

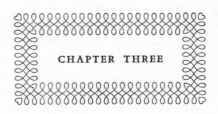

CHAPTER THREE

I N the spring of 1529 Surrey celebrated his twelfth birthday, was
given his own retinue of servants and treated as a young man in
his late teens would be today — still as a minor in law, and in
certain respects under the jurisdiction of parents and tutors, but in
all else as a responsible and adult person. When Norfolk was at
home Surrey accompanied him on local tours and business visits,
receiving the homage and adulation due to the heir of a potentate;
for at that time the figure of Henry VIII, unseen, mighty, terrible,
was a shadow behind that of the Duke; the King could not then be
visualized nor his power personally felt by the East Anglian people,
who were as much Norfolk's subjects as his tenants; and their
attitude towards Surrey was therefore one of reverential affection
and ecstatic loyalty. Yet there was an omission in Surrey's upbringing; his father entrusted the administration of his estates to a
staff of secretaries and agents with whom his sons had nothing to do.
Surrey was trained as a soldier and, later, as a courtier; it occurred
to no one to make him feel responsible for or interested in the lives
and fortunes of the people amongst whom he lived, although he
must have been aware, early in life, of their uses and of the need of
their adherence to his family. So he was sociologically isolated.

Meanwhile the fissures and cracks in what was then called the
body politic were developing into precipices and chasms. This civil
and religious revolution began before Surrey was born and continued during the first sixteen years of his life without immediately
affecting him. Yet because the so-called divorce of Katherine of
Aragon, Anne Boleyn's domination, Wolsey's fall, Cromwell's rise,

Henry VIII's supremacy over the church, and the dissolution of the monasteries, created the conditions that were to make his career, their sequence must be outlined. The fact that after four hundred years the rights and wrongs of the English Reformation are still almost as hotly discussed as they were when Surrey was alive, makes some bias unavoidable; but perhaps the accretions of anecdote, moral judgment and special pleading may be eliminated.

In 1514 Henry VIII had already begun to consider a separation from Katherine, but did nothing to further it; in 1516 the only child of theirs who was to survive, Mary, was born. In 1517, the year of Surrey's birth, Martin Luther pinned his ninety-five theses against the abuse of indulgence on the door of a church in Wittenberg, and his teaching gradually spread from the continent to the English universities. In 1518 Katherine had her last miscarriage: she was then forty. In 1521 Henry received the title of Defender of the Faith from the Pope as the reward for his anti-Lutheran book, the *Assertio Septem Sacramentorum*. In the same year Anne Boleyn returned from France and became lady-in-waiting to the Queen; in 1526 (according to his own account) Henry fell in love with her; primed by her father and Norfolk, she refused to become his mistress. This situation was to last several years.

In 1527 Henry broke up his alliance with Katherine's nephew, the Emperor Charles V, and in October of that year sent to Clement VII to ask for a dispensation to annul his marriage and take a second wife; he had decided that in the event of success he would marry Anne rather than one of the foreign princesses Wolsey was considering. Henry's hopes of an annulment appeared to be good; for a previous Pope had granted his elder sister, Margaret of Scotland, a dissolution, as he had to the Duke of Suffolk, who eventually married Henry's younger sister Mary, the widowed Queen of France. Henry's case rested on these points: that Katherine had been the wife of his elder brother Arthur; that during his father's reign, when he was still a minor, a proper dispensation on the grounds of consanguinity had not been granted himself and Katherine; that God had punished this negligence by the deaths of all their male children. (At that time the succession of a woman could not be contemplated. The general view was that if Henry died without a son to succeed him, another claimant to the throne would create a party, and that civil war, followed by invasion from Spain or France, would result.)

At this point Rome was sacked and occupied by Imperial troops, and Clement, now in the Emperor's power, gave Henry an officially non-committal answer. Privately he suggested that the King should get himself freed from Katherine and married to Anne in England without applying to Rome, an action that would then have amounted to bigamy; this Henry refused to do.

In May 1528, as a result of pressure from Wolsey and Henry, Cardinal Campeggio was sent into England to try what would now be called a nullity suit between Henry and Katherine; his secret instructions were to hold up the proceedings as long as possible, and in June he duly dissolved the hearings till the autumn of that year. Meanwhile he and Wolsey suggested to Katherine that she should enter a convent, a compromise she rejected, and Campeggio returned to Rome. The result of this deadlock was the disgrace of Wolsey and the promotion of his secretary, Thomas Cromwell.

In the autumn of 1529 Parliament passed certain laws curtailing the powers and privileges of the clergy; these were promulgated by Cromwell, with the aid of Thomas Cranmer, who had been attached to the household of Sir Thomas Boleyn. Cranmer then suggested that the universities of England and the continent should be consulted as to the validity of Henry's marriage, and a majority in the King's favour was obtained, except, naturally, in those countries under Spanish jurisdiction. In 1530 Wolsey died. In 1531 Henry was declared Supreme Head of the Church of England. In September 1532 he created Anne Marquess (not Marchioness) of Pembroke, and she was received by his most influential and untrustworthy ally, Francis I. In the same year the clergy submitted their authority to Henry.

A few months later the Duke of Richmond, Henry's bastard son by Elizabeth Blount, died of tuberculosis; Henry had considered legitimizing him, and he had been looked on by many as a possible heir to the throne. Anne, now pregnant, was secretly married to

Henry after Katherine's marriage had been annulled by Cranmer at a court that Katherine herself refused to attend.

The powers of the ministry were now in the hands of Norfolk, Suffolk and Sir Thomas Boleyn, recently made Earl of Wiltshire; it was observed that Anne (whose coronation was celebrated in June 1533) dominated them all. In September of that year she gave birth to the Princess Elizabeth. Henry's disappointment, freely expressed, widened the breach already existing between them. In 1534 the dissolution of the monasteries, the redistribution of property under Cromwell's aegis and the Catholic martyrdoms began. In 1536 Katherine died. By that time Surrey had reached the age of nineteen.

During the next decade the three religio-political parties into which the country was divided began to emerge as separate entities, and to intrigue and struggle against one another. The least powerful was that of the Papalists, who desired the return of the Pope's jurisdiction and the abolition of Henry's supremacy. The reforming section had split into two branches — that of the Moderates, sometimes described as the Henricians, of whom Norfolk and Gardiner were the most influential representatives, and that of the Extremists, headed by Cromwell, Cranmer and, later, Lord Hertford. Norfolk's party were Catholics but not Papalists; they supported Henry's supremacy, the divorce of Katherine and the dissolution of the monasteries. The Extremists did not describe themselves as Protestants until after the accession of Edward VI.

The connection of these events (and their resultant divisions) with Surrey's family, and the part in them played by his father, seem to have reinforced his belief that the patrician group to which he belonged was still, and must always be, supreme; and when, a few years later, he was given a share in the administration, he behaved as if the Howards would continue to dominate this group. Such an attitude was, by then, inevitable; for shortly after his thirteenth birthday Surrey left home for good in order to share his education with the Duke of Richmond, who was two years younger than himself; so he was given the status and privileges of a king's son.

It was some time since Norfolk had been angling for this arrangement in a characteristically devious manner. In the summer of 1529 he encouraged, he may even have given rise to, the rumour that the King might make a marriage between Surrey and Anne Boleyn, in the event of his not being able to marry her himself.[1] Having thus shown his potentialities, Norfolk approached Chapuys, the Spanish Ambassador, during a supper party at Whitehall, and opened the conversation with the request that the envoy would do him a favour. Consent given, Norfolk drew out a letter written in Latin that he had just received from Surrey; would His Excellency be so kind as to read it and give his opinion? Chapuys did so, and pronounced it admirable, not only to the anxious father, but in his report to the Emperor. Norfolk expressed his gratification, adding that Surrey's achievements would be a good beginning for a project that he proposed to discuss later. No more was said for some hours; at about midnight the Duke offered to take Chapuys back to his lodgings, although they were far out of his way, and came in for a talk. After touching again on Surrey's advancement in learning and his good behaviour, Norfolk spoke of his own warm feeling for and confidence in the Ambassador. Chapuys took this rather coolly; he had not forgotten his master's indignation when he heard that Norfolk had signed a ministerial letter to the Pope threatening the loss of his supremacy in England if he did not grant the King's divorce. 'As friends,' Norfolk resumed in his fluent French, 'should tell one another their most secret affairs, I do not hesitate to tell you that His Majesty hath entrusted to me the care of his bastard son, the Duke of Richmond, of whom my own son may become in time the tutor and preceptor.' (Perhaps Norfolk meant that Surrey would be a good example to Richmond, who had been over-indulged.) 'A friendship thus cemented,' he went on, 'promiseth fair – and will be further strengthened by alliance; for His Grace would have the Duke marry my daughter.'[2]

A few months later, in the spring of 1530, Surrey joined Richmond at Windsor, and they at once became close friends. The background of Richmond's upbringing had been as disturbed as Surrey's: perhaps more so; and they seem to have been alike in other ways.

Henry Fitzroy, Duke of Richmond and Somerset and Earl of Nottingham, was born in the village of Blackmore in Essex at the

Prior's house, then disguised, 'for the King's pleasure', under the name of Jericho. Thus, when Henry went there to visit Elizabeth Blount, whom he afterwards dowered and married to Sir Gilbert Tailbois, his courtiers would say that he had gone to Jericho. A few years later Richmond was removed from his mother and given his own household at Sheriff Hutton in Yorkshire; Norfolk was partly responsible for this establishment. By the time Richmond was eight he had become the subject of bitter disputes between his tutor, Dr Croke, and his chief gentleman-usher, George Cotton. Croke, a preceptor of the strict, old-fashioned sort, wrote a series of angry letters to Wolsey — who, with Norfolk, was Richmond's godfather — accusing Cotton of distracting Richmond from his studies in the most shocking manner. Cotton refused to call his young master at the proper hour of six, lured him away from his lessons, and was busily disrupting the routine arranged for the boy by Wolsey and his father. Worse still, Cotton, clearly a firebrand and innovator of the most dangerous type, forbade the use of the rod, admitted jesters, musicians and tumblers at all hours, and was crowning his attempted subversion of Richmond's character by constant criticisms of the clergy; it was therefore easy for him to encourage the Duke to disobey Croke whenever he felt inclined. To Wolsey's admonitions Cotton blandly replied that he had to think of the Duke's health and relaxation: he was over-worked, and needed more out-of-door amusements than the tutor allowed. Defeated, Croke fell back on Cotton's interference in the schoolroom; the usher was secretly teaching Richmond the 'Roman' hand-writing when he ought to be learning the more involute and decorative 'engrossing' style. So the battle continued, ending, in 1528, with the rout of Croke and the triumphant ascendancy of Cotton, who was still in Richmond's service when Surrey joined him at Windsor. By this time, Cotton had amassed a large fortune by becoming the Duke's purveyor. His influence prevailed in the household shared by the two boys; it may not have been altogether desirable.[3]

Richmond was a courteous, handsome and intelligent boy. With him Surrey spent the two happiest years of his life, recording them after his friend's death in one of his few autobiographical poems.

This evocation, although short, is remarkably, lovingly detailed; and here again outdoor pleasures dominate the theme. He begins with a description of 'proud Windsor, where I, in lust and joy, With a King's son my childish years did pass, In greater feast than Priam's son of Troy'. After the bleakness of the eastern counties the castle's luxuriant setting was a revelation, especially the 'large green courts', 'the wild forest', 'the silver mead' and the clearings, 'clothed with green', where 'with reins availed and swift y-breathèd horse, with cry of hounds and merry blasts between', he and Richmond 'chased the fearful hart' until dusk. Then there were the tournaments; on the 'gravelled ground' below the 'maiden's tower' they jousted like knights of the Round Table, 'with sleeves tied on the helm, On foaming horse, with swords, and friendly hearts'.

More alluring still was the call of romance; when the Court was in residence Windsor was full of ladies, whom Surrey and Richmond watched flitting about the galleries and antechambers, 'with eyes cast up, and easy sighs, such as folk draw in love'. Indeed these elegant creatures often distracted them from the 'palm-play' when, stripped to their shirts in the tennis-court, they glanced up to see the particular star of the moment with 'dazèd eyes' — and then — 'oft we, by gleams of love, Have missed the ball, and got sight of our dame, To bait her eyes' — although she sometimes pretended to be interested only in the game.

In the evening they danced; but this was an excuse for telling stories ('long tales of great delight') and flirtation. When the chosen lady was cold, 'with words and looks ... each of us did plead the other's right'. That was only fair; next day they would compare notes in 'secret groves, which oft we made resound Of pleasant plaint, and of our ladies' praise, Recording oft what grace each one had found, What hope of speed, what dread of long delays'. Then came night, and 'such sleeps as yet delight, The pleasant dreams, the quiet bed of rest'.

Most absorbing of all was the relationship with Richmond, their confidences, arguments and jokes, their 'sweet accord' and 'The secret thoughts, imparted with such trust, The wanton talk, the divers change of play, The friendship sworn, each promise kept so just, Wherewith we passed the winter night away'. Looking back, Surrey could not but idealize that wonderful time, that 'place of bliss', and the graceful, gay companion with whom he had shared 'the jolly woes, the hateless, short debate', the bursts of high spirits, the endless, entrancing self-discoveries of adolescence.

The two years that Surrey spent at Windsor seem to have had a more lasting effect on him than any other experience, not only because of his devotion to Richmond, but because at no other time in his life did he stay so long in one place. From the moment of his birth he had been on the move; although it is not certain that he was taken to Ireland when his father became Deputy there, the household books show that at that time his family changed residences according to the seasons, so that his background was never the same for more than a few months at a time. Besides providing a certain stability, life at Windsor gave Surrey his first taste of the world in which intrigue, festivity, scandal, politics and religious controversy combined to produce an atmosphere of suspense, excitement and frenzied competition. At this guerrilla warfare, fought out in presence chambers, galleries, state bedrooms and privy council meetings, Norfolk was the supreme expert. Surrey appears to have admired his father's skill and trusted his judgment: he never acquired either. All those subtle manœuvres, manipulations, counter-plots and pullings of strings had for him no interest and little meaning; the only kind of war he understood was that waged with soldiers, armaments and the gallant, chivalric, picturesque tactics that he and Richmond practised in the tilt-yard – a method so long out of date as to have become the attribute of the legendary, medieval heroes on whom Surrey eventually modelled himself.

So between the ages of twelve and fourteen Surrey's character matured. His intellectual tastes were advanced: extraordinarily so, as his poetry shows; his political and social outlook reverted to that of the fourteenth century, when the power of the great noble could – and sometimes did – overwhelm that of the king. This misapprehension of his circumstances was enhanced by the personal favour of Henry VIII and of that flashing, predatory, seductive cousin who had brought the great Cardinal to his ruin and whom even Surrey's father must now flatter and cajole. Naturally Henry liked the company of his son's gifted, exuberant, rather boisterous friend; the fact that he had executed Surrey's maternal grandfather made no difference to the interest he took in the boy; and at this time Surrey was probably too young to understand that his own nearness to the dynasty might be a source of danger to himself. He shone in the blazing light and warmth of royal bounty and of the richest and most splendid Court in Europe. Nothing else was required of him. While Richmond lived and Henry's marriage with Anne was in sight Surrey's position remained secure and his future settled.

Norfolk's plan for the marriage of Richmond to his daughter being temporarily in abeyance, he began to arrange an alliance for Surrey. Anne Boleyn wished him to wed the Princess Mary; then she changed her mind in favour of a match between the Princess and Francis I, who had recently become a widower. Norfolk at once adapted his tactics to those of his niece; he told Chapuys that he did not want to be accused of intriguing for the Lady Mary; he had other ideas for Surrey, and early in 1532 these were carried out.[4] In February of that year Surrey was contracted to a distant cousin, Lady Frances de Vere, the fourteen-year-old daughter of the Earl of Oxford, after a great deal of wrangling over her dowry and Surrey's settlement. Eventually Lady Frances received £2,500, to be paid by instalments, and Surrey was granted lands that would bring in £2,000 a year. Lady Frances was a shy, rather characterless girl of some beauty: her profile was marred by a slightly receding chin. The marriage was celebrated at Kenninghall in April 1532, and the young people separated at the altar, returning to their respective homes. A few weeks later Lady Frances entered the Princess Mary's household, and her husband went back to Windsor.[5]

During his time in Norfolk the fifteen-year-old bridegroom, perhaps exhilarated by his prospects and the indulgences of Court life, began what was to become a lifelong course of overspending that he dared not confess to his father. His situation was fantastic, as his first extant letter shows. The heir of the richest man in England had no one to turn to for ready cash but an old friend and tenant of the Duke's, Abbot John Reeve of Bury St Edmunds, to whom he now desperately wrote that 'notwithstanding that aforetime I have borrowed of you to the sum of £22 sterling, having not yet repaid it, yet, by *very need and extreme necessity*, I am again constrained, my known good lord, affectuously to desire yourself so much my cordial friend as to lend some over and above £22, in such haste as I may have it here tomorrow by eight of the clock, for such is my present need and thought.'

This appeal is followed by a few vague phrases about repayment, ending with — 'If I were so ingrate (which God defend!) to deny ye ... my lord my father will not so see your hearty kindness un-contented.' Surrey added that his father's absence accounted for this application, concluding, 'And thus, my very good lord, with hearty request of this my desire, I leave you to God.'

The Abbot kept the letter, scribbling on it a note of the first, second and third sums borrowed by his young friend; the whole amount came to just over £50.[6] No repayment is recorded: nor is it known who was pressing Surrey, or for what reason. By the time he left Kenninghall he seems to have forgotten all about this crisis; his later conduct indicates a magnificent disregard of such trivialities.

NOTES TO CHAPTER THREE

[1] Calendar of Spanish State Papers, vol. V, p. 228.
[2] Ibid.
[3] Nichols, *The Duke of Richmond*, pp. 1–50.
[4] Cal. Span. S.P., vol. V, p. 424.
[5] Howard, *Memorials of the Howards*, p. 22.
[6] Brenan and Statham, vol. I, p. 167.

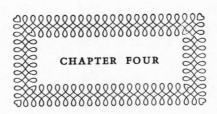

CHAPTER FOUR

I N October 1532 Henry VIII and Anne Boleyn with their entourage went to meet Francis I at Boulogne in order to conclude the
alliance against the Emperor. It had been decided to take this
opportunity of presenting Richmond and Surrey to the French King,
who had agreed to establish them in one of his households, so that
their education might be rounded off in the proper manner.

The festivities began with a supper party in one of Henry's French
castles that had been redecorated for the occasion with hangings of
silver tissue and wreaths of beaten gold.[1] No one expected that either
of the kings would attempt to exceed the glories of the Field of the
Cloth of Gold; that celebration had taken place twelve years before,
when the coffers of both were fuller; yet this meeting produced a
combination of splendour and fantasy characteristic of Henry's gift
for masking his diplomatic manœuvres with theatrical displays that
now appear rather childish and crude.

The King's share in the entertainment was part of a process that
this extraordinary man, now in his forty-third year and at the
height of his powers, had begun at his accession and long perfected.
The supper was designed to show his jovial side, just as another kind
of background would have been used for a semi-histrionic demonstration of wrath or sorrow. All were intended to bewilder and
deceive not only the audience, but the other actors. 'If a lion knew
his strength,' said Sir Thomas More, after one of Henry's planned
scenes, 'it were hard to rule him.' Astute though he was, More failed
to grasp the King's darker purposes. Henry always knew both his
strength and his weakness; his object was to prevent others guessing

HENRY HOWARD, EARL OF SURREY

their range and the use he might make of them. Wolsey, a more cunning and experienced victim, described him as 'a prince of royal courage and a princely heart', adding, 'Rather than he will either miss or want any part of his will or appetite, he will put the loss of one half of his realm in danger. I have often kneeled before him in his privy chamber,' he went on, ' ... the space of an hour or two, to persuade him ... but I could never ... dissuade him therefrom.'[2] Such obstinacy, if genuine, would have been habitual and, naturally, disastrous. When Henry decided to yield — as he often did — his timing was faultless and the impression he made unforgettable.

It was not possible that Surrey, young, ambitious, and high in royal favour, should have seen further than his more knowledgeable contemporaries did, or have grasped that Henry crowned the development of his many gifts with the exercise of his personal magic — a combination of good humour, frankness and informality that at any moment might be overcast by tigerish rage or icy sternness. While he used the technique of the political expert, the pious visionary or even of the buffoon, his intellect remained in control, interlacing one role with another, so that his animal spirits were sometimes tinged with poetic sensitivity, his piety with clowning, and his insight with brutal malice. When Surrey at last became aware that Henry's egoism could assume monstrous and terrible proportions, he was of course disgusted, but not afraid — indeed it seems doubtful whether he was ever afraid of anything — and it was partly this attitude that eventually made it necessary for Henry to destroy him.

On this occasion Surrey and Richmond were allotted minor parts in an elaborate charade designed by Henry for the exhibition of Anne Boleyn's status as his future wife. (Their marriage took place three months after the Calais-Boulogne meeting.) Surrey watched his patron dancing, jousting and playing host as if the struggle that for nine years convulsed the Courts of Europe had never been: as if this final phase — which included Anne's reception by the Queen of Navarre as well as by Francis I — was rather a pleasant interlude than a diplomatic victory. Indeed Henry so arranged the gaieties that all triumph was laid at the feet of the young woman whom Wolsey

39

had described as the night crow, whom shocked housewives called a goggle-eyed whore, and whom the Spanish Ambassador wrote of as the great harlot or, more bitterly still, the Lady.

Anne's first appearance took place after supper. She came in with seven of her gentlewomen, all masked and dressed alike in Oriental robes of crimson and gold striped with cloth of silver. The music struck up, and they invited the men to dance with them. Henry, still wearing the white damask gown that Francis had given him, would not consent until he had unmasked each lady in turn. Then Anne was presented to the French King and his sister.[3]

A few days later Surrey and Richmond escorted the French courtiers through the streets of Calais where the English soldiers were lined up for inspection. When the kings parted, the two young men accompanied Francis to Chantilly; here his sons — the Dauphin Francis, Henry, afterwards Henry II, and Charles — were awaiting them. Richmond, Francis I announced, was to be treated as if he were his fourth son.[4] During the weeks that followed, Henry, then Duke of Orleans, became very fond of Surrey; by the time they finished the tour that lasted several months and included Toulouse, Montpellier and Béziers, they were all on the best of terms. Surrey was rather subdued and reserved; he disliked the heat of southern France and seemed happier in Paris.[5] It was at Fontainebleau and the Louvre where he met Alemmani, a Florentine refugee poet, and read the work of Molza, one of the first translators of the *Aeneid*, that he found his inspiration and began to acquire the technique that was to revolutionize English poetry. There are no records of his personal life during this period. If he had had any adventures, they would have been remembered when, thirteen years later, it became necessary to find out every detail of his behaviour at this time. The lack of information indicates that he was completely given up to his new life and its cultural influences.

None of Surrey's poems was published till ten years after his death. By that time his tragic end called for additions and trimmings to his legend, with the result that a number of romances about his tour abroad began to circulate; these were epitomized in Thomas Nash's novel, *The Unfortunate Traveller*, published in 1594. Later historians and critics combined in sanctioning its authenticity with an autobiographical interpretation of nearly all Surrey's verse; and thus the story of the gallant Earl and his Fair Geraldine became an established belief, only recently refuted.

In fact, sentimentally, although not technically, Surrey affiliated himself with those poets who during the eleventh century had founded the Provençal school of Courtly Love — a school whose literary code survived until long after his own day. The rules were, roughly, these: The lover became the 'servant' or 'prisoner' of a relentlessly cruel mistress; having thus attached himself, his evocations sprang from the sufferings caused by her caprice; weeping and imploring, he submitted himself to tests of chivalry and self-sacrifice ordained by her; these entailed long and painful banishment from her favours, degradations and, naturally, dangers that might end in death. The mistress was generally the wife of another man, and had little or no contact with the lover, so that by the time Surrey began to write, the celebration of Courtly Love had become a formal tribute to a remote and shadowy ideal. Thus, although Surrey's Fair Geraldine did indeed exist — he met her after he returned from the French Court — she had no more personal connection with him than an artist's model might have with her employer. Her name was Elizabeth Fitzgerald; she was the daughter of the Earl of Kildare and became the third wife of Lord Clinton. She was a pretty child of nine when Surrey, living happily with his wife, decided to make her the subject of the verses that describe her charms. These are exercises in fancy and what came to be called Troubadourism.

Surrey's technical master was Petrarch, whose example of selecting a central thought, set off by a quantity of images and analogies, he copied in various ways. Surrey combined this practice with the exploitation, in a literary sense, of chivalry, courtesy, loyalty and honour, as understood in the aristocratic and knightly circles of the Middle Ages. There is no evidence that he was influenced by, or that he even read, such masters of this school as Chrétien de Troyes and Guillaume de Lorris; it is clear that all his life he remained under the spell of their great adapter, Sir Thomas Malory. Surrey was deeply moved by that writer's version of the Lancelot and

Guinevere legend, in which the concept of selfless and noble suffering for and through an adulterous relationship found its most perfect and thrilling expression.

In this respect, therefore, as well as through his educational and hereditary background, Surrey turned towards the medieval past — an attitude no more fitted to making one's way in the England of Henry VIII than it would have been in the England of the balloon, or of the steam-engine. The fact that the powers of the old nobility were yielding to those of a semi-middle-class government escaped him, because he had been born and brought up in an archaically privileged circle. He knew, as his actions and his literary output show, that his chief interests and the furthering of his career must derive from the Court; he therefore looked on a private, retired existence, however luxurious and easy, as an interlude, a time-wasting setback in the business of life.

Meanwhile the Howard ascendancy had been temporarily halted by the failure of Norfolk's efforts over the King's divorce. In the autumn of 1531 he had suggested to Parliament that all matrimonial causes should be judged by the laity; the rejection of this proposal weakened the alliance between Anne and her uncle, and their latent enmity was no longer concealed. In July 1533, while Surrey was at Fontainebleau recovering from an attack of malaria, the Pope declared Henry's divorce illegal and his marriage to Anne (her coronation, for which Surrey came over, had taken place a month earlier) null and void. Norfolk's embassy to His Holiness was withdrawn and he returned to England, not disgraced, but under a cloud of diplomatic defeat. The Pope, with a view to keeping Norfolk's adherence, had suggested to him that as Surrey's marriage had not been consummated, it should be annulled, so that he might marry the Lady Mary; the Duke knew better than to further this scheme.

In September of the same year Surrey and Richmond came home (they were just in time to attend the christening of the Princess Elizabeth), and with the marriage of Surrey's sister Mary to Richmond in November the Howard fortunes rose again. For the next two months the young men remained at Windsor; then Surrey left to take up married life at Kenninghall, where Frances joined him. A few months later they became involved in the quarrels between the Duke and Duchess about Bess Holland. The breach was now permanent and complete. The Duchess, appealing to Cromwell, accused her husband and his mistress of trying to kill her.*

From the remains of a voluminous correspondence one fact emerges; the Duchess was, at times, seized by what we now call persecution mania. There is no doubt that her husband treated her badly: but no worse than, and not as brutally as, many husbands in similar circumstances. The nature of the provocation she gave him may be conjectured; her letters are those of a shrew, a termagant and an egotist, who prefers the exploitation to the cessation of suffering. Through her tempestuous abuse the darker side of Surrey's early background and the partial cause of his wildness may be discerned; his behaviour in certain crises can be traced back to his mother's influence.

In the spring of 1534 Norfolk had to leave the Court and join his family at Kenninghall after a quarrel with the Queen, whose nerves were beginning to give way under the strain of Henry's displeasure at the birth of Elizabeth. She rightly suspected her uncle of having changed sides and of intriguing against her. The result was an outburst of hysterical vituperation that drove Norfolk from the palace. He must therefore have reached home in a bad temper, to be greeted by the demands of Bess Holland and the cataclysmic rage of his wife. (The Duchess's account of the scene was written some three years later and lost nothing, presumably, in recollection.) First, she told Cromwell, the Duke locked her up and gave all her jewels to 'that drab, Bess Holland'; then he threatened to turn her out of the house. She appealed to her brother, Lord Stafford, for redress; he wrote to Norfolk that that was out of the question. 'Her wild language', he explained, 'would undo me and all mine.'

The Duchess then agreed to remain at Kenninghall, and the quarrel was patched up by the temporary withdrawal of Bess Holland to the Queen's household, where Norfolk joined her as soon as his relations with his niece improved. The Duchess retaliated by dismissing the entire Holland contingent from her service. When the Duke, with his mistress, returned to Kenninghall, both ladies fell to it again, 'That harlot, Bess Holland,' the Duchess told Cromwell, 'and the residue of the harlots' (were these Bess's reinstalled relatives?) ' ... bound me and pinnacled me until I spat blood.'[7]

At this point Norfolk made an offer of settlement and separation, and the Duchess departed to his manor of Redbourne in Hertfordshire, where, she informed Cromwell, she dragged out a wretched existence on £50 a quarter and a staff of twenty servants. (The allowance was not lavish; its modern equivalent would perhaps be some £2,000 a year.) At the same time she tried to drive a wedge between Surrey and his father. He and Frances stayed on at Kenninghall; the Duchess of Richmond, whom her mother also set upon, was told to remain in attendance on the Queen until she and Richmond should be old enough to live together.[8]

The Duke now began to consider divorcing his wife; this was a complicated matter, involving her co-operation; the idea brought on another frenzy, and her letters to Cromwell redoubled in length and frequency. Redbourne was uninhabitable for one 'born and brought up daintily'. None of her children came near her – 'never woman bare so ungracious an eldest son and so ungracious a daughter and so unnatural.' Hearing that the King was at Dunstable, the Duchess rushed to throw herself at his feet. He listened gravely at first, then impatiently (he was on his way to hunt) and at last gave her a good talking-to on the sanctity of marriage and wifely duty – of which, it must be said, he had first-hand experience. Henry commanded the maddened creature to write 'gently' to Norfolk, to whom, as a Christian, she owed obedience and submission. Later on she assured the much tried Cromwell that she had done this; Cromwell left her letter unanswered, upon which she came to London in order to browbeat him personally and almost without intermission. Norfolk, hearing of her defiance, wrote to the minister in self-defence. He had never mishandled his 'wilful wife', whose story was a pack of lies, dating back to her lying-in of their daughter nearly fifteen years ago. Even then, Norfolk protested, she had accused him of 'pulling her out of her bed by the hair of the head about the house, and with my dagger [giving] her a wound on the head'. 'She had the scar', he went on, ' ... fifteen months before she was delivered of my said daughter, and that ... same was cut by a surgeon of London for a swelling she had of drawing of two teeth ... Surely I think there is no man on life that would handle a woman in child-bed of that sort,' he added virtuously, 'for my part I would not have so done for all that I am worth.'⁹

Surrey's judgment on this dispute was merciless; he did not see his mother again: and she did not forgive him his disloyalty. Whether he had always hated her will never be known.

The year that Surrey spent at Kenninghall with his wife was happy, as far as his relationship with her was concerned; they became very fond of one another, and he grew to rely on her devotion. It has been assumed that he was then writing continuously. As very few of his poems can be dated, and fewer still relate directly to his personal life, his work gives no clue as to what he felt during this period of inaction and obscurity.

So the year 1535 passed uneventfully. In 1536 a single piece of good fortune and a series of disasters came to the Howard family. In March Surrey's eldest son Thomas, afterwards fourth Duke of Norfolk, was born. In May the Queen, accused of adultery with four men and of incest with her brother, Lord Rochford, stood her trial in the great hall of the Tower. Norfolk presided as Lord High Steward; Surrey sat below him as Earl Marshal, his gold staff of office in his hand. On one side of him was Suffolk, on the other the Chancellor, Lord Audley. When Anne had been brought to the bar a chair was set for her and her indictment was read out. 'Where-unto', says one who was present, 'she made so wise and discreet answers to all things laid against her, excusing herself with her words so clearly, as though she had never been guilty to the same.' The verdict was unanimous. Surrey, as the youngest of the peers – he was nineteen – spoke first, laying his hand upon his breast and saying, 'Guilty, upon my honour.' Then Norfolk rose and addressed his niece. 'Because thou hast offended our Sovereign Lord the King's Grace in committing treason against his person, and here attainted of the same, the law of the realm is this, that thou hast deserved death. And thy judgment is this, that thou shalt be burnt here, within the Tower of London at the Green, [or] else to have thy head smitten off, as the King's pleasure shall be further known of the same.'[10]

The Queen, who had had several attacks of hysteria during her imprisonment, showed no emotion. She stood up, curtsied to the peers and was taken away. Four days later Surrey and Richmond were present at her execution. They did not attend the marriage of Henry and Jane Seymour which was privately performed during the same week. This connection was another setback to the Howard fortunes; the Seymours, recently ennobled (Jane's brother Edward was later created Earl of Hertford) leaned towards Protestantism, although at this time they still called themselves Catholics; they supported the reforming, anti-Spanish faction within the Court.

Hertford, a handsome, hard-working and accomplished courtier, was a dangerous rival. Surrey, resentful of the ease with which he had gained power and favour and contemptuous of what he later described as the new Earl's 'mean' origins (those of a country squire), took a dislike to him that he did not trouble to conceal. Norfolk was far too cunning to show his jealous hatred of the King's ambitious young brother-in-law.

A month after Henry's third marriage Surrey's uncle, Lord Thomas Howard, was imprisoned for secretly marrying the King's niece, Lady Margaret Douglas, the half-sister of James V. Within a few hours of Lord Thomas's arrest his bride followed him into the Tower, and there they remained until 1537, when he died and she was released.

In the first week of July the King and his new Queen, Surrey, Richmond and all the Court attended the triple marriage of Surrey's brother-in-law Lord John de Vere with Lady Dorothy Neville, of Lord Neville with Lady Anne Roos, and of Lord Roos with Lady Margaret Neville, in Shoreditch. Surrey escorted Lady Anne from the church after the ceremony.[11] The prolonged and splendid festivities, during which Henry took the opportunity to appear in a masque disguised as a Turk, were followed, three weeks later, by Richmond's death at St James's Palace. The news reached Surrey at Kenninghall, and he fell ill from grief. From this, the heaviest blow of all, he seems to have taken years to recover. The widowed Mary, who had never lived with her husband, joined him and her father, and a few weeks later they went to Thetford for the funeral. Henry had given instructions that Surrey should receive his friend's favourite horse, a black jennet, with the black velvet saddle and harness that had been made for the ceremony.[12] They then returned to Kenninghall, where Surrey abandoned himself to despair.

The Duchess of Norfolk's fury burst out again when she heard that Bess Holland had been established with her husband, her elder son and her daughter, and was ruling the household. Her complaints were ignored. Norfolk, having cemented his alliance, through his daughter-in-law, with the patrician families of Neville, Roos and de Vere, was now busy with a scheme for making a common front against the influence of the Seymours, of which Surrey was to be the figurehead; he stopped his ears to these echoes from the past. The Duchess therefore began to meditate a comprehensive and terrible revenge.

NOTES TO CHAPTER FOUR

[1] Hall, *Chronicle*, pp. 790-2.
[2] Cavendish, p. 245.
[3] Hall, p. 790.
[4] Ibid., p. 792.
[5] Casady, *Henry Howard, Earl of Surrey*, p. 57.
[6] Cal. D.S.P., vol. XIV, pt. I, p. 260.
[7] Ibid., pt. II, p. 200.
[8] Ibid.
[9] Ibid., pt. I, p. 160.
[10] Friedmann, vol. II, p. 201.
[11] Wriothesley, *Journal*, vol. I, p. 50.
[12] Ibid., p. 53.

CHAPTER FIVE

UNTIL he was twenty-one Surrey's career followed the lines ordained by his father, and was determined by the variations in Norfolk's social and political eminence. In the spring of 1537 he began to break out, not very creditably, from the mould of the dutiful and promising heir. This was partly because he became the subject of disagreement between the Duke and Henry VIII during the most serious rebellion of the reign, and partly because the preceding year of country life which had been darkened by Richmond's death and marred by family quarrels drove him into a studious and contemplative habit that did not suit his temperament.

Between 1535 and 1536 Surrey had leisure to produce his most important but not his best work, the translation of the Fourth and Eighth Books of the *Aeneid* into blank verse – the first blank verse written in English, and described as 'a strange metre' by the printer of the original edition. The expert view of these pieces is that they are stiff and inadequate, as poetry, and as translations; their importance in the history of our literature cannot of course be overrated. The spirit that evolved them was that of a daring and brilliant pioneer, who is now seen as ranking much higher than a student and a little lower than the forerunner acclaimed, imitated and outstripped by the Elizabethans. In these translations Surrey comes out better as a recorder of horror and bloodshed than as a rhetorician; this is the only reason for placing them in his early period: his adaptations from Petrarch are smoother and more pleasing. He deals adequately, though not in an inspired manner, with the passage in the Fourth Book that has become proverbial, when Laocoon, 'crying far off' to warn the Trojans against a too trusting acceptance of the wooden horse, exclaims —

> ' ... O wretched citizens!
> What so great kind of frenzy fretteth you?
> Deem ye the Greeks our enemies to be gone?
> Or any Greekish gifts can you suppose
> Devoid of guile? Is so Ulysses known?
> Either the Greeks are in this timber hid,
> Or this an engine to annoy our walls,
> To view our towers and overwhelm our town.
> Here lurks some craft. Good Troyans, give no trust
> Unto this horse, for whatsoever it be,
> I dread the Greeks — yea, when they offer gifts!'

'And but for Fates,' the translator goes on, 'and for our blind forecast, the Greeks' device and guile had he descried; Troy had yet stood, and Priam's towers so high.'

We may look on from this, Surrey's introduction of the unrhymed decasyllabic line, which was to prove the chief glory of English poetry, to the moment some thirty years later, when Christopher Marlowe and Thomas Nashe composed *The Tragedy of Dido*, published in 1594. Shakespeare seems to be paying homage to it when Hamlet speaks of 'an excellent play, well digested in the scenes, set down with as much modesty as cunning, which pleased not the million, but was caviare to the general'. A year or so later Shakespeare himself tried his hand at the 'tale of Troy divine'; and in the closing passages of *Troilus and Cressida*, which have a Virgilian quality, we can recall with gratitude Surrey's epoch-making innovation:

> 'Hector is gone:
> Who shall tell Priam so, or Hecuba?
> Let him that will a screech-owl aye be called
> Go in to Troy, and say there Hector's dead:
> There is a word will Priam turn to stone,
> Make wells and Niobes of the maids and wives,
> Cold statues of the youth; and, in a word,

Scare Troy out of itself. But march away:
Hector is dead; there is no more to say.'

From the rest of Surrey's poetry a few personal sidelights (as
opposed to autobiographical inspirations) can be discerned. Imagination and conjecture are tactless and dangerous guides; but here we
may so far trust them as to perceive in the opening 'Wrapt in my
careless cloak, as I walk to and fro – ' the impetuous movements of
a highly strung, hasty young man; and there is a similar glimpse in
the first lines of a Troubadourist sonnet, where he describes a lady
concealing her golden hair beneath her headdress, just as she with-
draws her 'smiling looks' from himself. 'I never saw you, Madam,
lay apart Your cornet black in cold, nor yet in heat – ' it begins; in
the quick, informal phrase Surrey's way of starting a conversation
can be faintly heard. In a studied and elegant pastoral poem he shows
a shepherd dying for love; and suddenly, again, he himself seems to
dash out of its stylized setting. 'Had been my heart of flint,' he says,
'it must have melted ... With tears I rashly to him ran, and in my
arms I caught him fast – '; but the afflicted lover 'cast on me a staring
look, with colour pale and dead – ' and fell to the ground. So
Surrey must have seen men die in battle. Lastly, in a poem already
quoted, on the Seven Ages of Man, Surrey recalls lying in bed sick
of the ague from which he often suffered, and thinking, 'The young
man, eke, that feels his bones with pains oppressed, How he would
be a rich old man, to live and lie at rest.' An oddly personal touch
and a paradoxical situation appear – why should the elder son of the
richest noble in England desire wealth, at the price of age, unless he
were desperately short of money?

In fact, a febrile impatience runs through much of Surrey's work;
the impression given is that he was incapable of putting up with the
minor setbacks and disappointments that most people learn to
accept early in life.

To such a young man leadership and responsibility, as much as
action in the field, are imperative. Surrey's chance came when
the Lincolnshire risings began in October 1536 and, spreading
to Yorkshire, became known as the Pilgrimage of Grace. His

eagerness to share in his father's command against the rebels was not ignored: nor was it assuaged; and this was due to the anomalies of Norfolk's position.

The grievances of the country people, to some extent shared by the local gentlemen and nobles, were set out in a proclamation issued at Horncastle in the first week of October. Henry VIII was asked to grant the remission of the land tax of 1534, the removal of the 'mean men' (Cromwell and Cranmer) from the Privy Council and the restoration of the monasteries. The last was the most important item, for the visitation of the houses and the redistribution of the abbey lands had been effected, in the northern districts at least, by corrupt and insolent officials, and the resultant distress was deeply felt and resented in all classes. For these abuses Cromwell rather than Henry was blamed. The King made it clear that he and Parliament were responsible for the new administration, in a reply that was a characteristic blend of scolding and paternalism. 'I have never heard, read nor known,' he declared, 'that princes' councillors and prelates should be appointed by rude, ignorant and common people. How presumptuous then, are ye, the rude commons of one shire, and that the most brute and beastly of the whole realm, and of least experience, to take upon you, contrary to God's law and to man's law, to rule your prince, whom ye are bound to obey and serve, and for no worldly cause to withstand.' He then pointed out that the suppression of the monasteries had been consented to and agreed on by the people's representatives, 'and not set forth by any councillor or councillors by their mere will and fantasy, as ye falsely would persuade our realm to believe ... There be none houses suppressed where God was well served, but where most vice, mischief and abomination of living was used ... Think ye that we be so faint-hearted that perforce ye would compel us ... to remit [the tax]? ... How unkindly and how untruly ye deal now with us! ... Remember your follies and traitorous demeanour, and shame not your native country ... Withdraw yourselves to your own houses, every man ... for doubt ye not else that we will not suffer this injury at your hands unrevenged; and we pray unto Almighty God to give you grace to do your duties ... rather than ... by your obstinacy and wilfulness to put yourselves, lives, wives, children, lands, goods and chattels ... in the utter adventure of total destruction.'¹

By the time the rebellion had spread over Yorkshire some 30,000 men were in arms against the state. Henry, who had already sent the Duke of Suffolk to meet them in Lincolnshire with a token force, all he could then raise, now called on Norfolk, his best general, whose name would bring awe and terror to the insurgents, to support Suffolk with his own East Anglian troops. Henry did not trust Norfolk; he had known him intimately for more than twenty years. The Duke was looked on by the whole country as the head of the ancient nobility and the most powerful representative of the régime that Henry and Cromwell had destroyed. If the rebels conquered the royalist forces — and at one point it looked as if they might well do so — their leaders would appeal to Norfolk to come over to them and reinstate the old order, and Norfolk knew this; if he accepted, the position of a dictator would be within his grasp: and from that position to the overthrow of the dynasty would be but one step. This, it seems, was what the King and Cromwell believed, and with some reason. Surrey, therefore, became, from their point of view, one of the most important actors in the drama.

On October 15th, 1536, Norfolk, who with Surrey was mustering his men in East Anglia, was desired by Henry to send the young man to Cambridge to collect more recruits, while he himself was to come to Windsor for his orders before going north. When he reached Cambridge Surrey was told to open any letters that arrived for the Duke; so the son was set to spy upon the father, on the old principle of dividing and conquering before taking any further action. When the Lincolnshire risings were subdued Surrey reported to Norfolk in a frenzy of impatience — what was he to do? If he did not soon advance northwards, his men would desert. He had not enough uniforms; he himself had ordered and paid for 1,500 leather jerkins without consulting the Privy Council. 'Judged by those here', he wrote triumphantly, 'who have seen many musters, [they are] the finest ever raised on state warrant.' He burned to set off; at last he did so, without waiting for permission. On his way to join his father, who had got as far as Welbeck, he heard and applauded a song against the Duke of Suffolk; this was reported to the rebels, some of whom began to say that he might be persuaded to change sides. On October 26th he and Norfolk arrived at Doncaster.[2]

By this time two leaders of the Pilgrimage had emerged from the turmoil of conflicting loyalties and turncoat intrigue — Lord Darcy, a nobleman in his seventies, and Robert Aske, a young lawyer practising at Westminster, who had returned to his father's manor in the West Riding for the summer vacation and had been swept into the movement almost, as he afterwards declared, against his will. The motives of both men were of the highest order; but politically, Darcy counted as a traitor, for he was so anxious to restore the old faith that he had been in touch with the exiled Cardinal Pole (one of Henry's Plantagenet cousins) and through him with Charles V, who at one moment had considered sending over an army to help the Pilgrims. In fact, Darcy was so torn between his loyalty to the crown and that to his religion, that he did not decide which side to take till the rebellion reached Pontefract Castle, which he was supposed to be defending for the King.

On October 26th 3,000 men and six pieces of field artillery were sent after Norfolk from London, and next day he held his first conference with the rebels at Doncaster. A truce was arranged. It suited Norfolk, who had fewer troops at his command than Darcy and Aske, to represent his situation as desperate, or nearly so — this was what he wrote to Henry — and to act as mediator between the Pilgrims and the King, thus playing for time. He was ordered to report to Windsor, and, leaving Surrey in Yorkshire, he arrived there on November 2nd with the statement of the rebels' terms. Henry was furious at what he regarded as a combination of treachery and insolence; but for once he was at a disadvantage, and had to agree to discuss the Pilgrims' demands. Norfolk returned with Henry's secret instructions and his public reply to the rebels on December 6th. As the negotiations wound on their slow course, with Norfolk acting as a go-between who might at any moment change sides, the Pilgrims' forces began to melt away. There was no fighting, and Surrey was given nothing to do but watch his father's manœuvres and sit silent during the conferences; finally he was sent back to Kenninghall.[3]

During the first months of 1537 Henry managed to collect enough men to dictate terms. At this point Cromwell's spies reported that Norfolk had sent for Surrey and was instructing him in the business of administration, so that he might be ready to take his place as ruler in the north, in the event of his father being sent elsewhere. Norfolk found it necessary to excuse himself. He had sent for Surrey to be near him, he wrote, 'partly because in truth I love him better than all my children, and would gladly have had him here to hunt, shoot, play cards and entertain my servants, so that they should be less desirous of leave to go home to their wives.' Henry replied amiably, but pointed out that Norfolk should have asked leave before sending for Surrey. Norfolk answered the implied reproach in his most pathetic strain. 'I trust the sending for me [to the north]', he wrote, 'is meant to good purpose, and if it chance to me to miscarry, most noble and gracious master, be good to my sons and my poor daughter.' Henry replied, 'We would you should perfectly know that if God should take you out of this transitory life before us, we should not fail to remember your children, being your lively images ... ' His orders for Surrey were, however, irrevocable. The Earl was to return once more to Kenninghall. The troops he had trained and equipped were to remain under his father's command.[4]

So there he was, back in the great palace, with his four hundred servants, in the familiar treadmill of getting up, going to Mass, dining, hunting, supping, giving orders, as if nothing had happened since he was a child, except that his wife and son were with him. It is not surprising that he at once fell ill, of what, or how seriously, is unknown. Sick at heart and powerless, he remained forgotten, while the rebellion reached its tragic and ignominious end.

In the spring of 1537 Henry consented to discuss the situation personally with Aske, on condition that all his followers laid down their arms. Aske went to London, and was well received by his inscrutable enemy and master. He returned to Yorkshire to find that, contrary to his orders, his side of the bargain had not been kept; Henry had guessed that this would happen, and that sporadic risings would continue. Aske and Darcy were now in the position of having, technically, at least, broken their oath to the King, with the result that Aske was executed at York and Darcy on Tower Hill; a few weeks later Norfolk was commanded to institute a reign of terror throughout the north. During one of Darcy's examinations by the Privy Council, he had accused Norfolk and Surrey of having been in sympathy with the Pilgrims and of having played a double game. Such evidence, from such a man, must carry weight, historically. Darcy had made no efforts to save his own life, and had nothing to gain by this declaration; of course he did not differentiate between the duplicity of the father and the victimization of the son.

Henry chose to ignore Darcy's statement. Norfolk had done, and was doing, what was required of him; the holocaust in the north would destroy his popularity with that section of the Catholic party. There were two hundred and sixteen executions, all of which Norfolk attended personally, reporting on the massacre of his fellow-Catholics with cynical disparagement of their useless sacrifice.

Meanwhile life at Kenninghall became almost as turbulent as if the Duke and Duchess had been in residence. Surrey took exception to Bess Holland's presence – she was not, after all, a fit companion for his wife – and quarrelled with Mary, whom he blamed for tolerating his father's mistress. The brother and sister then began a dispute about Mary's tendency towards Protestantism. Neither was pious: but Surrey regarded Mary's deviation as a breach of honour, and she resented his interference. The result was that he left Kenninghall for one of the family estates near Norwich, where he intended to build a mansion of his own, as soon as he could raise the money.[5]

In June 1537 Surrey joined the Court at Hampton Court Palace, presumably in a mood of the bitterest resentment that was intensified by the presence of Hertford and the realization of his increasing influence and power. There, for the first time, Surrey heard all the gossip about the aftermath of the rebellion. One day, in the park, he and Hertford began to argue – what about, is not known. Hertford repeated Darcy's accusation. It was the final outrage. Surrey struck him in the face. As the scene had taken place 'within the precincts',

Surrey was arrested. The punishment for an action of this kind was the loss of the offender's right arm.[6]

After interviewing Surrey, the Privy Council referred the matter to the King, and Surrey had time to think over the Act for 'malicious bloodshed within the Court', for which the 'sergeant-surgeon with his instruments' was called; then, 'the sergeant of the woodyard with a mallet and block whereupon the hand should lie; the master-cook for the King, with his knife; the sergeant of the larder, to set the knife right on the joint; the sergeant-farrier, to sear the veins ... the yeoman of the chandry, with sear-cloths; the yeoman of the scullery, with a pan of fire to heat the irons, a chafer of water to cool the irons, and two forms for all officers to set their stuff on: the sergeant of the cellar, with wine, ale and beer; the yeoman of the cellar ... with basin, ewer and towels'.[7] Meanwhile Norfolk was writing to Cromwell to plead for his son.

There was in fact no question of Henry allowing his dead boy's friend to be maimed, or even fined. He gave orders that Surrey was to be imprisoned in Windsor Castle at his pleasure, and there the culprit remained for a few weeks before rejoining his family at Shottisham near Norwich. He was allowed the freedom of the terraces and walks, but not that of the grounds. Windsor was full of memories of his life with Richmond; he recalled those happy times, not only in the detailed poem already quoted, but in a shorter piece, beginning, 'When Windsor walls sustained my wearied arm, My hand my chin, to ease my restless head ... The heavy charge of care,' he goes on, 'Heaped in my breast, breaks forth, against my will, In smoky sighs that overcast the air ... ' The longer poem concludes with an outburst of grief. 'Give me account, where is my noble fere [comrade] Whom in thy walls thou didst each night enclose?'

It is noticeable that none of these verses contains a single reference to religion or to eternal life. Surrey's deeper feelings and thoughts were generally confined to the present; occasionally the immediate past inspired him, as in a sonnet also written at this time, where he recalls his Fair Geraldine, whom he describes as 'bright of hue' (she had red hair) when he first saw her at Hunsdon.

The Duchess of Norfolk took no interest in her son's misfortunes, for she was now engaged on a new series of complaints to Cromwell, in which cringing, virulence and self-dramatization were characteristically blended. She would never, in any circumstances, go back to her husband: she was short of money, as usual. Norfolk was a gambler, as well as a lecher; also, he had broken up her marriage with the Earl of Westmoreland. (There is no record of this alliance ever having been considered.) He had had many other mistresses besides Bess Holland. Why had her daughter never received her dowry? The late Queen had promised Mary £1,000 a year if Richmond died. She herself continued 'poor and ailing' but — 'though my children be unkind unto me, I have always love unto them ... ' As for Norfolk, she would never trust him, although 'he can speak fair, as well to his enemy as to his friend ... He is so doting in love with that quean that he neither regardeth God nor his honour.'[8]

With a view to pacifying the Duchess the King began to consider arranging a second marriage for her daughter; it was at this point that Norfolk seems to have altered his plans for maintaining and increasing his own power, which had sunk perceptibly with the imprisonment of Lord William Howard and the execution of Queen Anne. The Neville—Roos—de Vere alliances, although useful, had done nothing to strengthen his position. The fact had to be faced that the Protestant party, headed by the Seymours, Cranmer and above all, Cromwell, were, under the King, in control of the political machine. The Seymour prestige had been further heightened by the defeat of the Pilgrims and by Queen Jane's pregnancy; if her child was a son, her family would become unassailable, and Norfolk believed that they would use any means to disgrace him, should the occasion arise. Indeed it may have been that Hertford had provoked Surrey deliberately, with the intention of forcing on the degradation of the Howards.

These were the liabilities. Norfolk's assets were Henry's affection for Surrey, his own long service, high position, great wealth and his qualifications as a general and an administrator; he was still indispensable to the King. He therefore decided to compromise (if only for a time) by allying himself with his rivals. He took no steps until, in October 1537, Jane Seymour gave birth to the boy who was to succeed as Edward VI. The Seymour influence was in no way diminished by her death twelve days later, for it was now clear that Henry would not live to see his son grow up, and was beginning more than ever to rely on Hertford who, with Cromwell, remained in the ascendant, and would probably become Regent during Edward's minority.

Norfolk therefore set about a marriage between his daughter and Hertford's younger brother, Sir Thomas Seymour, although he could not bring himself to show great personal enthusiasm for the alliance. Mary, when told of it, merely stipulated that her dowry from Richmond's estate should be paid first. She detested life at Kenninghall, and wanted to rejoin the Court. When the plague broke out in East Anglia she began to 'cry and wail' to her father, begging him to take her away.[9]

Having approached the King through Cromwell, Norfolk asked leave to proceed. Henry gave it, adding jocosely that Sir Thomas was a person 'of lust and youth, and able to satisfy her on all points', and Hertford declared himself ready to co-operate.

Then Surrey was told what was going forward. He at once went to Kenninghall, and made a scene with Mary, and with his father. An alliance with the family of the low-born, pushing upstart who had insulted him was out of the question. 'These new men love no nobility,' he warned his sister. 'If God called away the King, they shall smart for it. I hate them all,' he added fiercely. Norfolk tried to reason with his son; he himself, he said, was perfectly indifferent to the Seymours' ill-will.[10] Surrey was not self-confident enough to take this attitude; he remained obdurate. How he prevented his sister's marriage to Seymour is not known; but he did prevent it. His opposition infuriated her — Thomas Seymour was an attractive, gay young man, and she may well have taken a fancy to him — with the result that their former disagreements about Bess Holland and Mary's Protestantism helped to create a permanent feud. This finally resolved itself, on her side, into a violent and revengeful hatred. She never forgave Surrey his interference. Now his only supporter within the family circle was his father; his brother

Thomas's character was negligible, and he had no capacity for religious or political intrigue.

Surrey had made himself felt, at last; that it was to his own detriment probably did not occur to him. With the birth of his second son, Henry, and his return to Court in the spring of 1538, he was re-established, but still, from his point of view, unimportant politically – a courtier who carried no weight and whose opinion was not consulted.

NOTES TO CHAPTER FIVE

[1] Dodds, *The Pilgrimage of Grace*, vol. I, p. 100.
[2] Ibid., p. 200.
[3] Ibid., p. 250.
[4] Ibid., p. 231.
[5] Blomefield, *History of Norfolk*, vol. I, p. 289.
[6] Bapst, *Deux Gentilhommes-poètes de la Cour d'Henri VIII*, pp. 227-32.
[7] Hall, p. 801.
[8] Brenan and Statham, vol. I, p. 220.
[9] Ibid., p. 229.
[10] Ibid., p. 237.

CHAPTER SIX

In the summer of 1538 Surrey left the Court for Kenninghall. He now ceased to live at Shottisham; one reason for this was lack of money, another, health. At Kenninghall he could entertain at his father's expense and recuperate from what seems to have been either dysentery or malaria. Norfolk commented on his son's state in a letter to Cromwell, but gave no clue as to how ill he really was, merely adding, 'He was in that case a great part of last year, which came to him for thought of my lord of Richmond.' The Duke's next letter provides a more cheerful picture. Surrey had recovered, and Kenninghall was full of his friends and their retainers. Norfolk's expenses over the rebellion had been very great, and he was trying to put his affairs in order; he did not take at all kindly to Surrey's way of life. 'He doth not only cause many to resort to him at my charge', he complained, 'but doth also cause my deer not to be spared.'[1]

So Surrey alternated between the life of a country gentleman and that of a courtier until the spring of 1539, when the alliance of Spain, Scotland and France made it necessary to prepare for invasion from these countries. At last he was given the kind of work which he longed for and did well – the fortification of the Norfolk coast and the training of the local troops. He was busy with these plans until June; then he had to go to London to attend a memorial service for the Empress Isabella of Spain in St Paul's. Dressed in robes and hoods of black and preceded by their respective heralds, Surrey and a selected group of courtiers represented the King at a requiem Mass and had a buffet supper in the Lady Chapel.[2] He was on the point of departure for Norfolk when he heard that one of his relatives was guilty of the offence for which he himself had been imprisoned at Windsor. A relative of his mother's, Sir Edmund Knevett, had struck one of Surrey's Irish cousins, Thomas Cleere, within the precincts of Greenwich Palace during a dispute between Knevett and another Howard cousin, Sir Richard Southwell.

Lenient treatment of a man of Knevett's standing did not arise. He was condemned to lose his right hand. Surrey pleaded with the Privy Council to interview Knevett again and hear a suggestion he had to make. The King's affection for Surrey made it impossible for the Council to refuse, and Knevett was allowed to appear. (Surrey, it seems, was sensible enough not to accompany him.) Knevett knelt and said that he humbly accepted his punishment — but would their lordships consent to alter the sentence to the loss of his left hand, so that he might continue to serve His Majesty with his right? The result of a speech that had no doubt been planned and rehearsed by Surrey was the substitution of a fine and imprisonment for mutilation. Surrey was much attached to both Knevett and Cleere; their enmity was soon forgotten in their devotion to him.[3]

Although the danger of invasion from Scotland and the continent seemed now to diminish, it was still necessary to strengthen Henry's defences politically, and Cromwell's plan was to do so through a marriage with a bride from one of the states most likely to support England against the Emperor. At first it was hoped that Henry might drive a wedge between Francis and Charles by allying himself with a French princess, and he discussed his choice with Castillon, Francis's ambassador. The King's highly unconventional notion of meeting the lady before signing anything so shocked the envoy that he ventured a courteous reproof. It would not be honourable, he said, to trot out a series of gentlewomen for inspection as if they were so many hackneys. 'By God!' said Henry, 'I trust no one but myself. The thing touches me too near.' Castillon replied, *'Ne voudriez-vous point, Sire, encore monter sur toutes, l'une après l'autre, et après retenir pour votre personne celle qui irait le plus doux?'* Henry turned scarlet at this coarse rhetoric: then he laughed, and apologized for his odd suggestion; Castillon was able to boast to his master of his own boldness and wit.[4]

Henry might pass off a snub; he never forgot one. The result of this conversation was, that after many delays and hesitations, he fell in with Cromwell's plan for a marriage with the sister of the Duke of Cleves. And now at last Norfolk perceived his opportunity for the ruin of his greatest and most detested rival.

As the negotiations proceeded, doubts began to filter through about the suitability of the Lady Anne of Cleves as a companion for an accomplished and fastidious intellectual, the potentate of a brilliant Court, who spoke and read five languages, played four instruments, and whose principal recreation was the composition of songs and Masses to which he sometimes set his own words. Beauty was not essential if the bride were charming, witty and adaptable, or an expert musician or even a card-player. Rumour came back that the Princess spoke no tongue but her own, and that like most of her countrywomen she preferred needlework to reading, music and games. By this time the alliance had gone so far forward that something in her favour had to be produced; if her looks were only pleasing, that would suffice. On this point the reports so varied that a portrait was commissioned, Hans Holbein did his best – his worst, from Henry's point of view – and the picture of a handsome brunette arrived.

Norfolk was in touch with those who, having seen the sitter, dared not cross Cromwell nor disillusion the King. The moment had come for him to join in pressing on the marriage that might result in the minister's downfall. It was, of course, a gamble: but if Anne were as plain and dull as the resident envoys said she was, Cromwell, who alone was responsible for bringing her over, would receive the full weight of the bridegroom's displeasure.

In December 1539 she disembarked at Dover, where Surrey and a group of courtiers met her and escorted her to the Castle. Presently Henry arrived; and the effect on him was all and more than Norfolk could have desired. The King, appalled, protested ('Is there no remedy but I must needs against my will put my neck in the yoke?'), but it was too late.[5] To Anne he behaved well; she received his courtesies with placid indifference, and the wedding took place in January 1540, to the usual accompaniment of banquets, feasts, and a superb display of jousting, in which Surrey made a sensation. He was matched against one of the detested 'new men' — John Dudley, Viscount Lisle (son of a shady lawyer, executed nearly thirty years earlier) who had recently been created Governor of Calais. It was the kind of position that in pre-Tudor days could only have been given to a soldier of Surrey's breeding; and now Lisle crowned this odious triumph by appearing in the lists as if his new title put him on a level with the house of Howard.

Surrey's insolent bearing and fierce attack produced an answering rancour. Lisle also was an accomplished athlete, and an older, heavier expert in the art of tilting. At the first onset the clash was so violent that the mailed gloves of both combatants were shattered. This incident caused a great deal of talk. The chroniclers who were present or who heard of it from others recorded the scene in admiring wonder. During the momentary setback in which fresh gloves had to be provided, it seems as if Surrey and Lisle recollected that they were supposed to be part of an entertainment, and the match was formally concluded in seven courses.⁶ To Surrey, whose self-identification with the greatest Knight of the Round Table became part of his legend, the description of a more famous joust may have been recalled. 'And so Sir Lancelot or ever he stint, as fast he might get spears, he smote down thirty knights ... and ever the knights of his blood withdrew them, and made them ado in other places where Sir Lancelot came not. And then King Arthur was wroth when he saw Sir Lancelot do such deeds ... '

Henry VIII however was well pleased; such displays delighted him. Surrey's prestige was immensely heightened, and it looked as if he might at last obtain a post in which he would be able to use his energy and his gifts. If the Emperor or Francis I had invaded, he would have been given a command; but the strength of the English defences discouraged them, and they did not take the risk of a defeat. Their alliance weakened, then gradually dissolved; by the spring of 1540 it became clear to Henry that in marrying Anne of Cleves he had sacrificed his personal happiness for nothing — and for this Cromwell was to blame.

It was expected that Cromwell would be disgraced within a week or two of this discovery; in April Henry, inscrutable as ever, created him Earl of Essex, and their relationship appeared unchanged. Surrey must have found this time of waiting intolerable, for his hatred of Cromwell was as bitter as his father's; yet he seems not to have interfered with the Duke's machinations or to have subscribed to the evidence that Norfolk and his allies had been collecting for years, in order to convict Cromwell of high treason on the grounds of peculation and conspiracy against the royal power.

Just before the Council meeting of June 10th, 1540, Henry told Norfolk to proceed. In the early afternoon the Duke got up from the long table littered with papers and said, 'My lord of Essex, I arrest you of high treason.' Witnesses were then summoned to produce the main charges, followed by the Lieutenant of the Tower with the warrant for Cromwell's arrest. Snatching his cap from his head and throwing it on the floor, Cromwell burst into a passionate arraignment of his master's ingratitude.

Norfolk's moment of triumph had come. He went up to Cromwell and said, 'You are a traitor.' Then he tore the George from the minister's neck and trampled it underfoot. Another nobleman stripped him of his Garter. Cromwell began to struggle and protest. 'You shall be judged,' Norfolk shouted, 'by the bloody laws you yourself have made.' The Lieutenant of the Tower intervened, and Cromwell was removed. Surrey held back his epitaph until the execution had taken place. 'Now is that foul churl dead – so ambitious of others' blood,' he said. 'Now is he stricken with his own staff.'[7]

The next step was the divorce of Anne of Cleves, for which an embassy had to be sent to her brother to discuss terms. A rumour began that Surrey might go with it, and continued to circulate. George Constantine, formerly one of Cromwell's agents, said to Dean Barlow of Westbury, 'If there should be any pledges sent into Cleves, in good faith I would the Earl of Surrey should be one of them.' Barlow scoffed at the idea; his comment shows what sort of reputation Surrey had made for himself. 'It is the most foolish proud boy that is in England,' he said. Constantine was rather taken aback. 'What, man, he hath a wife and child, and call you him boy?'

'By God's mercy, methinks he exceedeth,' Barlow replied. 'What, then?' Constantine persisted, 'He is wise for all that, as I hear. As for pride, experience will correct that well enough. No marvel though a young man, so noble a man's son and heir apparent, be proud, for we be too proud ourselves without those qualities.' He added that if the Duke were in favour of the Reformation, 'he should do much good — for he is an earnest man, a bold man, and witty, in all his matters.' 'It is true, and ye say well in all that,' Barlow agreed.[8]

Constantine reported this conversation to the Privy Council, who had no intention of sending Surrey to Cleves or on any other mission of importance. So he continued to move rather aimlessly between Kenninghall and the Court, while the divorce proceeded, followed by the establishment of Anne of Cleves as 'fourth Lady of England'. She remained high in Henry's favour for the rest of his life, and visited him regularly.

Norfolk now began to look about for a fifth Queen among his younger relatives; his eye fell on another niece, the seventeen-year-old Katherine Howard, whom he produced at a banquet and a ball given by Bishop Gardiner and himself a few weeks before Cromwell's execution. It seems as if on this, or on some similar occasion, he took the opportunity to smooth over hostilities by inviting several members of the Seymour family; for, at about this time, a strange scene took place, described in one of Surrey's poems and entitled by his first editor, *Of A Lady That Refused To Dance With Him.*

By mingling allegory, personalities, rhetoric and narrative, Surrey, it seems purposely, has so veiled the real circumstances of this incident that they cannot be defined. As conjecture must therefore lead into romanticized interpretation, thus further confusing the issue, it is best to outline the story of the poem, which consists of thirty-eight rhyming couplets. Every beast, the author begins, has the right to choose his companion according to his nature. A short time ago he saw a white lion, gentle, noble and commanding, look for a mate; the lion came upon a white wolf, a beautiful but forbidding creature, before whom he bowed 'in humble wise'. Turning aside, she rejected him 'with spite and great disdain'. ' "Lion," she said, "If thou hadst known my mind before, Thou hadst not spent thy travail thus, nor all thy pain forbore." ' She then ordered him out of her way, refused to 'play' with him and told him to seek another companion. The lion 'beat his tail, his eyes began to flame. I might perceive his noble heart much movèd by the same.' He waited till his first rage had died down before answering. Then he embarked on a speech of reproach, defiance and abuse that occupies the second half of the poem. The wolf-lady is told about the great deeds of the lion's race and the advantages of the friendship she has so rudely thrown away; the contrast between her disagreeable attitude and the lion's kind and forgiving nature is emphasized; then, suddenly, the beast allegory is abandoned, and the poet speaks as a man to a woman. 'Wherefore I would you wist that for your coy looks, I am no man that will be trained, nor tangled by such hooks ... I will observe the law that nature gave to me, To conquer such as will resist, and let the rest go free ... While that I live and breathe, such shall my custom be.' Surrey then tells her that this cruel treatment will result in his revenging his hurt pride on those who have done him little or no wrong. 'I vow and swear thereto, A thousand spoils I shall commit I never thought to do. And if to light on you, my luck so good shall be. I shall be glad to feed on that that would have fed on me ... ' He himself, he adds, has now nothing to fear from her, because 'a lion's heart is for a wolf no prey.' Though he has brought on this rebuff through his own weakness, he no longer cares what she says or does.

Such an explosion of anger and pride can hardly be forced into the mould of Courtly Love or Troubadourism. That the poem records a personal experience is obvious, partly because of its manner, and partly because the cognizance of the Howards was a white lion. The majority of editors and commentators have identified the wolf-lady with Anne Stanhope, Countess of Hertford (with whose husband Surrey had already quarrelled, and who was renowned for her beauty and the hauteur of her address) because the Stanhope emblem was a wolf; it may be added that the country seat of the Seymours was called Wolf Hall. One of the historical references in the white lion's speech is to a former lion, 'of the race, That with his paws a crownèd king devourèd in the place' — i.e. to Surrey's grandfather, who defeated James IV at Flodden. The other family allusion is to Lord William Howard, who had just died in the Tower (it was supposed of a broken heart) during his imprisonment after his secret marriage with the Lady Margaret Douglas. 'It is not long ago,' Surrey reminds us, 'Sith that, for love, one of the race did end his life in woe, In tower both strong and high, for his assurèd truth, Whereas in tears he spent his breath, alas! the more the ruth. This gentle beast so died, whom nothing could remove, But willingly to lose his life for loss of his true love.'

The general effect of this very odd and rather immature poem is so intense and violent that to look on it as an exercise in fancy or technique is as absurd as to pin down the action to a ballroom quarrel in which Surrey and Lady Hertford are given the leading parts. There were other Seymour and Stanhope ladies who might have snubbed him, though none who was celebrated for being 'fierce and froward' as well as beautiful, and none so likely to have started away from him 'a foot or twain'. Lady Hertford constantly made scenes in public, and she was spitefully unforgiving. ('You your friends do threaten still with war ... You slay that seeks to you ... You kill where you subdue.') The word 'dance' is mentioned only in the title — evolved some fifteen years after the event — and never in the poem, although the phrase 'Thou shalt not play with me' might be thus construed.

The biographical value of the piece lies in the revelation of Surrey's temperament and in its glimpses of sixteenth-century Court life. To set it beside Dean Barlow's summing up of his character is to see 'the foolish proud boy' making an advance with the grave, high-bred courtesy for which he was noted, and throwing off his rejection with the almost maniacal fury that had earned him the reputation of a fire-eater long before he disgraced himself in other ways.

At this point in Surrey's career the inherited blend of his father's cold yet savage ruthlessness and his mother's hysterical tendencies may have fused, just when he himself had no serious work on which his bursting energy and corrosive ambitions could be expended. The picture is not pleasing, judged by contemporary or any other standards; it points to the conclusion that Surrey was a tragic rather than an appealing character — tragic, not because he eventually had to pay an unfairly high price for his own folly, but because he was misled by the flatteries of his father's hangers-on and by the King's indulgence into thinking that he could defy all the standards and escape most of the consequences.

Indeed, the standards of the Court of Henry VIII would have been hard to define, even by those who, unlike Surrey, had frequented it all their lives. It provided a curious blend of elegance, vulgarity, culture and intrigue. Coarse brawling alternated with formal grace; degraded and childish squabbles about precedence and privilege went hand in hand with subtle and sensitive appreciation of theology and the arts; arrogance was superimposed on sycophancy; an abject humility might be combined with a frenzied touchiness, so that a minor slight was sometimes revenged by death, while the grossest insults were accepted with cynical indifference. It is impossible to imagine what the social atmosphere of such a circle could have been; the effect on a young man of Surrey's heredity and environment was wholly and consistently detrimental.

A more rapidly destructive process was brought to bear on the pretty little cousin whom his father manœuvred into the glare of Henry's favour during the summer of 1540. Katherine Howard's brief career is the supreme example of *quem deus vult perdere primum dementat*. Ignorant but not innocent, poverty-stricken yet luxury-loving, feather-headed, excitable and sensuous, she was the victimized ninny, the prepared sacrifice to Norfolk's frigid scheming and Henry's last great passion. The least prejudiced picture of her character and appearance is provided by the French envoy, Marillac, who succeeded Castillon just before Cromwell's execution. At this time Marillac became Norfolk's confidant, but not his dupe. A keener and more disillusioned observer than his predecessor, he submitted to the exercise of the Duke's personal charm, while seeing through it, during the eighteen months of the King's fifth marriage; his account of Katherine's triumph and downfall and of Norfolk's and Henry's attitude to both can be supplemented by two poems of Surrey's.

When Norfolk and Gardiner decided to use Katherine Howard to undermine the Seymour influence and destroy the Protestant party that, after Cromwell's execution, was headed by Cranmer and Hertford, they found her sufficiently docile and teachable for their purposes. Her part in the scheme was the subjugation of the King; and this was so quickly effected that they had every reason to congratulate themselves. Anne Boleyn's adulteries (they were almost certainly no more than indiscretions used to get rid of her) and Anne of Cleves's coarseness had prepared the way for a wife who need only be attractive, healthy and, above all, chaste. It seemed as if they could not have done better than to produce this orphaned and penniless girl, who had been adopted by Norfolk's stepmother, the Dowager-Duchess, and who had spent nearly all her life in a household renowned for its strictness and piety. The reputed atmosphere of Horsham St Faith's was that of a convent school; although Katherine probably never learnt to write, she had been taught music and dancing, had acquired a certain elegance, and was an orthodox Catholic. The fact that she and her companions had been left very much to themselves – especially in the evenings – and that Katherine, seduced at fourteen, had had two lovers before Norfolk brought her to Court, was of course quite unknown to the Dowager-Duchess, whose notions of discipline were arbitrary and conventional. If she found one of her gentlemen talking alone with a young lady she boxed the girl's ears, gave the man a rating and went back to her needlework or her prayers.[9]

When Katherine Howard became Queen of England and the idol of the ageing, diseased and careworn King, he found in her all the unspoilt gaiety and freshness of a child; she had nothing to do but cover herself with jewels, wear new dresses every day, chatter, dance and parade her graces in the intervals of being primed by Norfolk and Gardiner as to how best to restore the supremacy of the Howards. Marillac, describing her beauty as mediocre (she was a tiny, plump brunette with large light eyes), soon succumbed to her naive charm, while observing Henry's infatuation with sophisticated wonder; he also noted that Katherine was not able to place her relations as Norfolk wished. Surrey got nothing at all, at first; nor did her younger uncles, Lord Charles and another Lord William Howard, receive the diplomatic posts Norfolk had designed for them. Meanwhile the Duke continued to assure Marillac of his support of the French alliance; but, the envoy reported, '*il y avait grande dissimulation, et, sous les douces paroles, beaucoup de venin.*'[10]

At last, in April 1541, Katherine's influence so far prevailed as to obtain leave for Surrey to go with his father to quell a guerrilla war on the outskirts of Calais and Boulogne; it was his first experience of real fighting. With a force of fifteen hundred men they marched through the neighbourhood, burning and destroying where necessary. But even on this minor expedition it was not possible for Surrey to escape the hated Seymour predominance; he was accompanied by his sister's rejected *prétendant*, Sir Thomas, who, although dashing and fiery enough, could not take a serious attitude towards any responsibility; the rumour reached Henry that the two young men had gone abroad 'only for their pastime'.[11] This was galling indeed; but Surrey insisted on proceeding alone to Guisnes, where he inspected and studied the defences; then he was summoned back for the feast of St George on May 22nd at Windsor, where the King invested him with the Order of the Garter. With this, the grant of the Stewardship of Cambridge University and of some small monastic properties in Norfolk and Suffolk, he had to be content. In the autumn of this year he accompanied Henry and Katherine on their triumphant progress through the north, as did Marillac, for whom Surrey and a party of young noblemen gave a banquet in York. At the end of November they all returned to London.

By this time, the gossip of those who had been privy to the Queen's affairs at Horsham St Faith's had reached the Court circle. Further inquiries revealed the extent of her deceptions, and it was decided that the news must be broken to the King. At first he refused to believe a word of the story; when it was verified by the confessions of her lovers, of several witnesses and, finally, of Katherine herself, he broke down completely, calling for a sword to kill himself and her; then he rode off to Windsor, taking a few musicians with him, and without telling anyone where he was going.[12] When he was able to take action, he had to consider a divorce; then he was told, and again the news was verified beyond question, that Katherine had become the mistress of a young cousin since her marriage; during her stay in York they had spent some of the nights together; their go-between had been Lady Rochford, the sister-in-law of Anne Boleyn.

Norfolk's powers of deceit and self-control did not at once rise to meet this appalling blow, although he soon pulled himself together in order to describe his niece's 'lubricity' to Marillac with tearful horror. He and Cranmer interviewed Katherine who, between bouts of agonized hysteria, at first denied and then admitted her guilt. The Duke, whose behaviour at his other niece's examination had been studiously mild and judicious — he had confined himself to exclamations of 'Tut! Tut!' at intervals — conducted this one with appropriate severity and harshness. (Indeed, he had been most cruelly deceived by the scatterbrained little chit he had raised to a throne.) He insisted on a complete and detailed revelation. At some point in the proceedings Henry offered Katherine the chance of defending herself in open trial. She refused it. She had acknowledged her guilt, and was now prepared to suffer the extreme penalty with a sudden courage that sustained her to the end.

Norfolk, attended by Surrey, then presided over the trial of the other prisoners. No evidence of any value could be obtained from Lady Rochford, who had become insane with terror. The Duke received the statements of the men with loud laughter and bawdy comments that sufficed to cover his own humiliation and clear him of suspicion.[13] His escape from disgrace and imprisonment was narrow enough, although he went in person to ransack his step-mother's coffers at the family mansion in Lambeth for written evidence of Katherine's guilt, and wrote to Henry disclaiming all responsibility for the wickedness of both his nieces. He seemed, Marillac thought, to rejoice at the Queen's downfall; that was all he could do, in view of the fact that the Dowager-Duchess and many of her servants, Lord William, Lord Charles and their wives were arrested and sent to the Tower for misprision of treason. Norfolk endured this martyrdom long enough to pronounce sentence on his niece; then he retired, exhausted, to Kenninghall, leaving Surrey to represent him at her execution on Tower Green, a precaution that disgusted Marillac more than any other aspect of the whole affair. (But the English were, after all, no better than savage beasts in such matters — he had always known it. '*Telle est la coûtume de ce pays,*'[14] was his summing-up.)

The eighteen-year-old Queen met her death as became a daughter of the white lion, practising how best to lay her head on the block the night before her execution, and apparently unaffected by the screams and maunderings of Lady Rochford, who was beheaded on the same scaffold.

The effect on Surrey of this scene may possibly be discerned in — although it should not be pinned down to — a short poem on Sardanapalus that has been traditionally associated with his feelings about Henry VIII. As the verses cannot be dated, the interpretation is questionable; they may simply have been an exercise on a classical theme. A much more obvious indication of Surrey's attitude and a far closer analogy with the circumstances can be found in his rhymed version of the third chapter of the Book of Ecclesiastes. Here, through the veil of scripture, he was able to record horror and disgust more succinctly. In the Sardanapalus poem he describes how the last Assyrian king, 'in peace, with foul desire, and filthy lusts that stained his regal heart', was vanquished in battle (a disaster that never happened in Henry's reign), and, recalling Sardanapalus's frequentation of his eunuchs, concludes that he 'scarce the name of manhood did retain, Feeble of spirit, unpatient of pain.' None of these failings could in any circumstances be ascribed to Henry. But in the Ecclesiastes poem Surrey gives a very significant rendering of the sixteenth verse, of which the original is — 'I saw under the sun the place of judgment, that wickedness was there, and the place of righteousness, that iniquity was there.' 'I saw a *royal throne,*' he says, 'whereas that Justice should have sat, Instead of whom I saw, with fierce and cruel mode, Where wrong was set, *that bloody beast, that drank the guiltless blood.*'

Such phraseology suggests, if it does not directly point to, the revulsion of a chivalric and in some ways sensitive young man from Henry's treatment of his two Howard queens. While Surrey had concurred in Anne Boleyn's condemnation as inevitable and a matter of state business, he may have disliked doing so. Katherine's youth and folly made her fate, although technically just, seem crueller and more pitiable than Anne's, even in that pitiless and cruel age.

Whatever Surrey felt about his cousins' deaths, he found his own situation more and more unendurable as the months went by, and he remained in the position of a courtier, with the result that, a year after Katherine's execution, he again broke out into violence.

NOTES TO CHAPTER SIX

[1] Cal. D.S.P., vol. XII, pt. II, p. 248.
[2] Wriothesley, vol. I, p. 97.
[3] Bapst, p. 256.
[4] Kaulek, *Correspondance de M. de Castillon*, p. 79.
[5] Herbert of Cherbury, *Henry VIII*, p. 300.
[6] Hall, p. 812.
[7] Merriman, *Life and Letters of Thomas Cromwell*, vol. I, p. 285.
[8] Brenan and Statham, vol. II, p. 309.
[9] Strickland, *Lives of the Queens of England*, vol. II, p. 248.
[10] Kaulek, p. 151.
[11] Bapst, p. 90.
[12] Strickland, vol. II, p. 285.
[13] Ibid., p. 289.
[14] Kaulek, p. 124.

During the spring of 1542 there was a pause in the struggle between the Howards and the Seymours. Norfolk, whose health had temporarily broken down, remained at Kenninghall; but he did not lose by absence, for the King, although very much aged since the tragedy of Katherine Howard, had the threads of the situation in his hands and rectified the balance of power by releasing all her relatives and replacing them in their former positions. This must have been extremely galling for Hertford, whose triumph had seemed so near; now the possibility of forcing Norfolk into second place was as far away as ever. The weakest point in the Duke's predominance was the lack of solidarity in his own family; long ago Cromwell had warned him that his wife would be his undoing, and since their separation it had become clear that she was ready to revenge herself by informing on him. The Duchess of Richmond, resenting her father's failure over the marriage between herself and Thomas Seymour, was on bad terms with him and Surrey; and Surrey's tendency to quarrel made him a constant source of anxiety. Yet none of these disadvantages affected Norfolk's military and political power. Henry still relied on him to the extent of entrusting him with the renewed negotiations for the marriage of the Princess Mary and the Duke of Orleans; as soon as these had been set in hand, he was sent to the Border to collect troops for the invasion of Scotland: for at last it seemed as if the enforced union of the kingdoms was within Henry's grasp.

Surrey was not allowed to accompany his father, although his recently disgraced uncles were given commands, with the result that, as soon as the Duke reached Newcastle-on-Tyne, news came that his son had been sent to the Fleet prison on a serious charge — that of challenging another courtier, John à Leigh, to a duel, within the precincts of the Court. Lack of detailed information and the necessity of remaining where he was made it impossible for Norfolk to intervene. This was a matter in which the Seymours must rejoice, and hope for a long imprisonment that might end — such were the conditions in the Fleet — in Surrey's death from gaol fever or the plague.

Varying reports reached Norfolk as to what the quarrel had been about; the evidence was not recorded: but the fact that Leigh had been accused of treasonable correspondence with some of the exiled Catholics, of whom one was Cardinal Pole, and had cleared himself by informing on another, unnamed, person, may partly account for Surrey's action. Whether Leigh accused Surrey himself, or one of his gentlemen, is not known. In Surrey's long and elaborately phrased letter of apology to the Privy Council this point was not raised; he was wise enough to make no excuses beyond that of 'the fury of reckless youth', and to acknowledge his fault without reservations of any kind. He pointed out that other young men had been pardoned for the same offence; and, choosing to ignore the incident that had caused his imprisonment at Windsor three years before, humbly referred their lordships to the 'quiet conversation of my past life'. He declared himself willing to wait patiently, although under duress, till he obtained the King's forgiveness, but to be 'quickly delivered, this heinous offence always unexcused, whereupon I was committed to this noisome prison, whose pestilent airs are not unlike to bring some alteration of health.' Would not His Majesty 'command me into the country, to some place of open air ... there to abide His Grace's pleasure'? Surrey continued with a plea to be allowed to serve — presumably in Scotland — and so to make up for his misdemeanours. 'Your grave heads', he concluded, 'should yet consider that neither am I the first young man that hath enterprised such things as he hath afterwards repented.'[1]

The tone of this apology is all that could be desired; yet beneath the courtesy and the self-abasement and the promises to do better, there is an undercurrent, not of arrogance but of an instinctive assumption that here the rules of punishment did not apply; and indeed, why should they have done so, in the case of a young man whom the King had treated more as a son than as a courtier, and who had always been in a privileged position? The Council also, perhaps unfortunately, subscribed to this view, and four days after Surrey's letter was written (July 25th) the Warden was empowered to bring him from the Fleet to the Court at Windsor. Here he renewed his promise of good behaviour and was set free after being fined. Then, at last, he was sent to join his father, and to take up the post of which he had been deprived during the Pilgrimage of Grace. At once he realized that this was to be warfare on a large scale. His references to the Scottish expedition and, it may be, to the conclusion of his quarrel with Lady Hertford, have been placed by some commentators in two poems, which are worth quoting rather for the light they throw on Surrey's character than for the possibility of their being autobiographical.

In the poem that is supposed to touch on his departure for Scotland — 'Spite drave me into Boreas' reign, Where hoary frosts the hills do bite, When hills were spread and every plain, With stormy winter's mantle white' — the influence, as so often, is Petrarch's; the verses themselves are original. Surrey begins with a reference to 'fortune's wrath' and a mysterious 'wealth' that 'fed mine eyes by stealth'. He ends with a description of crossing the sea that links up with his expedition to France in October 1543.

> Nor may the waves of the salt flood
> Quench that your beauty set on fire,
> For though mine eyes forbear the food
> That did relieve the hot desire,
> Such as I was, such will I be —
> Your own. What would ye more of me?

The other poem, one of the most dramatic and effective Surrey wrote, is based on the language of chess, a popular conceit of the day. Here again, the content is oddly personal, as of a man who has been insulted, yet scorns to wrangle or plead. 'Although I had a

76

check,' he begins, 'To give the mate is hard.' Describing himself as 'a man of war', Surrey then warns the person addressed to 'mark this foolish verse', for when their contest is over, 'Then shall yourself be glad, To end that you began.' He goes on:

> For if by chance I win
> Your person in the field,
> Too late then come you in
> Yourself to me to yield.
> For I will use my power,
> As captain full of might:
> And such I will devour
> As use to show me spite.
>
> And for because you gave
> The check in such degree,
> This vantage, lo! I have —
> Now check, and guard to thee!
> Defend it if thou may;
> Stand stiff in thine estate;
> For sure I will assay,
> If I can give thee mate.

To associate this poem with that of the wolf-lady and the white lion would be to run conjecture into the ground; for it might be addressed to a man, on whom the author was threatening to revenge himself; the vindictive, defiant note is highly characteristic of Surrey; it reveals his implacable side, and the inability to forget an injury, which he shared with all his family.

The Scottish campaign lasted from August till November, ending in the rout of the enemy at Solway Moss, the death of James V and the accession of the baby Queen of Scots. In October news came that Sir Thomas Wyatt, the only contemporary English poet who could have been Surrey's master and whose name is generally coupled with his, was dead. In fact, Surrey and Wyatt could not have known each other well, as Wyatt's career took him abroad a great deal. It was however suitable that the younger poet should mark the occasion by an elegy for private circulation, and Surrey produced three. Two are short, graceful and formal; the third is longer, intimately descriptive, and here and there almost colloquial, and contains one of Surrey's rare references to religion, of which the phrasing is curious in view of the fact that Wyatt was a Lutheran. 'But to the heavens', Surrey concludes, 'that simple soul is fled, Which left, with such as covet Christ to know, *Witness of faith that never shall be dead, Sent for our health, but not receivèd so.*' 'Covet Christ' sounds like a Protestant slogan; what spiritual influences, if any, were at work when Surrey wrote these lines, is unknown. As the poems were read the rumour went round that he had apostasized, but it was never confirmed. The solution probably lies in the fact that he had not the religious temperament, and indeed there had been nothing in his upbringing or his heredity to create it.

Surrey did not return to Court till early in the following year; he did so without any further acquisition of honours or rewards for the part he had played in his father's triumph. So he found himself again at a loose end; and again the pattern of violence — this time coupled with indiscretions that seem rather adolescent than fierce — was repeated. The circumstances in which Surrey now disgraced himself have a certain comic appeal.

On the morning of January 19th, 1543, a tailor, Richard Bourne, was in a butcher's shop in Old Jewry when a maidservant, Alice Flaner, came in for a knuckle of veal. He recognized her as an employee of Mrs Millicent Arundell, who had a tavern in St Lawrence Lane, Cheapside. Alice Flaner began by rating the butcher, whose name was Castell, for cheating her mistress over his last delivery. 'She desires to have the best,' Alice explained, 'for peers of the realm shall eat thereof, and, besides that, a prince.' 'What prince?' Castell asked. 'The Earl of Surrey,' Alice replied. 'He is no prince, but a man of honour — and of more like to be,' said Castell. 'Yes,' said Alice, 'and if aught other than good should come of the King, he is like to be King.' This treasonable talk appalled the butcher. 'It is not so!' he exclaimed. 'It is so — ' the girl persisted. She then proceeded to haggle with him over the meat her mistress had ordered, and went away.[2]

The veal was required for a special occasion. That same evening,

Surrey and a party of young men, among whom were Thomas Cleere, now his squire, Pickering, his body-servant, Thomas Wyatt, the late poet's son, and Hussey, Norfolk's treasurer, arrived for supper at Mrs Arundell's establishment. They ate and drank heartily, paid their bill, and at about nine o'clock went out into the city, making towards the riverside. As they did so Mrs Arundell and her servants noticed that they were carrying 'stone bows', i.e. the catapults generally used for shooting rabbits and birds.[3]

Mrs Arundell thought no more of the matter until the next morning — except that, although it was Lent, all the young men had eaten the meat she had bought from Castell; but then they often broke this rule when they supped at her house. She was hardly up before her neighbours came running in with news of a fine scandal. Surrey and his companions had begun by breaking the glass in the windows of the city merchants' houses (one of whom was Sir Richard Gresham, a 'new man' recently knighted) and also some of those of the neighbouring churches; then they hired wherries in which they had been rowed down the Thames. The left bank was a rendezvous for the women of the town and their pimps, who were accustomed to parade there. Surrey and his companions had fired off a few shots at these persons before going their separate ways.

Mrs Arundell, who was of course anxious to keep Surrey's custom, told her servants to say nothing about his party and to deny any rumours they might hear of his setting off from her house. Next evening Surrey appeared again, with some other friends, one of whom was Sir George Blagge, a favourite of the King's; this time he was in a soberer mood. Presently Mrs Arundell heard Blagge rebuke the Earl for his folly of the night before, to which Surrey replied, 'I had liever all the good in the world it were undone, for I am sure it will come before the King and his Council. But — ' he added, 'we shall [must] have a madding time in our youth, and therefore I am very sorry for it.'[4]

Surrey was right. The old excuse of reckless youth availed him nothing, and he was summoned before the Privy Council, of which Hertford was now a member. The first accusation was that of eating meat in Lent; for this Surrey was able to produce a dispensation.

Then the question of Alice Flaner's evidence arose – it had been reported by Richard Bourne – and was supplemented by the frightened maid's informing against her mistress. She had merely repeated, she said, what Mrs Arundell had told her. My lord of Surrey had complained to the hostess about the charge made for table-cloths in his own household; flattered by this democratic confidence, Mrs Arundell repeated their conversation to Alice, adding, 'I marvel they will thus mock a prince.' Alice was open-mouthed. 'Why, is he a prince?' she asked. 'Yea, Mary, is he,' her mistress replied, 'and if aught should come to the King but good, his father should stand for king.' Naturally this exciting piece of gossip could not be held back; Alice not only repeated it to the butcher, but also to Joan Whetnall, a servant in the Norfolk household at Lambeth, who added to it the information that the arms above the Earl's bed were 'very like the King's'. (The Howards had the right to bear the royal arms; their quarterings were their own, and quite different: but this had escaped Joan Whetnall's untutored eye.) When pressed, Alice, Joan and Mrs Arundell declared that they had not heard anyone else speak of Surrey or his father in these terms; nor could it be proved that Surrey had ever arrogated to himself the grandeurs they had placed upon him.[5]

It must have been with some disappointment that the Seymour faction in the Privy Council passed on to the window-breaking episode. 'I have every evil done therein,' was Surrey's answer.' I therefore submit myself to such punishment as should to your lordships be thought good.' He was committed to the Fleet, and Wyatt, Pickering and Cleere were committed to the Tower, while the Council considered their verdict.

Those among them who thought first of pleasing the King recommended lenient treatment – release and a fine. It seems as if this sentence might have been passed, if Hertford had not intervened. It would be, he objected, 'a secret and unobserved contempt of the law' to let the culprit off so lightly. He added cryptically, 'Undermining of authority must be either itself in indulging nothing, or be nothing in indulging all.' In other words, if the law was defied, it became meaningless, especially when privilege could so far prevail as to make this a possibility. 'Liberty knows no restraint, no limit, when winked at,' was his final comment.[6]

Henry decided not to interfere. Norfolk followed his master's example. And so, for two months, Surrey had to cool his heels in the 'noisome prison' where he had recently suffered.

This time he uttered no complaints, and sent out no pleas for transfer to a healthier place; in fact his mood seems to have been one of resignation tinged with sardonic amusement at the fuss made about his hooliganism; this was expressed in a poem that his first editor entitled 'A Satire on London'. Here Surrey showed up what he evidently considered the puritanical attitude of the Privy Council by an affected horror at the depravity of the city. He was so shocked, he begins, by the sight of the dissolute habits of the people that he resolved to enforce his disapproval, no matter what the cost. ('By unknown means it likèd me My hidden burden to express.') 'This made me', he goes on, 'with a reckless breast, To wake thy sluggards with my bow: A figure of the Lord's behest, Whose scourge for sin the Scriptures show.' He then explains that his demonstration against the citizens' sloth and lechery was completely disinterested. 'To stir to God, this was my mind, Thy windows had done me no spite.' That his call to a better life had been ignored was not his fault, because, unfortunately, 'indurèd hearts no warning feel'. He concludes with a pastiche of the Old Testament prophets. 'O! shameless whore! Is dread then gone? ... O! member of false Babylon! The shop of craft! The den of ire! Thy dreadful doom draws fast upon ... The flame of wrath shall on thee fall! ... Stricken shall be thy lechers all!'

The satire is neat, the caricature of the pious slogans excellently done. Yet here again, witty and good-humoured though the verses are, there is an undercurrent of total indifference to convention, and a touch of that same strange and fatal unawareness. The question of his having broken the law seems not to have arisen in Surrey's mind; it is as if he accepted his punishment with a contemptuous shrug of the shoulders and a pitying smile at the absurd eccentricities of his enemies on the Privy Council. To observe that this young man was perfectly sure of himself would be meiosis indeed.

After a short retirement to the country Surrey was allowed to go to France in October 1543, this time on a mission to the Emperor's camp at Valenciennes. (Charles V was now in alliance with Henry, and both were about to make war on France.) Here he and Sir Francis Bryan were received by the Emperor's sister, then Regent of the Netherlands, whom they found playing cards by the fire with the Duke of Lorraine. Surrey took little or no share in the conversation that ensued; no doubt he was angry and humiliated by still being in the position of an onlooker, a visitor. The reason for this — although he may not have known it — was that he had written what Chapuys described as a very foolish letter, of which no record remains, to another Spanish envoy, Cardinal Granvela; Granvela had complained of it to Henry VIII.[7] When Surrey returned a few days later he got a good report from the Emperor. 'He has natural intelligence, and a kind heart', Charles said. Shortly after this recommendation reached Henry he received another from Sir John Wallop, the captain of a small force then besieging Landrécy. 'My lord of Surrey', Wallop wrote, 'hath lost no time since his arrival at the army, for he visiteth all things that be meet for a man of war to look upon for his learning.' During one of Surrey's expeditions to the front line he had a narrow escape from the enemy gunfire. With Sir George Blagge and Thomas Cleere he was standing in a trench outside the town when a new weapon, described by Wallop as a 'mortar that shoots artificial bullets ... burst forth and shot off guns out of him, a hundred a shot, every one as loud to the hearing as a hackbutt ... whereof they counted well four score.'[8] Surrey's coolness and aptitude for military knowledge made a great impression on Wallop; his praise was supplemented by a second letter from Charles V, in which he described Surrey as upholding the warlike traditions of his family. 'One can teach him nothing,' he added, 'and whatever he is commanded to do he carries out well.'

Henry now decided to give Surrey the position he had earned; he had seen enough service in Scotland and on the continent to justify this step, apart from the fact that he seemed to be settling down. So again the fortunes of the Howards rose a little (although Henry's marriage to his sixth wife, Katherine Parr, had placed the Protestant party in the ascendant at Court) through the King's giving the command of all his armies in France to Norfolk. In January 1544 he partly paid for the Duke's expenses with the grant of some monastic lands near Norwich. Meanwhile Surrey received the post of 'Marshal of the Field in France' and the rank of Captain-General. He was to begin work on his father's staff. At last all his dreams of glory were to be realized – but not for several months, for the campaign could not open until the summer.

With a view, perhaps, to keeping his son out of mischief until then, Norfolk gave him the property of St Leonard's Hill, near Norwich, where the Earl began to build a great palace in what his contemporaries described as the classic style, which he called Mount Surrey. Here, when he was not soldiering or at Court, he planned to live in more splendid state than any of his forebears. Mount Surrey was to put Framlingham and Kenninghall completely in the shade. He was happily occupied with his building during the early part of 1544, returning every now and then to Court for some rather tedious duty. He headed the reception for a Spanish general, the Duke of Najera, whom he escorted to Paris Garden for the bull- and bear-baiting, and to the Tower, to inspect the lions and leopards of the royal menagerie; then he attended a state banquet given for Najera at Westminster. In April he was present at the Chapter of the Order of the Garter; in May he received another Spanish grandee; between these ceremonies he went back to Norwich.

Not a stone of Mount Surrey now remains; it was destroyed during the enclosure rebellion of 1549; no ground plans, drawings or designs survive. A single record of Surrey's taste may be found in a contemporary account of three banqueting-houses, or pavilions, that stood in the gardens; these were built like forts and crowned with ornamental cannon.[9]

Before the main structure was completed Surrey began to plan the interior; from what must have been a vast correspondence with stewards, builders and plasterers, a few letters are extant. The sum he had raised ran out before the palace was finished; and besides this debt, he now owed a great deal of money to local glaziers, carpenters and merchants. His father's treasurer wrote to him in despair. 'As concerning the provisions [furnishing] of the house,' Hussey protested, 'the same are not to be obtained at my lord's [Norfolk's] hand. We shall practise how to come by them, by such shift as may be made upon my credit in this town.'

Surrey pursued his schemes undeterred by these and other warnings. In the spring of 1544, during one of his visits to London, he sent for Sir Christopher Barker, then Garter-King-at-Arms, to come to him at the family mansion in Lambeth. Barker waited an hour. Then Surrey appeared with a design for an escutcheon which was to combine the quarterings of the Earls of Mowbray and Brotherton, of Edward the Confessor and of the Dukes of Anjou. 'I shall bear it,' he announced. Rather taken aback, Barker asked, 'By what title [right], my lord?' 'Brotherton [Surrey's maternal ancestor] bare it so,' was the reply. 'It is not in your lordship's pedigree,' Barker objected, who knew that though Surrey might be entitled to the Brotherton and Mowbray quarterings, the insertion of the arms of Edward the Confessor and of the Dukes of Anjou was now the prerogative of the heir to the throne, and to show them was a very dangerous departure from custom. Surrey replied sharply, 'I found it in a house in Norfolk in stone, graven so — and I will bear it.' 'It is not to your honour to do so,' said Barker, and a long argument ensued, in which Surrey seems to have shown his usual obstinacy and prepotence. Later on Barker told another herald to inform the Earl that he had no right to all these quarterings, and that he would be wise not to insist on using them.[10]

Having engaged a Dutch tutor, Hadrian Junius, for his two sons before he made his final preparations for departure to France, Surrey turned his attention to the state rooms of his new home. Richmond's portrait, one of his most valued possessions, must be reframed and placed in a more splendid setting, together with his own as a companion piece. Then, having found in a book of French romances the arms of Sir Lancelot du Lac, he added them to his escutcheon, of which the design was to form the major part of the interior decoration. Absorbed in these and similar plans, the question of payment seems not to have worried him. Hastily ordering a quantity of Turkey carpets, table-cloths bordered with designs of flowers and pomegranates, chairs of purple velvet and satin, crimson cushions embroidered in silver, and ten feather beds with linen quilts and bolsters to match, he set off for France.[11]

The turning-point in his life had come — a little late, according to the standards of the day. By this time his appearance had entirely changed, owing to the fashion that had developed from Henry's order of 1535, that his courtiers' beards 'should be knotted and no more shaven, and their heads polled.'[12] The last portrait of Surrey shows him as he was in the 1540s (it was painted in 1546) with a moustache, whiskers and a long, curling beard. His face has filled out; his slenderness is emphasized by the heavily embroidered, tightly fitting doublet and hose of the purple silk and gold tissue that only members of the royal family were allowed to wear. Height is added by the plumed cap, then known as a 'myllain bonnet'. (These cost eight shillings each, and were the invention of a tailor, Christopher Milloner, whose name has descended to his trade.)[13] Surrey's expression is one of deep melancholy, tinged with suspicion and uneasiness; he looks out of the canvas as if he were facing an enemy. Above the frame two cherubs support a large H. On one side are sculptured the three lions of England, on the other the Plantagenet lilies and leopards. On the base of the column against which Surrey leans is the motto, *Sat Superest* — 'It is enough to prevail.'

Surrey had prevailed at last, not only over the jealousy of his rivals, but over the setbacks caused by his own temperament. He was twenty-seven — and he had a little less than three years to live.

NOTES TO CHAPTER SEVEN

[1] Bapst, p. 256.
[2] Cal. D.S.P., vol. XVIII, pt. I, pp. 73-4.
[3] Ibid.
[4] Ibid.
[5] Ibid.
[6] Bapst, p. 269.
[7] Cal. Span. S.P., vol. XIII, p. 514.
[8] Cal. D.S.P., vol. XX, p. 728.
[9] Blomefield, p. 289.
[10] Cal. D.S.P., vol. XXI, pt. I, p. 1425.
[11] Nott, vol. I, Appendix p. xix.
[12] Stow, *Annals of England*, p. 571.
[13] Ibid.

CHAPTER EIGHT

THE alliance between Henry VIII and Charles V, secretly signed in April 1544, lasted less than six months; their combined attacks on the French armies extended over a period of ten weeks, during which the Emperor never put his full strength into the field. This lack of solidarity was partly due to religious differences and partly to divergence of aims. The Emperor wanted to recover Milan from Francis I, and Henry, still set on the subjugation of his nearest and most dangerous enemies, the Scots, was determined to break the bond between them and France. Henry and Charles had agreed to march together on Paris: neither intended to do so. Henry's intention was to acquire the fortresses and territory of Boulogne and to consolidate his hold on Calais. He realized that this would result in an occupation that he could not really afford; yet the expense would be justified by the deterrent to Francis's power on the continent, and the draining off of French men and arms from Scotland.

This was the international situation. The English policy, in so far as it related to the Howard fortunes in general and to Surrey in particular, was more complicated. For the first time in twenty years the Privy Council was united against the King on one point. They did not object to a short war, as such, nor to the capture of Boulogne; having concluded both, they did not want to occupy the new territory permanently, but to make a profitable deal with the French for its surrender. They believed that the maintenance of Calais alone was as much as the national finances would bear; the addition of Boulogne meant economic disaster — and their personal inconvenience. (They might even have to pay higher taxes, and that was unthinkable.) Henry, who had learnt from Cromwell that money could always, somehow, be raised, if he had national support, considered a larger foothold in France to be a safeguard, and a matter of prestige; on these points he had the whole country behind him.

Among the younger men now in authority, Surrey was the most enthusiastic of the King's supporters. He neither understood nor cared for money matters (like Henry, although with less reason, he thought that everything of that kind settled itself in the long run), and he saw the conquest and tenure of Boulogne as a partial return to the great days of Crécy, Poitiers and Agincourt, when the English bowmen had swept the French cavalry from the field, and his plumed and armoured ancestors had dictated terms from Paris and crowned their kings at Rheims.

In all matters of policy Henry's will was paramount, as long as he had his people's approval; his awareness of their mood was part of the Tudor genius. He stood, therefore, on the rock. Surrey, from the outset of the Boulogne campaign, was flung into the quicksands of Court and Council intrigue. The support of the nation availed him nothing; in any case he did not value it, although he may have presumed on his reputation for dash and vigour. Allied with the King against the Privy Council — against his own father — he seems to have felt that he could afford to be independent. In this frame of mind he crossed the Channel in the midsummer of 1544.

Surrey's military training and experience, although limited compared to those of such men as Hertford and Lisle, had been enough to qualify him for an important but subordinate post. In the nineteenth century he would have made an admirable quartermaster-general or a first-class adjutant, in the twentieth an ideal commando leader. In his day the equivalents of these positions were superimposed on or alternated with one another, and had to be combined with political flair, great self-control and complete lack of scruple. On these grounds Surrey was not up to his work. He had one other grave deficiency — his knowledge of the technical innovations of the last decade was slight: nor was he particularly interested in them; so he fell below the standards of the men he despised. Hertford, for instance, had already told Henry that archers must be supplemented by larger contingents of gunners; Wallop and other commanders were learning the use of trench-mortars; and Henry himself was now employing gunner-instructors from Flanders and Italy and gradually replacing the long-bow with hackbutts, hand-culverins and halberds, while combining all four for certain kinds of attack.[1] Cavalry was more subtly manipulated; and at sea large ships, such as the *Great Harry* and the *Mary Rose*, were supported by the smaller, more swiftly moving craft that were to be perfected in the 1580s.

Nevertheless the opening of the Boulogne campaign provided the best possible chance for an officer of Surrey's type. A month after he had reached the front, Henry VIII crossed with the main army, now modernized and re-equipped. Brass bands, and wagons that ground the corn for the stores as their wheels went round, accompanied each contingent, while flat-floored barges conveyed the cavalry across the Channel. The too conspicuous white coats of the infantry had been replaced by red and blue tunics guarded with yellow and by parti-coloured caps and hose.[2]

For the official entry of Henry and his troops Surrey left Calais to join them outside Boulogne, leading the rearguard as Marshal of the Field behind the King in his litter. Terrible, magnificent, undefeated by illness and care, the fierce old man still led his armies, although his riding days were over. The stalwart, genial, highly coloured King Hal of Holbein's famous portraits was now wrinkled, swollen, white-haired and shaky; yet the eyes, nearly hidden under their puffy lids, were as piercing as ever; the small, tight mouth, the square ringed hands, surrounded by folds of pallid flesh, looked as formidable as at any time in his days of health. The expression, so alarmingly made up of cunning, humour, sensuality and cynicism, had not diminished in its sharpness and vigour; nor had the range of temperament, that could change from majesty to uproariousness, from frank gaiety to cold and ominous withdrawal, become blurred in any of its variations; the staggering display of talents, accomplishments and intellectual power was still protean. And in the thirtieth year of his reign the loyalty and love of his soldiers for this capricious and tyrannical egotist had never been more deeply felt, more passionately expressed. The monster, the betrayer, the forsworn and outcast apostate of continental legend, the 'bloody beast' of Surrey's verse, the executioner and torturer of women, priests and monks, was for them not only their king, but England itself — an incalculable, semi-divine, semi-paternal figure to whom all, even the greatest, must turn in the worst danger, the most desperate moment. It seemed to the more unsophisticated of Henry's people that no mischance, no enemy, no earthly power could break, or frighten, or halt him. He could hardly walk; the pain from his ulcerous leg sometimes made him speechless and black in the face; he was asthmatic, dropsical, poisoned and rotting with a mixture of diseases that have never been diagnosed — but he was unconquerable; he was always to be found where he was most needed: and he always knew what to say, as well as what to do, in a crisis.

The nature of Surrey's feeling about Henry at this time is masked by the stately correctness and graceful courtesy of his letters, which, except on two occasions, he was sensible enough to confine to military matters. He was a loyal, courageous, but not subservient or sycophantic officer, of the kind indeed that the King most appreciated, however clearly he might see his favourite's limitations and weaknesses. From July till September 1544 Surrey did well, perhaps because he still had his way to make and was under his father's command.

Henry's plan was to begin war on the two fronts of France and Scotland. He had therefore sent Hertford to the Border and put Lisle in command of the Channel fleet, while reserving the bulk of his forces for the Boulogne campaign. The army council was headed by Norfolk and Surrey, who were detailed to organize an attack on Montreuil, a fortress some twenty miles inland from Boulogne, while Henry and the Duke of Suffolk besieged Boulogne itself, with the result that 'Muttrell and Bullen' became part of the English soldiers' vocabulary. Sitting down before Montreuil was of course a feint to draw off the enemy from the Boulogne area. Norfolk afterwards accused the Seymour faction on the Privy Council of keeping him short of men and armaments in order to discredit him with the King. No doubt they would have liked to do so; but Henry alone was responsible for this distribution, and his tactics were justified. Both sieges continued throughout August, that of Montreuil being withstood; in spite of Surrey's raids on the countryside, the fortress was well enough supplied to hold out. Henry and the Emperor therefore concentrated all their strength on Boulogne, and there Surrey joined them as Henry's aide-de-camp during the first week of September. On the 11th a breach was made, and the English troops poured into the town; after two days' fighting the French surrendered, and on the 14th Henry, attended by Surrey and Norfolk, received the keys of the city. Surrey was then sent back to Montreuil with reinforcements, while Norfolk remained with the King.

At this point Surrey's behaviour gives the impression that he was determined to take Montreuil at any cost and without delay, in order to show what he could do. The most sensible procedure would have been to continue the attrition of the city until the garrison was too weak to withstand an attack. Surrey would not wait to do so. On September 19th he attempted to breach the Abbeville gate of the fortress, where he was held up and repulsed. With Thomas Cleere and a small party of men he went on in advance of his troops; some of them began to retreat, and he was cut off. A shell burst, and he fell, wounded and concussed. Cleere thought he was seriously hurt; he managed to get to him, and was preparing to take over the command and receive Surrey's instructions; then he himself was hit. Somehow he dragged his unconscious leader from beneath the walls, and the attack was abandoned. A little later it was discovered that Surrey's wound was slight. Cleere's was incapacitating. He was sent home, and died in the spring of 1545.

Surrey's grief was deep and lasting. Cleere had been one of his dearest companions; besides helping him financially, Surrey had furthered Cleere's betrothal to Mary Shelton, a cousin of his own, writing verses to her on Cleere's behalf. Together, he and Cleere had attended the coronation of Anne Boleyn, escaped death at Landrécy, stormed Kelso during one of Norfolk's border raids, and got into trouble at Mrs Arundell's, parting only when different prisons engulfed them. After Cleere's death Surrey continued to look after Mary Shelton, and he arranged for Cleere to be buried in the Howard

vault at Lambeth. His tribute to their friendship is one of his best
poems — simple, dramatic and moving:

> Norfolk sprung thee, Lambeth holds thee dead,
> Cleere, of the County of Claremont though hight.
> Within the womb of Ormond's race thou bred,
> And saw'st thy cousin crownèd in thy sight.
> Shelton for love, Surrey for lord thou chase
> (Ay me! whilst life did last that league was tender),
> Tracing whose steps thou sawest Kelso blaze,
> Laundersey burnt, and battered Bullen render.
> At Muttrell gates, hopeless of all recure,
> Thine Earl, half dead, gave in thy hand his will;
> Which cause did thee this pining death procure,
> Ere summers four times seven thou couldst fulfil.
> Ah! Cleere! if love had booted, care or cost,
> Heaven had not won, nor earth so timely lost.

Henry made no comment on the risks taken by Surrey — he had
greater matters on his mind. On September 21st, a week after the
surrender of Boulogne, the Emperor signed a separate peace with
Francis I. So Henry had to face guerrilla warfare throughout
northern France, and the possibility of invasion at home by the
French army and navy. On the 26th he held a council and re-
arranged his forces. Norfolk was to remain in Boulogne, and
Surrey to alternate between there and Calais as liaison officer, while
the King made ready to return to England to prepare his coastal
defences.

Henry's departure was characteristic. Although his presence at
home was urgently needed, and he himself was exhausted by the
campaign, he staged a leisurely and triumphal farewell scene, thus
making it clear that England had nothing to fear from Scotland or
France and was already impregnable, which was very far from being
the case. Attended by Surrey, he progressed through the streets of
'battered Bullen' and embarked, as if for a pageant, on September
30th. He left Norfolk, Surrey and Sir Edward Poynings in charge
of the half-ruined fortresses above the city, with instructions to

rebuild them. Norfolk, who was now Governor of Calais instead of Lisle, retired there, taking Surrey with him and leaving Poynings with a small force in command. At once the French descended and made an entry; they were repulsed, but with the loss of eight hundred English soldiers, and Boulogne was saved by a hair's breadth. This carelessness shook Henry's faith in Norfolk as a commander. He wrote to him sternly, 'I marvel how you durst do so without knowledge of our pleasure ... excuse there is none', and thenceforth his attitude towards Surrey, as well as towards his father, changed; he was now much more liable to be influenced against them both, although Surrey had had no share in the Duke's military lapse.[3]

From October 1544 till February 1545 Surrey remained in France, mostly at Boulogne, making various sorties when the French showed signs of attacking in strength. This was the kind of work he did best. On October 11th he descended with a troop of horse on Requiers and Rieu, from which he removed all the stores; the men in these villages had gone, leaving the women and children, whom Surrey spared. This was a procedure that neither Hertford (who in the next reign became much beloved for his leniency) nor Henry would have allowed. The contemporary view was that the families of an enemy were so much vermin, to be destroyed as quickly and economically as possible. A few weeks later Surrey followed up this gesture with one still more typical. The French nobility, who were in command of the Dauphin's forces then encamped between Calais and Boulogne, sent Surrey's staff a challenge — would one of his captains care to 'break a lance' for the lady of his choice? Surrey was wise enough not to take up the gage himself (the temptation must have been severe) and allowed Captain Shelley, one of his gentlemen, to accept. Shelley killed the challenger, returning unhurt.[4] If this incident had come to Henry's knowledge it would have displeased and irritated him, and might have provided Surrey's enemies on the Privy Council with an excellent weapon; it was not reported until both the King and his *protégé* had done with gallantry for ever.

Although Henry's opinion of Norfolk's capabilities had sunk, there

was no one else who had enough local prestige to organize the East
Anglian coastal defences, and he was therefore recalled to set these
in hand, while Surrey and Poynings remained in charge of Boulogne. As it became clear that the French were preparing to take it
during the course of the invasion, Surrey also was recalled, to raise
more troops for its defence and to receive Henry's instructions, while
Hertford temporarily replaced him. This was humiliating enough;
then, in the first week of Hertford's occupation, the French attacked
again and were completely routed by the new general's brilliant
amphibious defence; he overtook the enemy from the rear with a
sea force, and descended on them from the fortress, thus cutting off
their army of 14,000 men with comparatively small loss to his
garrison. All this time Surrey remained in England, once more in a
subordinate position; it must have seemed to him as if his chance of
becoming a great leader had disappeared again, although he was
honourably and responsibly employed. Then at last he was allowed
to replace Hertford; but this tribute to his efficiency was, as it were,
back-handed. Hertford's absence from the Border had had fatal
results, so that he had to return to the Marches of Northumberland
in June 1545; thus Surrey's reoccupation of French territory (he now
took over the fortress of Guisnes, as well as those of Calais and
Boulogne) gave the impression that he was relegated to a less
important post than those given to Henry's other administrators. It
was something to have replaced Lord Grey, a nobleman of the
Seymour faction, to feel that in his determination to hold and keep
what had been won he had the King's support, and that some of the
Councillors were weakening about the tenure of Boulogne. 'There
is not one Englishman,' wrote Sir William Paget, now Henry's
Secretary of State and the most remarkable of the Protestant
Councillors, 'but will spend all that he hath with his blood, an'
Bullen shall again be French.'[5]

In that fierce resolve to keep their French possessions which sprang
from the atavistic dream of a continental empire, and their determination to cut down their ancient enemies from within their own
strongholds by land and sea, the English of all classes united in a
stubborn belligerence. It almost seemed as if they would have been

disappointed had the enemy called off the invasion. 'My lord,' said one East Anglian commander to Norfolk, 'if they come, for God's sake bring us between the sea and them.' Not only so: Henry's people were ready to risk what they rated far higher than their lives — their money. 'If it is not enough,' said one merchant when he made his contribution. 'His Majesty shall have more.' Eagerly they fitted themselves, each according to his degree, into the over-all scheme manipulated by the master hand that had guided them through thirty years of storm and tempest.

As the English spies reported that Francis's plan was to make Portsmouth his bridgehead, Henry established himself there. All his commanders were in their places. Hertford remained in the north: Norfolk held the Lincolnshire and Suffolk coasts, Lord Russell those of the west and the Duke of Suffolk Sussex and Kent, while Lisle and Sir Peter Carew occupied the Channel with a fleet of sixty sail. The fishermen had all been called up: their wives continued the industry. 'The women', Lord Russell wrote to the Privy Council, ' ... adventure to sail sixteen or twenty miles to sea, and are sometimes chased home by the Frenchmen.'⁶ It was the old pattern of enraged resistance, to be repeated in 1588 and in the early 1800s — and later still.

Henry found that to remain in Portsmouth and keep in touch with Lisle was impossible without an intelligent and resourceful messenger. He therefore sent for Surrey, who joined him in the third week of July. Whatever resentment still lingered between Lisle and Surrey was forgotten during the events of the next three days. On the night before he sailed, the French admiral, Claude d'Annebault, gave a party on board his flagship, which caught fire and sank. Standing off the Solent on July 20th, he had the satisfaction of seeing the *Mary Rose*, with seven hundred men on board, open her ports, turn out her guns for action, lie over, give to her weight and sink before a shot was fired. Almost at the same moment, *La Maîtresse*, opening fire, gave to the shock of her own cannon and was completely disabled. Undeterred, d'Annebault decided to land a storming party on the Isle of Wight. They proceeded a little way; many were killed by the bowmen hidden in the trees or behind the bushes.

Withdrawing to the open sands on the Bembridge coast, the rest were charged by a body of horse, deserted by their comrades in the boats that had been detailed to take them off, and so perished.

At eight o'clock in the evening of the 21st, d'Annebault's fleet stood off Selsea Bill, and Surrey was on board *The Great Harry* asking Lisle for a report. Lisle submitted it and his plan, which was to give chase; he would not take the risk without Henry's leave. To Surrey he said, 'These Frenchmen, which be here, if they land, they may happen to find such a blast that they should never see their own country again.'⁷

Surrey went ashore, then returned with the command to proceed. But d'Annebault had already slipped his anchor and retreated. Later he came back to attack Seaford, then Shoreham, without success. By the end of August plague had broken out in his ships, and he had to withdraw and disembark the remainder of his broken forces at the mouth of the Seine. So the naval attack failed before it had begun, and gradually, once more, the threat of invasion began to die away.

As soon as Surrey's liaison work came to an end he was sent back to Boulogne with a force of 5,000 men. By this time Suffolk and Poynings were dead; Norfolk was still employed in England; of Henry's younger high command only Hertford, Lisle, Surrey and Lord Grey remained. Surrey was put in charge of Guisnes, while Grey held Boulogne. By the end of September 1545, Surrey had done so well with his skirmishes and raids that he took over both fortresses from Grey and was created 'Lieutenant of the King on Sea and Land'. He at once began to reorganize his territory.

It is at this point that the tragedy of Surrey's career begins: where the phrases that start with 'if only' rise to the mind. Yet if the Greek dramatists were right in showing their heroes and heroines rather as victims of the gods than of their own misdeeds, then the story of his downfall might be differently introduced. Judged by the rules of what we may perhaps call the day before yesterday, Surrey appears as a pampered, headstrong young fool, who threw away all he had with both hands and rushed upon his doom, defying fate and tempting nemesis to the last. But now that the wheel of psychological diagnosis has come full circle, we can see him as Sophocles would have seen him — the prey of those unconquerable powers to which Sophocles' audiences gave names and kingdoms, and which we describe as environment, heredity, or the unconscious. Here was a young man who, as we say now, had everything, and did not value it: a young man of wealth, nobility, brilliance and charm. The antique deities did not permit such creatures to enjoy their advantages; they either destroyed or maimed them. The new gods (so we are told) destroy and maim from within the citadel of the personality. The result is the same.

If, on these grounds, Henry Howard is to be judged fairly, he should not be condemned, perhaps not even censured. But to trace the course of his actions from week to week, merely between October 1545 and March 1546, is to experience, at second hand, the irritation and dismay that those who tried to help or check him felt, while they protested either tactfully or angrily, always obtaining the same reaction — arrogance, heedlessness, irrelevant excuses. And Surrey's contemporaries had this reason for impatience and misapprehension; their God was the jealous God of the Old Testament and of the Christian Church. Judged by those standards, 'the most foolish proud boy in England' had no case at all.

From the moment that he took over the command of the French fortresses Surrey's administrative gifts were displayed to advantage. He saw to it that the troops were regularly paid; then he eliminated the most useless and dangerous of the camp-followers. During the first weeks of his lieutenancy he did not yield to the temptation of pitched battles, but confined himself to raiding expeditions, while so harrying the enemy that they were unable to build new strongholds, were chased from one encampment to another and kept short of supplies. This was admirable staff-work; equally sound, no doubt, were his personal relations with officers and men; what he did not grasp was the economic difference between the two. Skilled officers were few, and their lives correspondingly precious; the troops were expendable. Surrey took the view that the lives of those in command, his own included, could, in fact must, be risked, if the occasion arose. Such heroism was a fatal error, partly because only a limited number of officers had learned the technique of the new weapons; and since the deaths of Poynings and Suffolk a Lieutenant-General was almost irreplaceable.

It was therefore with considerable annoyance that on October 25th, 1545, Henry heard that the Earl of Surrey had risked his life by remaining on the bridge of one of the Boulogne fortresses, 'for the better viewing of the same', in spite of the fact that Captain Tomaso, an Italian mercenary-engineer, had begged him not to do so. Hussey, who was in touch with the Privy Council, wrote to warn his young master that His Majesty had taken his action 'in very ill part', and that his rout of a French attack a day or two earlier hardly counted against such censurable rashness, especially as the death of Cleere had been caused by a similar exploit the year before.[*]

Henry's tolerance of Surrey's excesses again prevailed, and Surrey himself took care not to offend any more in this respect, though he must have been irked by the enforced precautions. Meanwhile his absorption in his work mingled with his thoughts of home, of his wife and children (so far away, as he remarked in one poem, from 'base Bullen'), and with Mount Surrey, about which he was still corresponding with the patient and invaluable Hussey. Surrey's funds were running low: but the idea of adapting his standards to his finances did not occur to him. If need be, Hussey must borrow from the Duke; also, it would be a good plan for Norfolk to lend him some plate, so that his household might be suitably supplied until he had time to attend to such details personally.

Hussey replied to these suggestions in his most daunting strain. My lord's Grace would lend neither money nor silver vessels; he was in any case much vexed by Surrey's insistence on the retention of Boulogne, which he had been so rash as to describe to His Majesty as 'the chiefest jewel in his crown'. (This letter has not survived.) Why did he not heed the Council's opinion on that point? Did he know more of such affairs than his own father? After six days of argument, Norfolk and the Council had almost brought His Majesty to the point of making peace and a deal with the French, which Surrey's reports 'set back in six hours, such importance be your letters in the King's opinion at this time'. The Duke had told

Hussey to say that to hold Boulogne for another month might be expedient, 'but it cannot so continue', for His Majesty was already in debt for £300,000 which would have to be raised by subsidy, 'or other practices' — i.e. Norfolk and his fellows might be forced to disgorge. 'Moreover,' Hussey continued, 'I have heard the Duke say that he would rather bury you and the rest of his children before he should give his consent to the ruin of this realm, and that he has no doubt that ye should be removed [from the command of Boulogne] in spite of your head [obstinacy], work what ye could.' He added, 'To have my judgment of Boulogne, as I can learn, every Councillor saith "Away with it," and the King and your lordship saith "We will keep it." '[9] But Henry's decision was not now to be changed; Surrey was partly responsible for this, or considered to be so.

The new Lieutenant-General ignored these diatribes and repeated his request for a loan, if not from his father then from someone else. That was not possible, Hussey cautiously replied, 'except it be by Mrs Holland, whom I think ye would not trouble for the matter.' He added that Surrey was again in high favour with the King.[10]

The result of this correspondence was that Surrey's enemies on the Council began to say that self-interest was the reason for his determination to hold Boulogne and continue the war; if he lost his command, he would not be able to pay his debts; and indeed this aspect of the position may have entered into his calculations.

A complicated situation then arose. The browbeaten Council had officially to agree to keep Boulogne; but they desired to receive a contrary opinion from the fountainhead, thus bringing further pressure to bear on the King. Norfolk therefore wrote to Surrey 'not to animate the King too much for the keeping of Boulogne, for who so doth shall get small thanks ... Look well to what answer ye make to the letter from us of the Council. *Confirm not the enterprises contained therein.*'[11] Surrey took no notice of these instructions. Such double dealing was not in his nature, apart from the fact that he was as determined as Henry to have his own way, and even to enlarge his territory, if he could obtain the means to do so.

Sir William Paget then tried his hand at persuasion. He wrote to warn Surrey of the rising power of the Seymours; if he insisted on the tenure of Boulogne against their wishes, they would revenge themselves on him: in other words, deprive him of his command by working against him with the King. Then he would lose everything, even Henry's favour. Surrey could not visualize this last possibility. He continued his successful raids (this delighted the Commons) with the result that on November 24th, 1545, Henry got his subsidy from Parliament, one of 2s. 8d. in the pound on 'moveable goods' and one of 4s. on land, both to be paid over a period of two years.

The rage and disappointment of the Privy Council can be imagined, especially those of the newly enriched Seymour faction. On December 4th, Surrey, much heartened by the news of the subsidy and by Henry's gracious reception of his request for promotion and rewards for Captain Shelley and others of his staff, brought off an attack on the French supplies in which he used the amphibious tactics introduced by his predecessor. In his long and detailed report of this action to the King there is a significant and characteristic passage describing how 'Mr Marshall very honestly and headily brake his mace upon a Frenchman', and 'Mr Shelley brake his staff upon a tall young gentleman of M. Botyer's band, and took him prisoner; and, in effect, all the men-at-arms of this town brake their staves very honestly.'[12]

These are the terms of medieval chivalry. So Malory describes a tournament. For a hundred years at least, no English man-at-arms had used a mace in battle. Surrey was, as ever, living in the past, and conducting his campaign in a highly individualistic manner that ensured his predominance only while he was successful. He could not afford to make a single mistake; nor should he have presumed on such successes as he had made, as he did when he asked the King, through Paget, that his wife and their children (they now had four, two boys and two girls) might be allowed to join him. He missed them, and saw no reason why his occupation of enemy territory should not be provided with a domestic background; in fact, he seems to have seen himself rather in the position of a viceroy than of a general on active service. The request was refused, and Surrey spent a lonely Christmas.[13] By the beginning of January 1546, his situation had become slightly more precarious with regard to the King, who now realized that he might not live much longer, and was making plans for the eight-year-old Edward's minority.

In one sense Surrey was out of touch with English affairs, in spite of his correspondence with Hussey, Paget and the King. If he had remained at Court or had been given a position in Edward's house-hold, he would have realized the significance of Henry's putting the Prince's education into the hands of Protestant intellectuals of the middle class, all of whom were aligned with the Seymour family. Norfolk was already beginning to fit himself into this situation; if Surrey had been able to follow his father's example, he would have attained absolute security: for, apart from his only son, Henry loved few people, and of these, Surrey was one. Nothing else can account for the King's apparently inexhaustible patience with him. Surrey took Henry's attitude for granted; looking on Edward simply as a pawn in the political game, he disregarded him as an individual, while the Seymours and their allies made it their business to be friendly with Edward's tutors and to ingratiate themselves with this remarkably intelligent and responsive child. (Lisle, for instance, had already installed his second son, Robert Dudley, afterwards Earl of Leicester, in the Prince's household.) Such machinations were out of Surrey's sphere, apart from the fact that he was still bitterly resentful of Hertford, and set upon revenge at the earliest opportunity. All he knew was, that when Henry died there would be a struggle for the Regency in which the Howards must triumph. Henry also foresaw the struggle, and had decided to prevent it by giving the Seymours, Cranmer, Paget and Lisle the key positions; Norfolk was to sink into the background. Early in 1546 the Duke began to realize this, and made further plans to retain power, another manoeuvre of which Surrey was incapable. To him, Henry's favour was protection enough; he despised and underrated Hertford, and refused to recognize his influence.

This was the situation in the first week of January 1546. On the 5th, Surrey sent Sir Thomas Wyatt the Younger and another officer to discuss with Henry his long considered plan for capturing the fortress of Châtillon, near St Etienne, some ten miles from Boulogne. Henry gave him permission to proceed, upon which Surrey and his staff visited the terrain; his spies reported the garrison near starvation, and all promised well for the attack, which began on the morning of the 7th.

Surrey moved out of Boulogne with 2,000 foot and 600 cavalry, half his garrison, to join his outpost at St Etienne. The French at once advanced, were charged by Surrey's front line of infantry, and began to retire. The English cavalry pursued this advantage and, in Surrey's words, 'followed the victory, killing and slaying till they came to the carriages' – the commissariat wagons. He goes on, 'There they paused to destroy the French stores, whereof they brake and spoiled four score and ten carriages ... Our squadron then joined with the Almains [Flemish mercenaries], with a cry as of great courage and in as good order as we could wish.' By this time the second rank of infantry had come up behind the first, and the line of battle was confused. The cavalry, bent on destroying the wagons, were no longer in support, and it seemed to the newly arrived infantry that the first line was falling back, although this was not so. They fell back themselves – and thereupon, for reasons that have never become clear, panic seized them. They fled in disorder. Their officers' attempts to rally them were useless.

Now the French in their turn seized the advantage, and rode in, with terrible effect. 'Many of our gentlemen', Surrey says, 'were slain, although they gave as hearty an onset as hath been seen, and could but have had good success, *if they had been properly supported*' – his first damaging admission. 'So started,' he goes on, 'our fleeing foot-men ... could not be halted in any position that we could use [his defence becomes weaker and weaker] till they came to our trenches on St Etienne Hill. But ... our soldiers forsook those trenches and crossed the river. This gave the enemy courage to follow them. The fury of the English foot-men's flight was such that it booted little the travail that was taken ... to stop them ... In the meantime, our horsemen (who had been so successful, and thought all won) turned to find this disorder behind them ... having slain a great number of the enemy's ... Thus there was loss and victory on both sides.'

Surrey then gives the names of the officers killed – thirteen, of whom Shelley's was one. He continued, 'There were never gentlemen served more hardly. They should have had better fortune ... Beseeching Your Majesty, though the success hath not been such as we wished, to accept the good intent of us all' [of what use intentions, however excellent, were, Surrey did not pause to think], 'and consider that it seemed to us ... a necessary thing to present the fight' – i.e. to charge. After recommending several of his staff for rewards, he concludes: 'We beseech Your Majesty to consider that more of their [the enemy's] part were slain than of ours, that the fortress is in as great misery as before, and that only the sudden flight of our second line kept us from a full victory. And if any disorder there were, we assure Your Majesty it was no default in the rulers, nor lack of courage on their part. It was the fault of a humour that sometimes reigneth in Englishmen.'[14]

Surrey had condemned himself out of his own mouth, not only by his excuses, but by his assumption that the loss of his officers could not have been prevented, and that the disaster of St Etienne was a minor setback. On January 10th he sent Wyatt to explain the incident to the King. A few days later he received a stern rebuke from the Council, and a demand for more detailed information – why, for instance, had Sir George Pollard, a most valuable officer, and four Italian technicians (very expensive to replace) been omitted from the casualty list?

Surrey's defenders have pointed out that he did send a full report of the St Etienne action, and that his apparent negligence was probably caused by someone on the Council holding up his letter of January 8th, so as to prejudice the King against him. And indeed in their rebuke of January 12th the Council said that they had had no news at all from Surrey himself, adding, 'His Majesty cannot but marvel very much that in so many days [exactly four] you have advertised hither no part of that matter.' On the 18th Paget wrote to the same effect; he said that he had seen the King, who was not unduly displeased, for, 'like a prince of wisdom [he] knows that who plays at games of chance must sometimes lose' – but Surrey was to blame in not writing.[15] Whether purposely held up or not, Surrey's letter did eventually arrive, and Henry's reception of it was philo-sophical and sympathetic. What he really thought he kept to himself; as ever, his Councillors had to wait for the outcome: His Majesty gave nothing away. By this time, Surrey had made two more successful raids in the Guisnes and Hardelot area, for which he was praised. Meanwhile the English envoys at the Court of Charles V were told to inform the Emperor that the St Etienne action had been completely successful; but from London, Chapuys told his master of the real situation. 'Owing to the English losses in Bou-logne', he wrote, 'the Earl of Surrey has lost greatly in reputation.'[16] On the 20th two Italian mercenaries were sent to Boulogne as replacements and, from Surrey's point of view, St Etienne seemed to have been forgotten. During the first week in February he was informed that reinforcements were coming out, under the command of the Earl of Hertford. On February 21st, 1546, he received a long, carefully worded, superlatively tactful letter from Paget, who clearly anticipated an explosion and had been instructed by Henry to effect a compromise between Hertford and Surrey.

Having broken the news that Hertford was coming over as Lieutenant-General — 'whereby I fear that your authority as Lieu-tenant-General shall be touched' — Paget implored Surrey to behave sensibly; if he quarrelled with Hertford, then everyone would assume that he had been disgraced and he would be further humil-iated. Paget's advice, or rather Henry's, was, that Surrey should ask the King for another command, 'of the Foreward, or Rearward, or to other such place of honour as should be meet for you ... So ... you should the better be able hereafter to serve ... which should be to your reputation in the world, and in revenge of your men lost in the previous encounter.' In other words, Surrey was to be given a second chance. Paget went on to praise him for his bravery and good work, and again begged him to co-operate. 'If you should now tarry,' he explained, ' ... it would be thought ... that either you were desirous to tarry ... or else the credit of your courage and forward-ness to serve would be diminished ... ' Paget concluded with a promise that he would put Surrey's request to the King in such a manner that it could not be refused.[17]

For once — too late — Surrey was amenable. On February 25th Hertford was appointed Lieutenant-General, while the Marquis of Dorset (Suffolk's son-in-law) was made Captain of the Foreward, and Surrey Captain of the Rearward. Thus, although there is no record of his doing so, he must have applied for the post. The new forces were to arrive at the beginning of March; until then Surrey remained in command, corresponding with Paget and the Privy Council as usual. His letters are formal, detailed and courteous, showing great care for his men, no resentment about Hertford, and no anxiety for himself. In a letter dated March 15th he stresses his victory over the French in a skirmish near Etaples. 'I had the opportunity to see', he says, 'that the Frenchmen can run as fast away up the hill as the Englishmen not long ago ran down.'[18]

During the course of this apparently equable correspondence Surrey renewed his request for his wife, and their children, to join him in Boulogne. The reply came from the Privy Council that the King 'thinketh not best now that time of service, which will bring some trouble and disquietness unmeet for women's imbecilities [weakness] approacheth, that your Lordship should send for my Lady your wife'.[19] Surrey consoled himself by writing a poem, as from Frances, in which he represents her lamenting his absence, and describing a dream in which he seems to return to her, 'and to T., his little son'. In the dream, Surrey kisses her, and she exclaims — like a lady in the *Morte d'Arthur* — 'Now welcome home, my knight! Welcome, my sweet ... Thy presence bringeth forth a truce betwixt me and my care.' 'Then lively doth he look,' the supposed poetess goes on, 'And saith, "My dear, how is it now that you have all this pain?" ' She awakes, realizes that Surrey's return is a fantasy, and comforts herself by the thought of a real and imminent meeting, when 'But little time shall seem this pain, that joy shall be so sweet.'

Surrey would have done better to confine his need for his wife to his poetry; his assumption that he would be given everything he asked for increased the score against him. Although in fact his fate had already been decided, this was known only to the King. On March 21st he received a letter from the Privy Council telling him of Hertford's arrival and ordering him to submit himself to the new

Lieutenant-General. On the 22nd they wrote again, desiring Surrey to transfer the command to Hertford, to dismiss a certain number of his staff (presumably those who would have made difficulties about obeying Hertford), to cut down the garrisons to 5,000 in all, and to return to England to report to His Majesty. Meanwhile at Kenninghall, where his family were still waiting to move into Mount Surrey, the children's tutor was composing a Latin ode of welcome that contains the rather ominous phrase, 'You have commanded the waves – up to now.'[20]

On March 27th Surrey arrived at Whitehall. The King did not see him for a week. In April Lord Grey was given command of the Rearward. Surrey never set foot in France again.

NOTES TO CHAPTER EIGHT

[1] Fortescue, *History of the British Army*, vol. I, p. 101.
[2] Ibid.
[3] Cal. D.S.P., vol. XXI, pt. I, p. 742.
[4] Bapst, vol. I, p. 104.
[5] Cal. D.S.P., vol. XXI, pt. I, p. 758.
[6] Ibid.
[7] Haynes, *Burleigh MSS*, pp. 51-2.
[8] Bapst, p. 319.
[9] Ibid., p. 321.
[10] Ibid.
[11] Ibid., p. 340.
[12] Cal. D.S.P., vol. XXI, pt. I, p. 49.
[13] Ibid., p. 356.
[14] Cal. D.S.P., vol. XXI, pt. I, p. 394.
[15] Ibid., vol. XX, pt. I, p. 738.
[16] Cal. Span. S.P., vol. VIII, p. 292.
[17] Cal. D.S.P., vol. XX, pt. II, p. 738.
[18] Ibid., vol. XXI, pt. I, p. 438.
[19] Ibid., p. 470.
[20] Bapst, p. 326.

In Surrey's verse translation of chapter IV of the Book of Ecclesiastes, his view of the political situation in 1546 is clearly defined. He changes 'Better a poor and wise child than an old and foolish king, who will be no more admonished', to 'In better far estate stand children poor and wise, Than agèd kings, wedded to will, that work without advice.' Prince Edward was poor, or to be pitied, although intelligent, because his father had not made proper arrangements for his future; the implication was that with his accession the Howards would put that right.

The denigrating and arrogant attitude towards Henry VIII is highly characteristic; however much he may have come to dislike the King (who up to now had always been kind to him) Surrey was wilfully blinding himself to Henry's skill and experience; and his statement that he consulted no one is completely untrue. On this point, Surrey's greatest weakness, namely his inability to face an unpleasant situation, is revealed. He would not admit that Henry could reject Norfolk's advice for that of such 'mean men' as Hertford, Paget and Lisle. His comments on the King's behaviour during the last months of both their lives show a deliberate misinterpretation of the facts. According to Surrey, Henry had been turned against his real friends (he persuaded many people to believe this) by the insidious sycophancy of the Seymours, who were as inefficient as they were negligible. To correct this deplorable but temporary change of heart it was only necessary for Norfolk to attack the upstarts by showing the King his mistake, and producing the requisite evidence for a charge of high treason: an easy matter for one who had destroyed such potentates as Wolsey and Cromwell. When Hertford, and those of his followers who seemed likely to give any trouble, had been executed, then Norfolk and Surrey would take over, and everything would go on as before. Surrey had a second plan. This was, to wait until Henry died; then the power of the Seymours would crumble, Hertford's attainder and execution must follow automatically, and with them the ruin of his party.

It was in accordance with contemporary standards that Surrey should plan a campaign of revenge on these lines; he deviated from custom and common sense in his almost insane indiscretion. Instead of preparing his trap secretly, while keeping up an appearance of amity, in the manner that his father had perfected, he spoke of his intentions to several people, not only before, but after, his return from Boulogne, thus losing such supporters as remained to him, and placing more and deadlier weapons in the hands of his enemies. If Surrey had been able to hold his tongue, Henry would probably have continued to protect, although not to trust him; within six months of the loss of his command, he destroyed the King's belief in his loyalty, by threatening to disrupt the arrangements made for the regency. Yet Surrey was not disloyal; he brought on his own death and the ruin of his family by his belief in the possibility of a return to the pre-Reformation régime that Henry had discarded for ever, and that he could not have resuscitated, even if he had wanted to do so. The fact that Surrey had risked his life for his country half a dozen times counted as nothing against his resolve to recreate the past. If he had succeeded, or even begun to succeed, civil war would have ensued. It was therefore expedient that the man who had fought for the national security should die for it, although it is possible that he was guilty of little more than foolish talk and insolent tactlessness.

Hertford, Lisle and Paget have been accused by contemporary and other historians of conspiring against Surrey. There is no written evidence to show that they did so before he was arrested for high treason. By that time he himself had provided enough evidence for his condemnation; they therefore used it, without hesitation and without mercy, according to the custom of the age. Before then, between March and November 1546, Paget did his best to curb

Surrey's excesses, partly because it was this astute statesman's practice to keep an ally in every camp. It is almost certain that Paget held in his mind the possibility of what did in fact happen: that Edward might die before reaching his majority, and that Mary would try to set the clock back as soon as she succeeded; in that case, the Howards would turn to Paget, and he would work with them. Far from being grateful to Paget for his help and advice, from whatever motives they derived, Surrey despised him as a climber and a self-made man (Paget's father had been a 'catchpole', or bailiff) although, in his letters, he observed the forms of courtesy towards the King's Secretary of State.

Hertford, whose lead was followed by Lisle, had a low opinion of Surrey, and wanted, naturally, to push him out of the privileged position he had so often abused. The other Councillors seem to have looked on him rather as a nuisance than as an enemy. At this point, Norfolk's attitude and behaviour show an energy, adaptability and sense remarkable in a man of seventy-two, who might have been expected to want to retire from the struggle. He was not present at Surrey's interview with the King, of which no record survives: he was sitting in Council when Surrey made his report on Calais and Boulogne. Norfolk's subsequent actions show that he had decided to treat Surrey as a political liability, setting him outside his plans for retaining power. Surrey made this impossible.

Henry seems to have offered Surrey the chance of working under Hertford in Boulogne, for in April Sir William Paget wrote of his going back there to wind up his accounts, which Hertford later reported to be in a 'raw and uncertain' state.[1] Hertford was determined to make it as difficult as possible for Surrey to return to France, in any capacity; but Surrey himself put an end to his military career by retiring to the country, where he remained during April, May and June, dividing his time between Kenninghall and Mount Surrey, to which he was now putting the finishing touches.

In June Lady Surrey became pregnant of her fifth and posthumous child. Throughout Surrey's story she remains a curiously indefinite figure. That he loved her is clear from his poems; whether she returned that love to the same degree may be doubted. She took no part at all in his Court life, which he resumed, momentarily, in August, when he was summoned to London for the reception of the new French Ambassador, de la Garde, taking precedence over all the other nobles.[1]

A few weeks earlier Surrey had been corresponding with Paget about Hertford's dismissal of some of his officers from Boulogne. His letter shows that he was making an effort to resign himself to private life, but that he was, as ever, in financial difficulties. His officers' 'necessity' had cost him a good deal, and he had received no help from Lord Grey in recompensing them. Grey's accusation that Surrey had used his position for his own gain was untrue. 'As to the charge that I retained the office to my private profit,' Surrey declared, 'there are in Boulogne too many witnesses that Henry of Surrey was never for singular [personal] profit corrupted, nor never yet bribe closed his hand; which lesson I learnt of my father, and wish to succeed him, as in the rest.' This dignified refutation does not quite match with the writer's request in the following autumn for the grant of the clock-tower and cloister of Christ Church in Norwich, which were, Surrey pointed out, 'unserviceable to their church save as a memory of the old superstition, and will extend to discharge me out of the misery of debt.'[2] His conclusion shows a dawning doubt of the continuance of Henry's favour. 'If it were his most excellent Majesty's pleasure to give it me, I will faithfully promise never to trouble His Majesty with any suit of profit to myself hereafter, and spend that and the rest in His Majesty's service with the old zeal that I have served with always ... I expect success in this suit,' he goes on, 'the thing itself being such that the King shall forbear nothing.' This letter shows signs of having been dashed off: and indeed it might have been better phrased.

Those quiet summer months in the country gave Surrey too much time to brood, not only over the debts that he now realized would not be paid until his father died, but over the monstrous injustice, as it must have seemed to him, with which he had been treated. It was not in his nature to keep his furious resentment to himself, or even to attempt to do so; and as soon as he returned to London he began talking of his plans for rehabilitation to his old comrade, Sir George Blagge. Whether their conversation took place in the Howard mansion or at Whitehall, is not clear; the measure of Surrey's indiscretion is shown by the fact that they were not alone, and that some of their talk was overheard and reported.

Blagge seems to have interrupted Surrey's attacks on his enemies by reminding him that 'those the King shall appoint shall be meetest to rule the Prince in the event of the King's death', to which Surrey replied, 'My father is meetest, both for good services done, and for estate.' Blagge, irritated by this haughty assumption – and no doubt frightened at his own indiscretion, for to speak of Henry's death bordered on treason – answered in a manner designed to show his loyalty. 'Then the Prince shall be but evil taught,' he said. 'Rather than that it shall come to pass that the Prince should be under the government of your father or you, I would bide the adventure to thrust this dagger in you.' 'You are very hasty,' said Surrey. 'God sends a shrewd cow short horns.' 'Yea, my lord,' replied Blagge, 'and I trust your horns also shall be kept so short as you shall not be able to do any hurt with them.'

Blagge then walked out of the room. Surrey, who was unarmed, caught up his sword and dagger, and followed him to his house. There he began, 'Of late you have been very hasty with me – ' and at that point they withdrew.[4] Their quarrel ended amicably, from Surrey's point of view, with an apology for his rashness that he embodied in a short poem – the prologue to his versification of the Seventy-Third Psalm. He explains away his outburst in the opening lines – 'The sudden storms that heave me to and fro, Had well-nigh piercèd faith, my guiding sail' – and after a brief description of the ill fortune that had almost brought him to despair ('Then I 'gan faint, and all my courage fail') he goes on, 'But now, my Blagge, mine error well I see, Such goodly light King David giveth me.'

The light provided by the Jewish king reveals Surrey's hatred of the Seymours and their supporters in a passage of splendid vitupera-tion of which the original runs, 'But as for me, my feet were almost gone; my steps had well nigh slipped ... I saw the prosperity of the wicked ... their strength is firm. They are not in trouble as other men; neither are they plagued like other men ... Behold, these are the ungodly, who prosper in the world; they increase in riches ... When I thought to know this, it was too painful for me; until I went into the sanctuary of God; then understood I their end. Surely thou didst set them in slippery places; thou castedst them down into destruction ... As a dream when one awaketh; so, O Lord, when thou awakest, thou shalt despise their image ... For, lo, they ... shall perish ... I have put my trust in the Lord God.'

Surrey was incapable of trusting in God's vengeance; in fact, he would only have had five years to wait for Hertford's execution, two for Thomas Seymour's, and six for Lisle's. Thirsting for his rivals' blood, he preferred to put his faith in his own violence; and its edge was turning against him.

Meanwhile Norfolk had embarked on a change of tactics that would have reversed the process planned by Surrey. Accepting the Seymours' status as unassailable, the Duke approached Lord Hertford with a suggestion for what he described as cross-marriages that would combine their powers and put an end to rivalry. Admiral Seymour's marriage to the Duchess of Richmond was to be reconsidered, and contracts made between Norfolk's two elder grandsons (Surrey's children) and his grandson by Lord Thomas Howard to three of Hertford's daughters.[5] Norfolk rightly guessed that Hertford's hostility would be overborne by the advantages of these four alliances. The King's approval was obtained some time in May, while Surrey was in the country. It seems that Norfolk had decided not to inform his son of these plans until he himself had come to terms with Hertford. Surrey might then be tempted to give his consent by the prospect of paying his debts out of the income accruing from the settlements on which he would be able to draw during his sons' minority. Until their marriages were consummated there remained the possibility of dissolution in favour of more profitable matches. No arrangement could have been more satisfactory from Norfolk's point of view, or more pleasing to the Seymours, who were anxious to ally themselves with patrician families of great possessions; that Hertford's grandchildren would thereby be able to claim descent from Mowbrays and Plantagenets was another inducement, for he was acquisitive and ambitious in more ways than one.

The preliminaries to these arrangements were common knowledge at Court when on June 6th Surrey appeared at Whitehall for the feast of St George. As soon as he realized what had been going on, he went to his father and told him that he would not for an instant consider such marriages for his sons. Norfolk expostulated. 'You will lose as much as ye have gathered together,' he said. In a towering rage, Surrey went to find his sister, to whom he protested with even greater violence; he was more than ever determined to prevent her marrying Admiral Seymour.

This scene seems to have taken place in one of the ante-rooms of the palace, in the presence of several courtiers, whose versions of it bear out one another. Surrey began by abusing the Council, and then, according to a witness whose evidence is not supported on this point, taxed his sister with the rumours of her loose behaviour. 'If it be true,' he said, 'I will be your mortal enemy.' To this the Duchess made no reply, and Surrey turned to the question of the Admiral. 'Your fantasy will not serve to marry with him,' he declared, and added something about a pretence of a marriage. The assumption that Mary could not possibly like Seymour (a shallow but very attractive young man) is highly characteristic.

Something in the Duchess's manner and expression must have enraged Surrey further, for now, at the top of his voice, he burst into a bitterly satirical harangue that was as insulting as it was treasonous. 'You should dissemble the matter,' he said, 'and I will find the means that the King's Majesty shall speak with you himself. Ye should in no wise utterly make refusal of him [Seymour], but leave the matter so diffusely [uncertainly] that the King's Majesty will speak with you again – and thus, by length of time, it is possible the King should take such a fantasy unto you that you shall be able to govern, like Madame d'Estampes [Francis I's mistress], which should not only be a means to help yourself, but all your friends shall receive a commodity by the same.' The Duchess replied passionately, 'I would rather we should all perish, and cut my own throat than consent to such a villainy!' and Surrey flung out of the room.[6]

His behaviour during this interview shows a crudity and high-handedness from which the modern reader recoils; his suggestion that the Duchess should become the King's mistress was of course ironical, and his strongest form of protest. Many of his contemporaries, while ostensibly shocked by his references to Henry — whose mistresses had never had any official standing, as in the case of Francis I — sympathized with his care for his sister's reputation, and with his hatred of the Seymours. The Duchess, pitied for being 'neither wife nor maid', since Richmond's death, was a beautiful, lively and now embittered girl, who had been deprived of her rights through her widowhood, and of a household of her own by the fact that Norfolk and Henry had not been able to make up their minds about her next husband. That she should remain chaste was therefore of the greatest importance to her relatives, not only in respect of her eligibility (Norfolk's chief concern) but also in that of the family honour, a matter that Surrey rated higher than anything else. The report that she was free with her favours did not reach him until his return from France; this, combined with her inclination towards heresy, and her frequentation of Bess Holland, was more horrifying to him than any imputation on his own integrity. It was therefore natural, and, according to contemporary standards, right, that he should speak as he did; his mistake was in doing so publicly, and in allowing his satire to touch the sacrosanctity of Henry's person. Surrey may not have realized that Mary was bitterly hostile to him, no doubt because he persisted in preventing her marriage — from her point of view, quite a profitable one — to a man whom almost every lady in the Court circle found irresistible. The impression created by such dialogues as these contrasts oddly with the fact that many persons who worked for and with Surrey were deeply attached to him. He never forgot an obligation, or the care of those less privileged than himself; he was incapable of deceit or cowardice; and his social address had a natural gaiety that was extremely endearing to his associates, even when they disapproved of or were alarmed by, his impulsiveness, obstinacy and pride. This side of his character is lovingly described by Thomas Churchyard in a very indifferent poem published after Surrey's death. Churchyard was attached to Surrey's household for a short time, and he cherished the memory of his kindness, his wit and the distinction of manner that even his outbursts of violence could not entirely spoil.

So Surrey's virtues as well as his faults helped to bring him down. Surrounded by such admirers as Churchyard, whom he subjugated in spite of themselves, and who were not in a position to warn or check him, he could not remould his life after he ceased to be a soldier. If he had been able to settle at Mount Surrey, he would have been remembered as a great poet and the star of a magnificent Court; he would have continued the idyll of his love for his wife on a solid basis of domesticity; he would have inherited, with the premier dukedom of England, the accumulated love and loyalty of those who looked on him as their protector; his financial position might have become stabilized; his appearances at the Court of Edward VI would have been greeted with ceremonious respect, and his children's careers woven into the fabric of the state to the enhancement of his own power.

Surrey could no more have shaped his course of life on these lines than he could have cringed to Hertford for a place, or shown cowardice in the field. His poetry was a hobby, privately shared with a small group of intellectuals; his domestic impulses, although deep and sincere, were intermittent. As he saw it, his whole existence had its being in the glittering gambling-hell of political intrigue, where such a player as he must stake life as well as fortune on every throw: where impulse, honour, chivalry and pride had no place: where the subtlest cunning and the most highly evolved forms of lying and prevarication were the only safeguards. Surrey turned his back on the privacy, and what he must have felt to be the intolerable monotony, of his country home, because he had been conditioned to do so; in this respect he followed the example of his contemporaries.

Before he left his new home for London in July 1546, Surrey was busy with certain details of its interior decoration that were to become the hinges of the trap in which he was caught and held. In the last weeks of his command at Boulogne he had discovered, and may have brought back into England, some craftsman who still possessed the art of staining glass that had reached its apotheosis during the

Middle Ages. Such work was exactly what Surrey desired for his new mansion. Having evolved designs and colours for his escutcheon with this French glazier, he sent one of his servants, John Spencer, to install the result in his rooms at Lambeth, while he had copies made for Mount Surrey. At the time that this work was in progress his secretary, Hugh Ellis, noticed that the arms of Edward the Confessor were incorporated in the glass panels, and that they were also engraved on some table silver that Surrey had commissioned from another craftsman. Some protest or warning was made. Surrey replied, as he had two years before to Barker, the King's herald, that Richard II had given his Mowbray ancestors the right to bear those arms, and that, although his immediate forebears had ceased to do so, he was going to revive the practice.[7] In making this decision Surrey again deliberately ignored the fact that since the accession of Henry VII the arms of St Edward had formed part of the escutcheon of the heir to the throne and had been borne by no other family after the last Plantagenet king perished on Bosworth Field. The Tudors then assumed them; Surrey had already been warned that for anyone else to do so amounted to a breach of the law, and an insult to the crown. He felt, as his speeches and actions show, defiant, embittered and resentful, and he was determined not only to express but to record those emotions, in the face of convention, good manners and common sense. It was the only gesture he could make that relieved his feelings and for which he could produce a precedent, if not an excuse. He did not realize that this form of consolation would be invaluable to his enemies, and of ominous importance to his sole protector and ally — the dying Henry VIII, who was using all that remained of his energies to establish the undisputed inheritance of his son.

Again, if Surrey had been content to claim a privilege that was no longer his, while staying outside political strife, he would probably have been reproved and his impertinence forgiven; but he combined the alteration of his escutcheon with hints and threats that seemed to indicate the organization of a plot against the government. This welding of two forms of rebellion appeared highly dangerous to the majority of the onlookers; Surrey himself was unaware of the impression he was making.

Detailed study of a contemporary drawing entitled *Howard, Earl of Surrey for Which He Was Attainted*, now in the British Museum, shows some interesting differences between his version of the Howard arms and that preceding it. The escutcheon has twelve quarterings; the fifth is that of Edward the Confessor, and the second that of the Brothertons. The three Brotherton points, or 'labels', of silver, have been transferred by Surrey from the Brotherton quartering to that of Edward the Confessor. Surrey thus implied that his Brotherton ancestors were directly descended from Edward the Confessor, and that he himself was in the line of succession; in fact, to follow his process of heraldic reasoning to its limits would be tantamount to placing the Howard claim above that of the Tudors.

What we should now consider a trivial alteration in a semi-private code, and the concern of the owner alone had, in Surrey's day, and especially at that particular moment of unrest and anxiety, enormous and sinister significance. His shifting the 'three labels silver' is remarked on over and over again in the contemporary records of his trial; for it came near to being a declaration of war against the dynasty; and very few persons then looked on it as a perversion of justice when he was arrested partly because he moved three symbols from one place in his escutcheon to another.

Surrey effected this final change in his arms just after the treaty of Boulogne had been signed, when he was asked by Lisle to supply certain information about the fortresses of Calais and Guisnes. He seems to have replied at random, with the result that Lisle, a far more venomous and spiteful intriguer than Hertford, was able to report to Paget that his lordship's letter contained 'so many parables that I do not perfectly understand it; which letter (if you think it meet) I advise you to show to the King's Majesty, with also to send me your advice, touching an answer ... ' Surrey's letter to Lisle has not survived.[8]

Surrey then followed up the installation of his new escutcheon at Lambeth and Mount Surrey — where the Duchess of Richmond and Bess Holland duly noted the changes he had made — by commissioning the portrait of himself already described. In addition to the *Sat Superest* motto on the column, he caused to be inscribed on his

Garter the words, *Tel Dandus*, which, freely translated by himself a few months later, meant 'Till then, thus.' It was at this point that Norfolk heard what he was doing, and expostulated with him, in vain. The Duke went so far as to tell Bess Holland that she 'should take no pattern of his son's arms to work them with her needle in his [Norfolk's] house'.* Bess seems to have proposed to do this for her own purpose (the implication of Norfolk, of whom she had tired) at the Duchess of Richmond's suggestion; for the Duchess was now preparing to work against her father and her brother, in order to ally herself with the Seymours.

Norfolk then ordered Surrey to obliterate both the mottoes on the portrait, and to restore the escutcheons to their original forms. Surrey told the painter, an Italian, to remove the *Tel Dandus* from his picture.[10] (The *Sat Superest* is still there.) Surrey must have sent the artist back to his own country, for he was not called upon to give evidence. In any case, both mottoes had already been noted and recorded. Surrey, who was again at Court, then began to try to collect allies likely to support him against the Seymours; what practical plans of attack, if any, he had formed, will never be known.

The Duchess of Richmond's methods were forthright and simple – she went to the King and told him about Surrey's picture and the escutcheon. She weakened her case by adding that in some of the shields he had incorporated the arms of Sir Lancelot du Lac, placing on top of these a cap of maintenance and the crown of England; she was unaware that Surrey was entitled to the last two additions and that the first was a private fantasy. It seems that she had not the courage to repeat the far more damning evidence of Surrey's remarks about her becoming Henry's mistress. The King himself remained non-committal.[11]

Meanwhile the installation of Surrey's new escutcheons had been reported to Garter-King-at-Arms by Sir Edward Warner and Devereux, another herald. They may have felt that they should have prevented his assumptions of two years before, and that they would now be censured for their negligence, so they said nothing to the Privy Council, although they were very uneasy. 'I like not the doing thereof,' Warner said. Devereux began to inveigh against

Surrey's 'pride and vain-glory'. 'It may be abated one day,' he added significantly. 'What mean you?' Warner asked. 'What if he should be accused to the King that he should say [has said], "If God should call the King to His mercy, who were so meet to govern the Prince as my lord my father?" ' said Devereux. 'Is there any such thing?' Warner exclaimed. 'It may be so,' Devereux replied.[12]

The gossip caused by Surrey's behaviour died down a little when he left for the country at the beginning of November. A week or so later the King, who was at Windsor, became very ill; it was assumed by those who had not seen him that he would die during the next few days, and that his powers had failed him, which meant that Hertford and Paget would be in control of the government. In fact the attack, although severe, was temporary; by the time Surrey had hurried up to London, Henry was transacting business as usual.

Surrey, believing that the moment to act had come, brought with him a cousin who had been his companion since boyhood, Sir Richard Southwell. Then and since, some confusion has arisen between Richard Southwell and his brother Robert. Robert had nothing to do with the events that took place between the middle of November and December 2nd, 1546; his descendants averred that he was ashamed of the part Richard played in them; it is therefore possible that it was he who destroyed the evidence that was to form the greater part of the charge against Surrey and that was provided by Richard. In any case Richard, not Robert, was present when Surrey said to Sir Edmund Knevett, whose right arm he had saved by pleading with the King eight years before, 'My lord of Hertford shall smart for replacing me in France.'[13]

Surrey then made a statement which later on was set aside from the other charges, and given into the keeping of Robert Southwell; it was last heard of as being in his possession, and thereafter disappeared. Bishop Burnet may have seen it, but does not record it in detail: he says, 'Sir Robert Southwell knew certain things of the Earl that touched his fidelity to the King,' thus further obscuring the issue; for Burnet does not make it clear whose fidelity to the King was in question, Southwell's, or Surrey's.[14] Rightly or wrongly, from this Southwell evidence the conclusion was drawn that Surrey planned to seize and murder certain members of the Privy Council as a preliminary to a *coup d'état*; whether he had actually set in hand such a scheme will never be known; it is more than likely that he was preparing to do so: but even that cannot now be proved.

At about the same time, Knevett taxed Surrey with having 'borne him malice' about some dispute that had taken place between them in Boulogne. Surrey replied, 'No, no, Cousin Knevett, I malice not so low — my malice is higher, my malice climbs higher — ' and then reverted to his father's destruction of Wolsey and Cromwell. Knevett reminded him that it was sin to speak ill of dead men. Surrey burst out, 'These new erected men would by their wills leave no nobleman on life!' He added that Wolsey and Cromwell had sought the death of his father, as their low-born successors now sought his, and went on to explain that the King had never forgiven him for his failure in France. 'This displeasure,' Surrey declared, 'was set forward by them who hate me, for setting up an altar [it had been to the Virgin] in the church at Boulogne. God long save my father's life — for if he were dead, they would shortly have my head.'[15]

Richard Southwell then began to keep a watch on Surrey's movements, and noted that through one of his servants he was corresponding with that potentially dangerous, because Plantagenet, exile, Cardinal Pole, who had been supposed to help organize the Catholic renaissance at the time of the Pilgrimage of Grace. Richard Southwell also believed, or afterwards said he believed, that Surrey was employing his jester, an Italian, as a spy. In this suspicion he was supported by Sir Gawain Carew, who had been present during Surrey's dispute with his sister; he and Richard Southwell were together when Surrey said to them, 'Note these men which are made by the King's Majesty of vile birth — [they] have been the destruction of all the nobility of this realm. These are they that now slight me — ' he added fiercely, 'but one day I shall make them look small.'[16]

Meanwhile Norfolk, bitterly resentful of being left out of what he described as the '*privy* Privy Council' during Henry's illness, was confiding in Elizabeth Holland, unaware that both she and his daughter had turned against him. He told Bess that the King was 'much grown of his body, and that he could not go up and down the stairs, but was let up and down by a device.' None of the King's Council loved him, he added, 'because they are no noblemen born themselves — as also, because I believe too truly in the Sacrament of the altar. Moreover, the King loves me not, because I am too much loved in my country. His Majesty is sickly,' he concluded darkly, 'and cannot long endure.'[17]

This speech was one of Norfolk's few indiscretions, and may be accounted for by the fact that Bess Holland, who had now been his mistress for more than twenty years, was the last person he was likely to mistrust; he did not guess that this far-sighted lady was planning to change sides as soon as the Duchess of Richmond gave the signal. Norfolk's attitude towards Surrey shows a similar unawareness; he had put an end, as he thought, to his son's folly over his arms; he knew nothing of the plot against the Council that Surrey had been organizing: or if he did, he shut his eyes to it. Norfolk, who had extricated himself from so many difficulties, had perhaps become over-confident, in spite of his complaints about the withdrawal of the King's favour; and he had no conception of the lengths to which Surrey had gone, and was going. Surrey had written several times to him when the King fell ill; Norfolk ignored these letters, and destroyed them.

Surrey's final gesture, a threatening letter to Admiral Seymour, which was shown to the Privy Council and has not survived, was, in the writer's view, a legitimate expression of the candour on which he had always prided himself. 'Pardon my frankness,' he had once written to Paget, 'as you do know it is my nature to use such frankness with such as I do hold my friends.'[18] The frankness Surrey used towards an enemy was enough to complete the case against him. By the end of November this letter and Richard Southwell's evidence had been collated with the statements of Sir Edward Warner, Knevett and Blagge, and submitted to the King, who came to the conclusion that Surrey — and possibly also his father — was guilty of high treason and of conspiracy of murder. Henry therefore made the decision which he had probably been considering for some time.

Surrey must die. Any discrepancies in the evidence must be disposed of by the usual means, that of supplementary charges based on hearsay, and information obtained through terror or bribery. Those who could reveal anything, however trivial, against Surrey and Norfolk were promised impunity. Meanwhile Henry told Paget that he intended to hamstring Norfolk by taking away his properties and handing them over to the Seymours, giving Hertford the largest share. A number of eighteenth- and nineteenth-century historians and biographers have recorded their disgust at these methods. They were accepted by Surrey's contemporaries (although some of them sympathized with him) as part of the judicial procedure and as a safeguard against civil war.

On December 1st Surrey was at Whitehall. Henry had given orders that his arrest was to be made privately, and that he was to be conveyed not to the Tower but to the Lord Chancellor's house in Holborn — a last extension of favour, for from there it would be easier for him to call upon his friends for help and advice. A Spanish merchant who was in the palace has described how he saw the captain of the guard come into the great hall in the early afternoon of that day with twelve halberdiers, whom he told to wait in an adjoining corridor. When Surrey came out from dinner, the captain approached him. 'My lord,' he began, 'I would your lordship should intercede for me with the Duke your father in a matter in which I need his favour, if you will deign to listen to me — ' and so led him towards the corridor. There the halberdiers took charge, and Surrey was escorted to Whitehall stairs where a boat was in readiness; thence he was conveyed to Holborn without attracting attention. No one missed him until that night.[19]

Next day Surrey was brought up before the Privy Council, who had summoned Richard Southwell to hear his evidence read out; this is the evidence that has disappeared. Bishop Burnet, who may have seen it (for Southwell's descendant was one of his friends), says that it contained some 'points that were of a higher [graver] nature' than those of the escutcheon and the portrait, although these formed part of Southwell's accusations. When the reading came to an end Surrey burst into a passionate speech of self-exculpation, denial and defence. He offered, then and there, to fight Southwell, 'in his shirt', according to the medieval custom. Southwell became equally belligerent, and a violent scene took place, with the result that both accuser and accused were taken into custody, Southwell to the Tower and Surrey to the Lord Chancellor's. Here he was allowed to remain for the next ten days, in order, presumably, to work on his defence. On December 12th Norfolk, who was at Kenninghall, was arrested and sent up to London; from his residence at Lambeth he was conveyed by water to the Tower.[20]

On the same day Henry gave orders that Surrey, whose arrest had not been made public, should be taken through the streets on foot from Holborn to the Tower.[21] This departure from custom caused much comment; that the privacy of a covered barge should have been denied a man of Surrey's rank implied, from the citizens' point of view, the intent to degrade. Crowds followed Surrey all the way – in silence. In their eyes he was no longer to be pitied, or a hero, because all they knew was that he had threatened the inheritance of the boy whom they spoke of as England's Treasure, the little Prince whose reign was to inaugurate 'a golden world'. According to an eye-witness, Surrey made 'great lamentation' during the course of his journey.[22] This last word had then another connotation that may be here applied. Surrey did not weep, or ask for pity. He protested and stormed, cursing and defying his enemies. In his own eyes, he was a loyal servant of the crown, whose only crime was that of trying to correct abuses and punish the villains who were bent on destroying him.

As soon as Surrey reached the Tower he wrote to the Privy Council. His letter shows that his attitude was unchanged. He was disgraced, and his enemies had triumphed – for a time. He had nothing to fear, because he had done no wrong. As on other occasions, he had only to put his case in order to be released.

NOTES TO CHAPTER NINE

[1] State Papers of Henry VIII, vol. II, p. 18.
[2] Bapst, p. 350.
[3] Cal. D.S.P., vol. XXI, pt. I, p. 1274.
[4] Ibid., pt. II, pp. 555-6.
[5] Ibid.
[6] Ibid.
[7] *Chronicle of Henry VIII*, pp. 143-8.
[8] Cal. D.S.P., vol. XXI, pt. II, p. 1263.
[9] Herbert, p. 562.
[10] *Chronicle of Henry VIII*, p. 159.
[11] Ibid.
[12] Cal. D.S.P., vol. XXI, pt. II, p. 555.
[13] Burnet, *History of the Reformation*, vol. I, pt. I, pp. 533-8.
[14] Ibid.
[15] Cal. D.S.P., vol. XXI, pt. II, p. 555.
[16] Ibid.
[17] Herbert, p. 569.
[18] Cal. D.S.P., vol. XXI, pt. I, p. 1274.
[19] *Chronicle of Henry VIII*, pp. 143-8.
[20] Cal. D.S.P., vol. XXI, pt. II, p. 605.
[21] Ibid.
[22] Greyfriars' *Chronicle*, p. 52.

IN the reign of Henry VIII a public trial in open court was a
formal demonstration of the prisoner's guilt, of the sacrosanctity
of the state and of the sovereign's duty to protect himself and his
people against their enemies. The real trial, as we now understand
the word, with its very faint chances of defence and ultimate
freedom, took place privately, in the council chamber of the
Chancellor's house or of the Tower; an open hearing was therefore
dreaded and if possible postponed by those who had offended.
Their best hope was to prolong and amplify the private hearings,
so that they had time to collect as many defending witnesses as
were allowed them.

In this respect Surrey was leniently treated. His witnesses may
have been to some degree intimidated, but they were neither
terrorized nor silenced, as their evidence shows. His greatest danger,
which he seems not to have realized, lay in his father's power and
status. As Norfolk's heir and pupil — as the descendant, both
through his mother and through his Mowbray and Brotherton
ancestors, of Edward III — rather than as a rebel and a conspirator,
Surrey was on a knife-edge. Nevertheless he was allowed five weeks'
interviewing and the right to object to certain examiners as being
unduly prejudiced against him. According to the standards of the
day, the first stage of his condemnation was achieved by careful, fair
and orthodox methods, as his letter to the Council proves. Surrey
would have complained and protested if he had been unjustly used,
as far as his defence was concerned. He did not do so. He asked for a
further and more private examination than those already granted;

in other words, an interview with a few personally selected Council-lors, which might then be considered in full Council and so reported to the King. His letter, highly characteristic in its lack of reference to the major issue, is not dated, but was probably written on or about December 13th, 1546, and begins with an exculpation of Norfolk, of whose arrest he had just heard.

'Since the beginning of my durance,' he says, 'my master's displeasure, much loss of blood and sorrow to see the long approved truth of mine old father brought into question by any stir between Southwell and me has sore enfeebled me.' Having thus indicated that a recurrence of the dysentery from which he had suffered on other occasions had made it impossible for him to defend himself adequately, Surrey goes on, 'And therefore, lest my wits should not be fresh to unburden my conscience of a matter which I have re-served in expectation of your being sent from the King to examine me, I make this suit.' He then refers to his first examination by four members of the Privy Council – Sir Thomas Wriothesley, Gardiner, the Marquis of Winchester and Sir Anthony Browne – when he had been arrested for brawling after the supper-party at Mrs Arundell's. 'Wherein', he says, 'God knoweth with what danger I escaped, notwithstanding mine innocency, for the which I humbly confess to have conceived no small jealousy [prejudice] in your favour, and ask your pardon therefor. My desire is, you four, and only you, may be sent to me, for so it should be best for His Majesty's service, to whom I intend to discharge my conscience in such matter of importance as dependeth unto the formal examination, trusting in your honourable lordships that with respect of my particular deserts to you, ye will make report of my tale to His Majesty, according as ye shall hear. If this request seem too bold, I trust His Majesty shall be content when I am heard.'[1]

It is almost unbelievable, and indeed tragic, that Surrey could affiliate a trivial act of hooliganism, by which he had seriously injured no one, with the change in his escutcheon and his threats and plans against the state; and his belief that he would be able to eliminate Hertford, Paget and Lisle from the interviews on which his life depended, shows an unawareness of his circumstances that now calls for compassion; surely mercy might have been extended to a young man so completely out of touch with the facts? It could not be. The situation was too precarious. If Prince Edward had reached his majority, or if the King had been in reasonable health, Surrey might have ended his days in more or less comfortable confinement or in exile. His final request to the Privy Council is another proof of his unrealistic attitude. 'And albeit Mr Barker [a mistake for Sir Christopher Barker, Garter-King-at-Arms] was present at the formal examination, he should not be at this. Nevertheless my matter [request] is prejudicial to no creature, unless to myself.' Evidently Surrey thought that Barker's censure, dating from three years before, of the alterations in his escutcheon, would form the greater part of the charge against him. This was not so, as some of the questions put to him prove, although naturally his recent advertising of his Plantagenet ancestry and his shifting of the Brotherton arms from one quartering to another were later dealt with in full.

Surrey did not know that while he was writing this letter Sir Richard Southwell had been released from the Tower and sent to Kenninghall with two other informers to tell Lady Surrey and the Duchess of Richmond of Surrey's and Norfolk's arrest, and to collect further evidence. As soon as Southwell and his companions arrived they placed men at all the doors and sent for the Duchess of Richmond and Bess Holland, 'who were only just risen,' Southwell reported, 'but came to us without delay in the dining-chamber.' When she heard their errand, the Duchess fainted. Revived, she fell on her knees and said, 'Though I love my father, and my brother – whom I note to be a rash man – I will conceal nothing. I will declare in writing all I can remember against them.' 'Use truth and frankness, and do not despair,' Southwell told her.[2]

The Duchess's statements against Norfolk and Surrey were then taken down. She dwelt at some length, not only on Surrey's satirical suggestion that she should become Henry's mistress, but on the portrait of himself in which the two mottoes, *Sat Superest* and *Tel Dandus*, had been incorporated, adding that Norfolk knew of these and thus implying that he had let them pass. She said also that

Surrey had warned her against individual interpretations of the Scriptures.[3]

Her cupboards were then searched; nothing of value being found, she was asked for an explanation, and replied that she had had to sell all her jewels to pay her debts. Her servants' evidence supported this statement. Bess Holland's treasure-chests revealed nothing either. She herself was stripped, and was found to have concealed on her person a quantity of jewelled belts, beads, gold buttons, pearl necklaces and rings. An inventory was made of these, and another of all the contents of Kenninghall. Lady Surrey was not called on to give evidence, and was allowed to remain under house arrest, while the Duchess and Bess were escorted to London, with a selected number of Surrey's servants, to repeat and amplify their statements to the Privy Council.[4]

Bess Holland confined her evidence to information against Norfolk, adding that Surrey had always hated both herself and his sister of Richmond. The Duchess repeated her account, which was verified by others, of Surrey's conversation with her about becoming the King's mistress, and of his threats against the Council.

And then at last the Duchess of Norfolk was given the chance of revenge for which she had craved in solitude and obscurity; but the evidence she had treasured up against her husband was rejected as confused, out of date and valueless, and she was left to long for his death — in vain. She survived him by four years, dying at their house in Lambeth in 1558. Meanwhile another commission was sent down to Bindon in Dorset to arrest Lord Thomas Howard, Surrey's younger brother. He was released shortly after Surrey's execution.

Having collated the evidence of the Duchess of Richmond, Bess Holland, Southwell, Knevett, Blagge and several other courtiers and officers of heraldry, the Council then examined the witnesses for Surrey's defence, of whom the principal — and the only one of value — was his secretary, Hugh Ellis. Ellis maintained his denials of his master's guilt, but his replies show that he did not grasp the extent to which Surrey had offended in altering his escutcheon.

'Have you heard,' he was asked, 'the Earl of Surrey wish or devise that his sister of Richmond might rule about the King as Madame d'Estampes does?'

Ellis replied, 'I never knew them so great together as to wish her so good a turn, nor saw in him the countenance of any such purpose.'

'Have you heard him speak of the governance of the Prince in the event of the King's death?'

'Never.'

'Have you heard him deprave [run down] any of the King's Council?'

'I know only of a discord between him and my Lord Admiral, to whom he wrote his mind in a letter.'

'Have you heard him speak of flying out of the realm?'

'Never. But he has said that if he survived his father he should have enough and never covet more.'

'Has he lately taken into his arms any of the ancient coats of the crown, why and by whose counsel, and where are the patterns?'

'I heard him say that King Edward [the Confessor] gave the arms of England to his predecessors; and at Boulogne, in presence of the King's Council there [Ellis is here trying to throw the responsibility on to the authorities] he devised of painting the same among other coats in escutcheons sent thence to Norwich, and still remaining in the house of John Spencer, his servant. And since, at Lambeth, he drew other arms for windows which a glazier of Norwich has to work in glass for his new house. There is a stamp of the same for vessels.'

'Have you seen writing touching these matters?'

'Only of the descent of his ancestors – for placing their coats in escutcheons and windows.'

'What letters did he write from Lambeth to his father when the King was sick, and what were the contents?'

'The letters were of his own writing, and I did not read them.'

'Have you heard him speak of selling or yielding up Boulogne?'

'I never saw a spot of any likelihood thereof.'[5]

Some minor points were then gone into, with which witnesses is not clear. These were Surrey's armoured 'pavilions' at Mount Surrey, his correspondence with Cardinal Pole, his assumption of the 'gown of gold' that was the prerogative of royalty, his negligence

during the Hardelot raid and his poetical satire on London. The
answers to them were satisfactory, from Surrey's point of view, and
not incorporated into the charges against him.[6]

Surrey was then called upon for a series of formal and informal (or
public and private) examinations. All his answers have not survived;
no doubt they amounted to categorical denials; they may have been
destroyed with the Southwell evidence. His statements during the
trial, however, his father's defence and Ellis's evidence provide a
fragmentary portion of his replies. Thus supplemented and slightly
simplified, a typical dialogue between Surrey and his accusers would
run as follows:

'Do you bear in your arms the escutcheon and arms of Edward
the Confessor?'

'King Richard II hath given the Mowbrays, my ancestors, the
right to bear the arms of Edward the Confessor.'

'How long have you borne them?'

'Your lordships know that all my ancestors have borne these arms,
and that King Henry VII took them away from the Duke my
father.'

'By what authority have you borne them?'

'King Edward [the Confessor] gave the arms of England to my
predecessors.'

'Are you next heir or akin to St Edward, and if so, how?'

(No surviving answer.)

'Did your father or grandfather bear those arms?'

'My Brotherton ancestors bare it so.'

'Did William the Conqueror do your ancestors any wrong at the
time of the Conquest?'

(No surviving answer.)

'Why did you put these arms in your coat?'

'Go to the church of East Winch in Norfolk, and you will see
them there, for they have been ours for five hundred years.'

'Why do you bear them at this time more than you or your
father at other times before?'

'I never sought to usurp the King's arms, for all know that my
ancestors bore them.'

'Have you any inheritance from Edward the Saint?'
(No surviving answer.)
'If so, where is it, and what do you call it?'
(No surviving answer.)
'If the King should die in the Prince's tender age, have you devised who should govern him and the realm?'
(No surviving answer.)
'What have you devised or done whereby you might rule the King in his own time [life] or the Prince, if God should dispose of His Majesty?'
(No surviving answer.)
'Did you procure any person to dissemble in anything with the King's Majesty, to the intent that the same might grow in his favour for the better compassing of your purposes, or procure your sister or any other woman to be the King's concubine?'
(No surviving answer.)
'What words of reproach or slander had you of the King's Council, and what were the words, and against whom?'
(No surviving answer.)
'What arms [weapons] have you given to any man, English, or stranger, what, and to whom?'
(No surviving answer.)
'Do you acknowledge yourself the King's true subject?'
'I do. But I have had the King's displeasure after the overthrow at St Etienne.'
'Of what degree do ye take yourself to be in this realm?'
(No surviving answer.)
'What inheritance do ye think ye ought to have therein?'
(No surviving answer.)
'What person of what estate is there to whom ye suppose yourself inheritor after the death of your father?'
(No surviving answer.)
'What person, and of what estate ye suppose to be of the best blood that ye come of, and to be inheritor thereunto?'
(No surviving answer.)'
It is noticeable that Surrey's rashest action in the matter of his

arms — that of shifting the 'three labels silver' of the Brotherton quartering to that of Edward the Confessor — is not dealt with in this part of his examination; it must therefore have come under a separate heading, as did the question of the mottoes on his portrait, which was resuscitated at his public trial.

Before this could take place the Privy Council had to submit the result of the examinations to the King. Their statement shows that though they had not officially come to the conclusion that Surrey was guilty, they were putting forward a recommendation for his trial for high treason; they resolved their findings into six questions. The ultimate decision rested with Henry; his interpolations, shakily written in his own hand, show that he had made up his mind as to Surrey's fate. In the first question Henry emphasized the fact that although Surrey had inherited the right to bear the royal arms, his changing over the Brotherton 'labels' had 'altered the true difference of the ancestry' by his arrogation of them 'in the very place of the heir apparent'. Henry added, 'How [is] this man's intent to be judged, and whether this impute any danger, peril or slander to the title of the Prince, and how it weigheth in our laws?' After amplifying this point in the second question, Henry associated Norfolk with Surrey in the fourth, thus: 'If a man say these words, "If the King die, who should have the rule of the Prince but my father or I?" what it importeth?' The third and fifth questions deal with Surrey's threats against the Council and his conversation with the Duchess of Richmond. The sixth question is the most important, for it touches on the lost Southwell evidence through which Surrey was eventually condemned, and which had nothing to do with his heraldic and other offences. 'If a man, provoked or compelled by his duty of allegiance [this refers to Southwell and possibly to other informers] shall declare such matters as he heareth touching the King [i.e. Surrey's plans for a *coup d'état*] and shall after be continually threatened by the person accused to be killed or hurt for it, what it importeth?'[8] This paragraph seems to indicate, not only that Surrey had offered to fight Southwell 'in his shirt' for informing against him, but also that he had actually set in hand a scheme for overthrowing the régime, and that he had determined to destroy anyone who tried to circumvent him. Whether Surrey had really gone to these lengths or not was irrelevant. He might have done so: he had threatened to do so: he had the power to do so. According to the law, as then embodied in the famous statute of Edward III, he was guilty.

It now only remained to find out the extent and nature of Norfolk's collaboration with Surrey. As a peer by courtesy, Surrey was to be tried by a special jury. Before Norfolk could be condemned, he must be deprived of his Garter and attainted by act of Parliament; this could not be effected till the Houses met on January 14th, 1547. Surrey's trial was fixed for the 13th, at the Guildhall. These arrangements made it clear to Norfolk that he had a faint, a very faint, chance of escape; he seized it by informing against his son in a written declaration of their common guilt.

The Duke's acknowledgment of his and Surrey's crimes, interlaced with cringing pleas for mercy for himself, frenzied outcries of loyalty and the recapitulation of his least creditable exploits on the state's behalf, makes curious reading. The writer's character is here stripped down to its essentials. Without the wealth, power and distinction that for nearly forty years had informed and graced his public and private utterances, his appeal resolves itself into a mixture of poltroonery, treachery and histrionics. It is in fact rather more disgusting than the majority of such appeals, in which the contemporary records abound, and contrasts strangely with Surrey's attempt to absolve his father in his letter to the Council. After drawing attention to his sustained hostility to the 'Bishop of Rome', Norfolk declares that 'if I had twenty lives, I would have spent them all than that he should have power in this realm ... I am a true poor gentleman,' he goes on, 'never gold was tried better by fire and water than I have been.' He then enumerates some of his services, including that of laying information against his stepmother, the Dowager-Duchess Agnes, for which, he triumphantly points out, 'she was attainted with misprision of treason – who can think that I should now be false?' – reminds Henry of their kinship through his first Duchess (when he became the King's uncle by marriage), stresses the second Duchess's slanderous hatred of himself, and recalls his share in the destruction of Anne Boleyn and Katherine

Howard. Then he comes to the heart of the matter. 'I have concealed', he says, 'the high treason of my son, Henry Howard Earl of Surrey ... and have, against all right, unjustly and without authority, borne in the first and principal quarter of mine arms ... the arms of England, with a difference of the three labels silver, which are the arms of my Lord Prince, which I know and confess to be high treason ... I admit this without compulsion.' He then offers to settle all his lands on Prince Edward, and concludes, 'I humbly beseech you to show this scribble to His Majesty, beg him to grant its petition and remit out of his noble, gentle heart the displeasure conceived against me. His Highness's poor prisoner, T. Norfolk.'⁹

By the time Norfolk's letter reached Henry, Surrey had already been condemned. Whether the Duke knew this is uncertain.

There was an interval of some ten days between the winding up of the examinations and Surrey's trial. During this time the King, who was at Westminster, began to sink and never again left his bed. Although he saw no one but his physicians, Cranmer and a few of the Council, he was transacting business and in perfect command of his faculties. Henry may have decided to give Surrey this respite in the hope that he would produce conclusive information against Norfolk, who if he had been involved in his son's plots was a much more dangerous enemy to the Regency and the Prince's succession. Surrey, having, as he thought, exonerated his father, and unaware that Norfolk was trying for a pardon by betraying him, must have realized, as soon as he was told that he was to stand upon his trial, that he was doomed. He therefore began to plan an escape from the Tower.

The circumstances of this attempt are obscure, and not all the details provided in the single contemporary account of it are acceptable. That it was made, is clear from the fact that it was referred to during Surrey's trial and used as further evidence against him. For a prisoner who tried to escape the penalty was death.

The recorder of this incident is that same Spanish merchant who was constantly at the Court of Henry VIII and who saw Surrey's arrest and removal to the Chancellor's house at Holborn. A proportion of his memoirs has been verified from reliable sources: but he himself makes his accounts appear more suspect than they really are by supplementing them with conversations that he could not possibly have overheard, as in the case of Surrey's efforts at escape. He probably obtained the main facts from Lord Thomas Howard, who seems to have been concerned in it; the circumstantial background is borne out by contemporary and official records.

In accordance with the custom of the day, Surrey and Norfolk were allotted separate suites of rooms in the Tower, and allowed their own servants, Surrey being given one man and Norfolk two.[10] The care of these privileged and more comfortable quarters was not only exercised in a hugger-mugger fashion, but apt to be relegated to minor officials who might be suborned, and whose sympathies with the prisoners were sometimes shown in ways of which the Lieutenant of the Tower, at this time Sir Walter Stonor, a Catholic of the old nobility, knew nothing. Thus, relations between Surrey's servant Martin and the warders may have been friendly enough for Martin to pass in and out of his master's rooms without very strict surveillance.

Surrey's suite overlooked the river and consisted of a bedroom and a privy leading out of it. This privy was really a bottomless well in the floor, so placed that the tide rose and fell beneath it, thus making it into a primitive water-closet. Surrey was guarded by men-at-arms, some of whom, with Martin, slept and ate in his room, at intervals leaving it to go the rounds.

If the Spanish memoirist is to be believed, Martin was instructed by Surrey to obtain a dagger, which he hid at the head of his master's bed. During another expedition into the outside world he hired or bought a boat from a wherryman at St Katherine's Wharf (this still lies just beyond the principal gateway of the Tower) and the services of two rowers, whom he told to be ready at midnight, when the tide would have fallen, and a drop from the privy would be possible for a slender, agile and courageous person. Martin had to borrow a large sum from Lord Thomas Howard for these purposes; and this fits in with the contemporary records of Surrey's penniless state during his imprisonment, which was intensified by the fact that all his goods had been seized.

As soon as the guards left to go on their rounds Surrey went to the privy and began to let himself down. He may have had to wait longer than he expected for the water to recede; he was on the point of dropping when the guards returned, and gave the alarm. After a fierce struggle Surrey was disarmed, overpowered, and thereafter chained. Martin, having waited in vain for his master, disappeared, taking the money with him. (He may have re-entered the family service later on and so provided Lord Thomas Howard with the details of his brother's penultimate attempt to save himself.)[11]

According to the Spanish chronicler, the news of Surrey's desperate adventure swept over London, and created a revulsion in his favour. This is to some extent borne out by the fact that he was escorted to the Guildhall by three hundred halberdiers. Evidently the Council were afraid that the people, hitherto hostile to Surrey although not to his father, might try to rescue him.

The revival of Surrey's reputation as an heroic and now victimized figure made it necessary for the government to put out conclusively damning propaganda against him and his father. The foreign ambassadors, the Courts of Europe and the English public were informed that Surrey and Norfolk were conspirators of murder, that they had planned to seize the Prince (and thereafter the throne itself) and that both had confessed to these crimes. That their 'abominable and detestable practices' had been brought to light by a happy chance was the conclusion of the statements made by the resident envoys to Francis I and the Emperor. Francis, remembering Surrey's friendship with his sons, refused to believe a word of the story; the Emperor, not very much interested, but sympathetic over Henry's difficulties, let fall a vague comment on Surrey's pride and arrogance.[12] In London the rumour began to circulate that Norfolk had been privately executed within the Tower. Nothing that the government could say now affected the citizens' attitude. All danger of Surrey harming Prince Edward having been removed, they could afford to pity him, romanticize his dash for freedom, and condemn the pitilessness of his enemies.

Surrey, who had determined to make a last struggle for his life (he had no defence but his own certainty that he had acted rightly) realized, within a few days of his trial, that he had not the black doublet and hose that the occasion required, and no money with which to buy them. Sir Walter Stonor came to his help with a loan, and he obtained the right clothes just in time.[13]

Surrey's one faint hope of mercy — and for the lenient treatment of his family in the event of his death — was to follow the accepted pattern of behaviour by acknowledging his guilt and throwing himself upon the King's favour by sending him the kind of letter that Norfolk had written. It is very doubtful whether Henry, who when the day of Surrey's trial dawned, had a fortnight to live, would have consented to commute his sentence: but there was a chance of his doing so. This Surrey refused to take. He scorned to plead as a traitor and a murderer: he was neither. As soon as he was permitted to speak, the Guildhall — crowded with such members of the public as had been able to bribe or wheedle their way in, some of whom have left an account of the trial — echoed with his declarations of innocence. For eight hours without a break, from nine in the morning till five in the afternoon, Surrey reasoned, argued and recapitulated in his own defence.[14]

It was a strange scene, and extremely disturbing for the judges, of whom there were twelve, most of them members of the Privy Council. For as the hours went by, it began to dawn on them that the jury, who in accordance with custom had been selected from the Norfolk and Suffolk areas and were personally acquainted with the prisoner, might be constrained in the face of all precedent and usage to bring in a verdict of not guilty.

No verbatim report of Surrey's trial exists; such fragments of his and his accusers' interchanges as are extant come from a handful of eye-witnesses, who were so staggered by the prisoner's pride, courage and belligerence that their recollection of his forensic methods is extremely meagre.[15] It is, however, consistent. The outbursts of contemptuous and haughty derision, the obstinate and inflexible asseverations that he had right, custom and privilege on his side remained long afterwards in the memories of those who saw the Earl of Surrey stand before God and his country to defy his enemies — alone. He was allowed to call two witnesses in his defence; either he could not obtain them, or would not stoop thus to justify his actions. No one, not even Hugh Ellis, spoke for him; and one may be sure that he neither expected nor desired a single supporter.

Behind the slight, black-clad figure stood the headsman with his axe — its edge as yet turned away from him. As the dull winter light began to give way to the uncertain flicker of candles and torches, Surrey's statements, some of them many times reiterated, became curter, more sharply phrased. Now each reply came out like an insult; and presently his impatient bitterness turned to enraged abuse.

The summing-up of one chronicler shows shocked disapproval. 'If he had tempered his answers with such modesty as he showed token of a right perfect and ready wit, his praise had been the greater', says Holinshed, adding: 'Some things he flatly denied, seeking to weaken the credit of his accusers by certain circumstances; others he excused with interpretations of his meaning, to prove the same to be far otherwise than was alleged against him.'[16] Lord Herbert of Cherbury, who had access to contemporary records since lost, is less critical of Surrey's manners, and much admires the brilliance and ingenuity of his replies. 'As the Earl was of a deep understanding, sharp wit and deep courage [he] defended himself in many ways,' is his conclusion, 'sometimes denying their accusations as false, and together weakening his adversaries.'[17] Part of an anonymous witness's evidence consisted in his description of how he had argued with Surrey, whose 'high words' he repeated, with his own 'braving', or insulting, answer. The prisoner at once interrupted — 'Is it probable this man should speak thus to the Earl of Surrey, and he not strike him again?' he demanded, and so disposed of that particular charge.[18]

When the question of Surrey's inserting the mottoes in his latest picture was raised — possibly by Hertford, whom he considered his bitterest enemy — his answer was calmly given. 'Your sister hath accused you,' said Hertford, 'of having the picture with the arms of the King and an inscription of your own. What meant you by this?' Surrey replied, as before, with a reference to his ancestral rights, and again spoke of the inscription on the tomb of his forebears in

East Winch. 'Why did you put the inscription [*Tel Dandus*] on the Garter, and what does it mean?' asked another Councillor. Surrey answered that he had not put His Majesty's motto for fear of offending him; the words *Tel Dandus* ('Till then, thus') were a hint that his work for the state should be better rewarded. 'It means,' he explained, 'that so it [his service to the crown] will remain till it comes to light.'[19]

Lisle now interposed. 'If you be not guilty and meant no ill, why did you bedaub [obliterate] the motto, and why did you break out of prison?' Surrey did not trouble himself with the triviality of the first question. He said, 'I tried to break guard to prevent myself coming to the pass in which I now stand. And you, my lord,' he added angrily, 'know well that however true a man may be, they always find the fallen guilty.' Here Paget burst out in defence of his master's justice. 'Hold your peace, my lord! You would have committed treason, and as His Majesty is old, you thought to become King.' Surrey turned upon him savagely. 'And thou, catchpole! What hast thou to do with this? For the kingdom hath never been well since the King put mean creatures like thee into government!'[20]

A confused and prolonged dispute seems to have ensued, interrupted by another Councillor summing up before any question of the jury's retirement had arisen; this practice was then customary and taken for granted. 'My lords,' he said, 'for either [any] of the offences the Earl hath committed he deserves death — first, for usurping the royal arms, and the other for escaping from prison, whereby he hath showed his guilt,' 'You are false!' Surrey replied fiercely, 'and for a piece of gold would condemn your own father.' And he repeated, for perhaps the twentieth time, 'I never sought to usurp the King's arms, for all know that my ancestors bore them.'[21]

At five the jury retired. To the dismay of the judges, they were still in debate at seven. Eight o'clock came — and nine — and ten. Still they remained in consultation. Then Paget, who had been instructed by the King to inform him of the progress of the trial, slipped out of the Guildhall and took a boat to Westminster. An hour later he came back; it is believed, although it cannot be proved, that he brought the jury a message from Henry.[22] At eleven o'clock they returned. The Lord Chief Justice bade them stand and look upon Surrey. He said, 'Do you find the prisoner guilty or not guilty?' The answer came in a loud voice, 'Guilty, and he should die!'

Slowly the headsman turned the edge of his axe towards the figure in the dock. Surrey was silenced by the uproar of the crowd, some of whom had observed Paget's withdrawal and re-entry, and suspected Henry's interference; they were outraged by the injustice of the whole procedure. The heralds and tipstaffs shouted in vain for order; as they began to force the people towards the doors their tumult died away. Then the Lord Chief Justice rose and pronounced sentence of death either by the axe or the rope, according to His Majesty's pleasure. He said that the offence for which the Earl of Surrey was condemned was not that of assuming the royal arms — for this he was acquitted — but of conspiracy of murder. It was so entered in the official records, where it can still be seen.[23]

Surrey was asked if he had anything to say. He burst into a torrent of words. 'Of what have you found me guilty? Surely you will find no law — but I know well the King would deny the noble blood around him, and employ none but mean creatures — ' he began, and was still in a flood of furious protest when he was taken away. According to one shocked onlooker, it was terrible to hear the things he said; he braved it out to the last, declaring his innocence and inveighing against his judges during the whole course of his journey from the Guildhall to the Tower.[24] So the day of his final public appearance ended in a tornado of hatred, insane courage and wild bravado. His execution was fixed for January 10th.

When he returned to the Tower he had time, at last, to feel as well as to know what had happened. For a little while he experienced all the bitterness of death, its terror and despair. He has left a record of these contrasting phases in three sets of verses; two are rhymed versions of the 55th and 88th Psalms, and the other is a short poem declared by his younger son to have been written the night before his execution.

In his adaptation of the 55th Psalm Surrey's cry to the God he had so often relegated or ignored is loud and agonized, the cry of a man whose existence in the world has been a frenzied pursuit of glory; for he had loved life, even when he held it lightly enough to stake it on the hazards of battle or intrigue. Yet his choice of this Psalm shows the same unassailable sense of his own innocence and of his enemies' wickedness that had sustained his defence in the Council chambers of the Tower and in the Guildhall. After a reference to 'the grisly fear of death', he describes the hideous malice of Hertford, Southwell, Blagge and the Duchess of Richmond as being fatal, not only to himself, but to the country for which he had fought and was now to die. 'Rein those unbridled tongues! Break that conjured league!' he exclaims, adding that 'Guile and wrong kept the walls, they ward both day and night.' 'It was a friendly foe,' he goes on, 'by shadow of good will, Mine old fere and dear friend, my guide, that trappèd me.' The vengeance of which the headsman is to deprive him is then required of the Almighty. 'The everlasting God, Whose kingdom hath no end' will defend Surrey's reputation from his slanderers, and His wrath, 'more sharp than any tool can file', will one day destroy 'those false wolves' who had betrayed him to his death.

In the 88th Psalm Surrey found the perfect expression of his longings for his wife and children, and for the friends — Richmond, Cleere, Sir Thomas Shelley — 'which in their graves remain'.

He expresses regret, not of course for the crimes of which he had been condemned, but for 'follies past' — 'yet', he pleads, 'did I never cease Thine aid for to desire, With humble heart and stretchèd hands for to appease Thine ire.' It is now too late. 'The flesh that feedeth worms cannot Thy love declare ... nor blazèd may Thy name be by the mouth of those Whom death hath shut in silence ... Why dost Thou not appear, O Lord? ... My wretched state behold, whom death shall straight assail ... ' This poem ends with an evocation of the patient, gentle creature who was carrying the child he would never see. 'For they whom no mischance could from my love divide, Are forcèd, for my greater grief, from me their face to hide.'

So the tempest raged and the waves broke over his head. Then, in those last, awful hours of realization, knowing himself for what he was, and for what he might have been, the tormented, hounded victim of his own obsessions found peace, and knew the strange serenity of the dying. The Furies that had driven him from one disaster to another had been exorcized. He was safe, free, almost happy, when he wrote:

> The storms are past, the clouds are overblown,
> And humble cheer great rigour hath repressed.
> For the default, is set a pain foreknown,
> And patience graft in a determined breast.
> And in the heart, where heaps of grief were grown,
> The sweet revenge hath planted mirth and rest.
> No company so pleasant as mine own.
>
> Thraldom at large hath made this prison free.
> Danger well past, remembered, works delight.
> Of lingering doubts such hope is sprung, perdie!
> That nought I find displeasant in my sight,
> But when my glass presenteth unto me
> The cureless wound that bleedeth day and night.
> To think, alas, such hap should granted be
> Unto a wretch that hath no heart to fight,
> To spill that blood that hath so oft been shed
> For Britain's sake, alas, and now is dead!

On the morning that he was to die his mood changed. When he came out of the tranquil remoteness of his cell into the concourse of men-at-arms, sheriffs and ministers of religion – when he saw the masked headsman and his assistant – as he passed through the ranks of officials to mount the steps of the scaffold – that terrible, corrosive rage seized him again. The memory of his wrongs swelled within him like a poisonous growth. A passion of resentment and bitterness filled his heart and mind.

No verbatim report of Surrey's dying words survives, for his execution was private. It was said that to the last he maintained his right, and utterly denied any intention of treason. The impression his violence created was conveyed through the gossip of a few eye-witnesses to the world by their disjointed comments on the vociferations and protests that had to be forcibly silenced. 'On the scaffold he spoke a great deal,' says one chronicler, 'but they would not let him talk any more ... '[25] His hatred was keener than the axe, his fury hotter than the blood that streamed out over the sawdust.

So Surrey died — to some a traitor, to others an obstacle removed with difficulty, to many a martyr in a moribund cause: the cause of that splendid, medieval past which perhaps existed only in his imagination. Over a gulf of four hundred years, he appears as a picturesque anomaly in a world that had no time for him: where the chase after new wealth, new greatness and extended power could not be halted for the spectacles, fantasies and visions in which he had his being, and whence his inspiration came. He may be pitied; he can never be loved, and not often admired.

NOTES TO CHAPTER TEN

[1] Cal. D.S.P., vol. XXI, pt. II, p. 555.
[2] Ibid., p. 548.
[3] Ibid.
[4] Ibid.
[5] Ibid., p. 555.
[6] Ibid.
[7] Ibid.
[8] Ibid.
[9] Ibid., p. 695
[10] Chronicle of Henry VIII, pp. 152-3.
[11] Ibid.
[12] Cal. Span. S.P., vol. VIII, p. 526.
[13] Bapst, p. 356.
[14] Herbert, p. 567.
[15] Ibid.
[16] Ibid., p. 531
[17] Ibid.
[18] Ibid.
[19] Chronicle of Henry VIII, p. 148.
[20] Ibid.; Holinshed, p. 861.
[21] Chronicle of Henry VIII, p. 160.
[22] Ibid.
[23] Fisher, History of England, p. 391.
[24] Chronicle of Henry VIII, p. 160.
[25] Ibid.

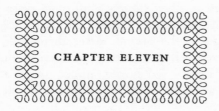

CHAPTER ELEVEN

IT has long been agreed that Surrey's turbulent and disastrous career is of almost no interest compared with the effect of his poetry on English literature. He left behind him an indestructible possession that he himself did not greatly value and that might have disappeared if he had not lived in a circle where the product of such a gift as his was considered worthy of preservation. As a pioneer, he is enshrined; as the prototype of unwitting and involuntary self-destruction, he has been forgotten. It is therefore desirable to continue his story a little beyond the moment of his execution; for nothing in his short life was more characteristic than its sequel. The forces of violence and treachery swept over Surrey's grave, obliterating his blunders and degrading his fame in a welter of failed ambition, useless intrigue and mistaken betrayal.

His head and trunk were bundled into an unsealed coffin, and remained in the chapel of the Tower until those of his relatives who were still free to take action had decided about their disposal. He was then embalmed, and buried in the vault of All Hallows, Barking.[1] Meanwhile, the legatees who had helped to destroy him and to whom Henry VIII had given his property, descended upon Kenning-hall and Mount Surrey. Of these, Hertford was the principal, and the most thorough. With the bulk of Surrey's estates, but not, presumably, his debts, he inherited and seized a quantity of personal possessions that might have been treasured by Lady Surrey and her children and that to Hertford were merely the accretions of the spoil.

The Garter robe of purple velvet, the caps set with jewels and feathers, the knitted hose, the daggers and rapiers, the famous 'gown of gold' trimmed with sables, the doublets of orange and crimson satin embroidered in silver filigree — all these were packed up and sent off with the furniture, carpets and household plate to the Hertford mansion in the Strand. After them followed the black jennet with the velvet trappings that had been Richmond's, and the rest of the live stock — led horses, mules, sheep and cows — and finally the wagons loaded with salted meat and fish and the jars of preserved fruit. Nothing was forgotten, not even the embroidered linen pillow-cases and the bed-hangings of silk and brocade.[2]

When Norfolk heard of this clean sweep he made no plea for his helpless, ailing daughter-in-law, or for his four Surrey grandchildren, of whom the eldest, his namesake, was nine years old. As his cries for mercy to the King and the Privy Council remained unanswered, he began to prepare himself for death with calculated resignation and piety. His next letter to the men who had outstripped him in the race for power was in the style of one who has done with this world and is making ready for the next in the manner most likely to please and impress. He asked that a priest might be sent him, and for various works on religion, especially for those of Sabellicus, 'who doth declare', he explained, 'most of any book that I have read, how the Bishop of Rome from time to time hath usurped his power against all princes.' It seems that these requests were granted.[3]

With the meeting of the Houses of Parliament on January 14th the procedure for Norfolk's attainder and his condemnation for high treason and conspiracy of murder began. By the afternoon of the 27th the act for the supreme penalty had been engrossed, stamped with the King's signature (he could no longer write), witnessed by Hertford and Paget, presented to the members and passed. They rose; and Norfolk must have told himself that he had lost the last throw. Between the end of that day's sitting and the drawing up of the necessary instructions for the sheriffs and the Lieutenant of the Tower — at two o'clock on the morning of January 28th, 1547 — Henry died. For thirty-six hours Norfolk's fate hung on a thread swayed by the winds of divided faction in the Council. Then Hertford, with Paget's help, obtained absolute control by his concealment and subversion of Henry's will, and was proclaimed Lord Protector, Duke of Somerset and Governor of the nine-year-old Edward VI. He was lenient in his triumph. Norfolk's trial and execution were indefinitely postponed. Attainted, ruined and disgraced, he remained in the Tower for the five years of Edward's reign.

When Edward died, Surrey's old enemy, Lisle, now Duke of Northumberland, who had sent Hertford to the block in 1552, attempted a *coup d'état* in favour of his daughter-in-law, Lady Jane Grey, the great-niece of Henry VIII. Norfolk was told that he had three days to live. Nine days later Lisle's revolution failed, and Mary was proclaimed. Entering the Tower in triumph, she greeted the eighty-year-old Duke with a smile, raised him from his knees and gave him her hand to kiss. Lisle and his collaborators were executed, and Mary restored all Norfolk's honours and most of his estates. In the following year, 1554, he led a small force against Surrey's former comrade in arms, Sir Thomas Wyatt the Younger, who routed the Duke at Rochester, and was thereafter himself defeated and beheaded as a result of his attempt to raise the City of London in the Protestant cause. Lady Jane, her husband and her father followed Wyatt to the scaffold. Norfolk lived peacefully at Kenninghall for another year. He died at the age of eighty-two, and was buried at Framlingham. To the end of his life, and long after it, he was described locally as the good Duke, whom his tenants had delighted to honour and to serve.

Lady Surrey gave birth to her third daughter and fifth child in February 1547. Her two eldest children, Thomas and Henry, were taken away from her and put in the care of the Duchess of Richmond, who was given £100 a year for their keep. She engaged Foxe, the martyrologist, as their tutor, and their upbringing was scrupulously Protestant. The Duchess died in 1557. Surrey's daughters married into the old nobility. In 1553 his widow became the wife of Mr Francis Steyning; she died in 1558.

Surrey's elder son, the 'little T.' of his poems, succeeded his grandfather as fourth Duke of Norfolk at the age of eighteen. As Queen Elizabeth's cousin and one of the wealthiest and most favoured of her subjects, he was the principal ornament of her Court.

And then his father's story was repeated. Norfolk's ambitions outsoared his capabilities. In the 1570s he headed a Catholic plot for Mary Stuart's release and accession to the throne. Again and again, Elizabeth, disregarding her ministers' advice, warned him, threatened him, told him sharply to take heed, much as her father, through Paget, had tried to prevent Surrey dashing to his ruin. It was useless. Norfolk, discovered at last to have secretly betrothed himself to the Queen of Scots and to have set in hand an organization for a general Catholic rising, followed his father to the scaffold in 1572. The dukedom of Norfolk then remained in abeyance for ninety-two years.

Surrey's second son Henry, Earl of Northampton, inheriting much of his father's brilliance and all his grandfather's cunning, was imprisoned for corresponding with Mary Queen of Scots. By 1600 he had re-established himself, was recalled to Court, and restored the Howard fortunes by intrigues and manœuvres that reached their apotheosis in the reign of James I. Northampton had the family passion for power: power garlanded with seemliness and respectability. In 1614 he removed Surrey's body from Barking and re-interred it beside that of Lady Surrey and the third Duke at Framlingham, under a splendid monument, with a pompous and euphemistic inscription. According to Northampton, his noble father died 'prematurely' (*abrepto*), reverenced and admired by all.

Surrey's eldest grandson, the fourth Duke's heir, was called Philip; after his father's attainder and execution, he was allowed to retain the title of Earl of Arundel, and in his turn was much favoured by Queen Elizabeth. Then the pattern of disloyalty, arrogance and maniacal rashness emerged again. In the 1580s Arundel became involved in new schemes for Mary Stuart's seizure of the throne; he died in the Tower in 1595, after twenty years' captivity.

For two hundred and twenty years Surrey's remains lay undisturbed beneath the recumbent figures of himself and his wife. In 1835 it became necessary to repair the foundations of the church, and his coffin was removed from the vault. The parson of Framlingham, an amateur archaeologist and historian, was interested in his distinguished parishioner's story, and, observing that the coffin was in poor condition, gave orders for the skeleton to be taken out as soon as another was ready. The bones crumbled into dust — but the scraps of clothing, and the evidence of the head having been severed from the body made it possible for the clergyman to verify Surrey's identity.[4]

And there the fragments of his earthly beauty lie, under an inscription as absurd as it is false. That hardly matters; for few visit his tomb; and fewer still trouble themselves with his epitaph.

NOTES TO CHAPTER ELEVEN

[1] Bapst, p. 356.
[2] Nott, vol. I, Appendix.
[3] Cal. D.S.P., vol. XXI, pt. II, p. 648.
[4] Richardson, *The Lion and the Rose*, p. 80.

LADY KATHERINE GREY
(1540-68)

The marriage night
Is the entrance into some prison.
And those joys,
Those lustful pleasures, are like heavy sleeps
Which do fore-run men's mischief.

'The Duchess of Malfi'

LADY KATHERINE GREY

by Marc Geerarts

CHAPTER ONE

IN the summer of 1660 Charles II restored to William Seymour,
Earl and Marquis of Hertford, the dukedom of Somerset, which
had been in abeyance since the attainder and execution of his great-
grandfather, Edward Seymour, in 1552. This grant concluded the
public rehabilitation of his family which Lord Hertford had set in
hand some twenty years earlier by putting up a vast and elaborate
monument to his father, his uncle and his paternal grandparents in
Salisbury Cathedral. Before he could thus commemorate his
immediate forebears, Lord Hertford had to remove the body of his
grandmother, Katherine Grey Countess of Hertford, from the
cemetery of Yoxford in Suffolk, where it had lain for more than
sixty years, and place it beside that of her husband. This reunion,
surmounted by the baroque splendours of a tomb some thirty feet
high, was intended to crown, and also to immortalize, the story of
their marriage. According to seventeenth-century standards, the
act was fittingly pious and the scale on which it was carried out
suitable and justified. The result has an ironic side. In death, as in life,
this husband and wife were partially misrepresented and wilfully
misunderstood.

The Hertford monument is, as it were, symphonically constructed,
opening on a theme of medieval chivalry, thereafter developed in a
series of Renaissance variations; it culminates in a fully orchestrated
recapitulation of Jacobean honours and distinctions that recall and
amplify the glories of the Seymour, Tudor and Plantagenet dynasties.
It occupies the whole height of the Lady Chapel, and is topped by
the plumed and gilded helmet of a fourteenth-century warrior.

Below this a lion and a unicorn support an escutcheon of six quarterings in red, blue and gold that includes Tudor roses, Plantagenet
lilies and lions, and the wings, 'joined in lure', of that Sir Roger de
St Maur who was made Lord of the Manor of Woundy in Mon-
mouthshire by Henry III. As the eye travels downward it is confronted by a second lion and unicorn who surmount a pair of angels
displaying a gilt inscription on black marble. Underneath these is a
large arched canopy flanked by shields and coronets and lined with
fifteen cognizances; it encloses the recumbent alabaster effigy of
Lady Katherine Grey, slightly raised above that of her husband,
Edward Seymour, second Earl of Hertford. A golden phoenix lies at
her feet, a cap of maintenance at his; on either side of the Earl and
his Countess are the kneeling figures of their sons, Edward Viscount
Beauchamp and Lord Thomas Seymour, a pair of tapered alabaster
obelisks decorated with trophies in bas-relief, and two more angels
holding palms of victory. Below them is another Latin inscription,
so spaced out as to form a lengthy and intricate pattern; this enumerates the Hertfords' titles and outlines their history in the following terms.

Lord Hertford was the eldest son of 'the most illustrious prince',
Edward Seymour Duke of Somerset, brother-in-law of Henry
VIII, uncle of Edward VI and 'most worthy Protector of his dom-
inions and dependencies'. Lord Hertford's 'most dear and beloved
consort', Katherine Grey, was the daughter of Henry and Frances
Grey, Duke and Duchess of Suffolk, and granddaughter of Charles
Brandon Duke of Suffolk and Mary Tudor, Queen-Dowager of
France and younger sister of Henry VIII. To emphasize Lady Kathe-
rine's lineage, it is added that she was the great-granddaughter of
Henry VII.

The memorialist then launches into the accepted strain of melan-
cholic eulogy. 'An incomparable pair', he says, 'who, after having
experienced alternate changes of fortune, here at length rest together
in the same concord in which they lived. She, distinguished as an
example of uprightness, piety, beauty and faith, the best and most
illustrious, not only of her own but of every age, calmly and piously
breathed her last on January 22nd, in the year 1567. He, the most

perfect pattern of nobility, the preserver of pristine manners and discipline, endowed with eloquence, wisdom, innocence, gravity ... and splendour of birth, as one who had pursued his studies with Prince Edward ... a most determined defender of religion ... having filled the office of Ambassador for His Britannic Majesty King James ... yielded to nature in his eighty-third year on April 6th, 1620. By the heroine of this epitaph he had two sons.'

So presented, Lady Katherine does indeed appear a heroine – of romance. The falsification of her and her husband's characters and careers is contained in a number of misstatements. She and Lord Hertford never lived together, in concord or otherwise, for they separated on their wedding day, thereafter meeting at infrequent intervals. Lady Katherine can hardly be regarded as an example of uprightness, for she temporarily apostatized from the faith in which she had been brought up, and was guilty of gross deception over her marriage. Nor was she in any sense more illustrious than her Tudor cousins, her sisters or her mother; their birth was equal to hers, and her intellect and accomplishments ranked far below those of the Lady Jane Grey or of Queen Elizabeth. She did not die on January 27th, 1567, but on January 22nd, 1568.

As to Hertford, he was neither disciplined nor wise; in his early years at least, his behaviour alternated between rashness and pusillanimity; several of his contemporaries described him as an outrageously spoilt and conceited young man. The fact that he and Lady Katherine fell so desperately in love as to abjure prudence, self-control and custom may now, after four hundred years, excuse them and evoke our pity. To the authorities of their own day their misdemeanour appeared criminal and monstrous, as indeed, on belated reflection, it did to themselves. Those who had to punish them for their transgressions would probably have agreed that they were lucky to escape the block; under Henry VIII they might not have done so, for the fact that Lady Katherine was Henry's great-niece and her husband his nephew by marriage would have been no safeguard. Her descent was her misfortune, and from her inability to grasp this aspect of the political situation her tragedy developed. It began twenty-six years before her birth, with the marriage of her grandmother, Henry's favourite sister Mary, to Louis XII of France.

In 1514 the contract was made between the high-spirited sixteen-year-old Princess and the infirm King of sixty. The bride, who some months before had fallen in love with Charles Brandon Duke of Suffolk, Henry's closest friend, made her brother promise that her next husband should be her own choice, and departed, weeping, to Abbeville, where the marriage was celebrated. She had not long to wait. Three months of feasting, dancing and late nights in Paris relieved her of Louis. Some eight weeks later she was once more in England and married to Suffolk, a dashing, worthless, handsome young man of mean descent, who had been divorced from one wife and whose second had died. In 1517 Suffolk's and Mary's elder daughter, Frances, was born; in 1520 they had another, Eleanor. In 1533 Mary died and Suffolk married his fourth wife, Lady Katherine Willoughby d'Eresby, by whom he had two sons. In the same year Frances married Henry Grey, Marquis of Dorset, and they settled at Bradgate in Leicestershire, where in 1537 Frances gave birth to their first daughter, Lady Jane Grey. Katherine was born in August 1540, and Mary five years later. In 1545 the Duke of Suffolk died, and his elder son by his fourth marriage, Frances Dorset's eight-year-old half-brother Henry, succeeded to the dukedom.

The remarkable character and dramatic martyrdom of Lady Jane Grey made her as famous in her own generation as she is today. Many of those who had to do with her recorded their memories of her background and behaviour, and it is through their information that a picture of her younger sisters' earliest years may be discerned. Katherine and Mary Grey were brought up in the shadow of Jane's superior intellect and stronger personality. Their resultant relegation, and the fact that the Dorsets' over-ambitious schemes for Jane were constantly changing or falling through must have had a lasting effect on Katherine's temperament and attitude. She shared Jane's setting and education; but Jane's seniority, its burdens and demands, seem to have created in Katherine what might now be described as an unconscious rebellion, resulting in an impulse to compete with, and even, later, to outstrip, her super-eminent elder sister, whose short life — Jane was sixteen and a half when her head fell from the block on Tower Green — became a favourite theme with Protestant historians over a period of three hundred years.

This theme generally opens with an account of the high standard of learning imposed by the Dorsets on their children. In this respect all three received the same advantages: and all developed differently. In a later age Jane would have been described as the clever sister, Katherine as the pretty, frivolous one, and Mary as that poor little creature for whom nothing could be done: for she was a dwarf, and very ugly. Mary's misfortune did not affect her parents' attitude; they loved her neither more nor less for her disability, for they were incapable of affection, or of differentiating, emotionally, between their girls. Jane's brilliance, Katherine's looks, Mary's deformity — these counted as nothing to the Dorsets against their daughters' uses as political and dynastic catspaws. The three princesses grew up unloved, often, it would seem, disliked, by their father and mother, who treated them with a sternness that in Jane's case developed into brutality. In other ways they were privileged; they had first-class tutors, luxurious living and a beautiful home.

The mansion of Bradgate had been built by Dorset's father on and out of the ruins of an abbey bought from Henry VIII. The oaks of Charnwood Forest surrounded the valley in which it stood; the manor was enclosed by rocky hills covered with ferns and moss. The house was square, of red brick, with a stone-faced turret at each corner. It confronted a huge, unfinished gatehouse, flanked by dwellings in which the outdoor servants lived. A stream ran through the garden, which looked over a lake; beyond this stretched a park, and beyond that a huddle of cottages occupied by the tenantry.[1] The Dorsets were bad landlords, always in debt and often on the verge of financial disaster; but they were optimistic, perhaps with reason, about their prospects.

They were well matched; they can seldom have disagreed about their next move. Frances, as became the daughter of a Tudor princess and a scheming and unscrupulous climber, was cleverer and more consistently forceful than her husband. Bold, vital, insensitive and coarsely handsome, she marred such charm as she had by her violent temper. Most people were afraid of her. Sir Richard Morrison, a contemporary and friend, who often suffered from her outbursts of rage, deplored her 'heats', adding, 'It is a great pity that so goodly a wit waiteth upon so froward a will.'² Dorset, described by another statesman as gay, headstrong and self-indulgent, was a gambler in more than one sense. A 'great dicer and swearer' according to his widowed mother, whom he treated abominably,³ he annulled his first marriage on the chance of marrying Frances; as soon as he had brought off this coup, he affiliated himself with the most influential 'new men' at the Court of Henry VIII. That he never had a son was his greatest disappointment, and might partly account for the harshness with which he and Lady Dorset treated their daughters; by the time the youngest was born the dynastic situation had so developed as to place the three girls in the line of succession; if the Dorsets had had a boy, their position would have been immeasurably stronger, and their resentment against fate may well have turned upon their children.

When Henry VIII made the will that raised the Grey sisters one step nearer the throne, he knew that he would not live to see his only son grow up, and that the boy must succeed under a regency. Henry can hardly have anticipated that his children — Edward VI, Mary and Elizabeth I — would leave no heirs: yet he arranged the order of their successors as if he had done so. He cut out the descendants of his elder sister, Margaret Tudor, who had married James IV of Scotland (and whose granddaughter, the infant Mary Stuart, became Queen of Scotland in 1542), transferring her rights to the Greys. Thus when Henry died in January 1547 and the nine-year-old Edward succeeded, the Dorsets' prospects rose. The Regency Council was dominated within thirty-six hours of Henry's death by the King's uncle, Edward Seymour, Earl of Hertford, who became Duke of Somerset and Protector of the realm and of his nephew's person. The Council was chiefly composed of his and Dorset's friends and allies. They were Protestants; it was with their support in mind, and not from any spiritual convictions, that Dorset and his wife had educated their daughters in the reformed religion.

When Edward VI became king, Jane Grey was nine years old,

Katherine seven, and Mary three. Jane and Katherine had completed the first stage of their education. The absence of comment on Katherine's progress is an indication of the light-mindedness that no severity seems to have eradicated. She was brought up far from the Court and seldom stayed at the Dorsets' palace in Southwark. Her tutors were selected from a circle of Protestant intellectuals whose standards were exacting and in a theological sense revolutionary. The most influential was Thomas Aylmer, formerly Dorset's tutor, now his chaplain, and one of a group that at Cambridge had included Cheke, Edward VI's much loved governor, Ascham, the favourite instructor of Princess Elizabeth (in whose reign he published *Toxophilus* and *The Schoolmaster*), and William Cecil, afterwards Lord Burleigh. Ascham's and Cheke's methods were unconventional and humane; Aylmer, although equally advanced in his views on female education, inclined to an exigence that fitted in very well with his employers' plans for their daughters. Jane and Katherine became very fond of him; his critical, uncompromising methods stimulated Jane's intellectual ambitions: and his stern Protestantism created in Katherine a piety that her circumstances were to shake yet could not destroy. Their devotion to Aylmer was enhanced by the contrast between his treatment and that of their parents, whom they learned to fear and obey but never to love.

It was not until Katherine was eleven that the famous, much quoted conversation between Ascham and Jane took place, which ten years later he recorded in an amplified and possibly idealized form. Her reply to his question about her preference for the study of Plato's *Phaedo* to a day's hunting gives an unforgettable picture of the Dorsets' domestic manners and customs. 'When I am in presence of either father or mother,' she said, 'whether I speak, keep silence, sit, stand or go, eat, drink, be merry or sad, be sewing, playing, dancing or doing anything else, I must do it as it were in such weight, measure and number, even so perfectly as God made the world, or else I am so sharply taunted, so cruelly threatened, yea, presently [now] sometimes with pinches, nips and bobs [blows] and other ways — which I will not name for the honour I bear them — that I think myself in hell till the time come that I must go to Mr Aylmer, who teacheth me so pleasantly ... that I think nothing all the time whilst I am with him. And when I am called from him, I fall on weeping, because whatsoever I do else but learning is full of grief, trouble, fear and whole misliking ... '[4]

It is possible that the Dorsets treated Jane more unkindly than Katherine and Mary, for two reasons. One was that Jane's force of character was shown, as in this talk with Ascham, by an extreme and daunting articulacy; she never faltered for a phrase, and was apt to express herself at great length and with an abrupt frankness that sometimes bordered on insolence. Furthermore, she had disappointed her parents. Soon after Edward's accession, they had made her the ward of the Protector's brother, Lord Seymour of Sudely, High Admiral of England; they gave him a large sum of money, on the understanding that he would arrange a marriage between her and the King. This plan having failed, Seymour, then high in Edward's favour, began to consider marrying Jane himself. His schemes ended with his attempt to kidnap Edward, and he was executed in February 1549. So the twelve-year-old Jane had returned to Bradgate branded, in the Dorsets' eyes, as a failure, and they used her accordingly. Thereafter, her and Katherine's education continued under Aylmer on the lines laid down in Luis Vives's celebrated *De Ratione Studii Puerilis Epistolae*, originally dedicated to Katherine of Aragon and recently translated.

The fact that Vives was a Spanish Catholic did not affect his popularity as a guide in Protestant circles. In England, that part of his work dealing with female education became the companion volume to Sir Thomas Elyot's *Book of the Governor*, a manual of training for upper-class boys. Vives's ideas were as advanced, and as puritanical, as Aylmer's. He recommended the direction of young ladies by men, as the best way of teaching them to write quickly and elegantly, to express themselves accurately, to speak Latin and Greek, to learn long passages of prose and poetry by heart, and to keep a commonplace book, in which they might copy their favourite excerpts from classical authors. Vives goes on to censure painted faces and dyed hair ('If it were to please herself, it is a vain thing, if it be to please Christ, it is a folly'), and warned his readers about the fatal disillusionment of a young husband seeing his wife as she really was, at bed-time, or in the early morning, when the 'crust of paint' was washed off, and her complexion, hitherto 'slubbered and starched' by its highly dangerous mask of white-lead, was revealed. 'Ovid', he adds, 'called these things venomous, and not without a cause.' It was all so obvious. Men never had, and never would, take to girls who painted, or who decked themselves with 'ouches and brooches' and then topped this odious display by drenching themselves with scent. 'Weenest thou', he demanded, 'to seem fairer, nobler or wiser, if thou have so much metal upon thee? Nay, never a whit!' Also — 'A woman smelleth best when she smelleth of nothing.' After a passage on chastity and modest behaviour, Vives concludes with an attack on modern dancing, as being over-intimate to the point of lechery. 'What good', he exclaims, 'doth all that dancing of young women, holden upon men's arms, that they may hop the higher?' It reminded one of Salome; and again, men did not really care for it, however much they might appear to do so.[5]

Aylmer's reports on his pupils' progress to his friend Bullinger, a Swiss reformer, show his affiliation with Vives, as does his encouragement of the correspondence which Jane and her father carried on with the Zwinglian pastor. The tutor's difficulties with the girls (why did they not copy the Lady Elizabeth in the simplicity of their attire? — and the hours they spent practising their music would have been better occupied with a more intensive study of Hebrew) were enhanced by his struggles with their parents. The Dorsets' fervour about the 'true religion' and the evils of Popery were frequently expressed; yet this conviction did not weaken their adherence to their usual relaxations, of which gambling was the principal. Not only the Dorsets themselves, but all their servants, continued to dice and play cards for high stakes. Aylmer, appalled, called upon Haddon, another Cambridge divine, now chaplain to the household, to remonstrate with their employer. Dorset listened amiably enough; then he suggested that he should forbid his servants to play, while continuing to do so himself in his and his wife's private apartments. Haddon protested. Dorset explained that he did not wish to venture great sums: but without stakes, the game lost all interest. 'I must in this yield to fashion,' he added, 'and not act with so much strictness.' Haddon's answer was reasonable, but unacceptable. 'Let the game be cold and lifeless,' he urged, 'and the prize a garland of praise.' This ingenuous suggestion appealed to neither of the Dorsets. They continued to gamble behind closed doors, and the shocked clergymen resigned themselves to the unavoidable.[6]

At about this time Dorset, who was again in financial difficulties, began to look round for a rich husband for his eldest daughter, and started negotiations with the Duke of Somerset for a marriage between Jane and Somerset's heir, Lord Hertford, who was then in his fifteenth year. The match was not so profitable as it would have been when the boy King succeeded and Somerset was at the height of his power; but the Duke was still very wealthy, and eager to strengthen his Tudor connections. As these arrangements made it necessary for Dorset to stay in London, he removed his family to Southwark; there Hertford visited them, and the contract between him and the Lady Jane was drawn up and signed. So he and Katherine first met. It is unlikely that the eleven-year-old girl made much impression on a boy who would then have thought of himself as grown up, and the accredited suitor of her elder sister. Frances Dorset took a fancy to Hertford, and he was treated as a son of the house.[7]

The negotiations for this marriage were not quite completed when the Dorsets took their three daughters on a round of visits that lasted from November 1551 till January 1552. Lady Dorset had been seriously ill; she was well enough to spend Christmas at Tylsey with her husband's nephew and ward, Lord Willoughby. Here the Princess Mary joined them; the two younger girls — the diminutive Mary Grey was in her fifth year — were formally introduced to her, and presents were exchanged. In honour of the Princess, Katherine and Mary, as well as Jane, were allowed to stay up to supper and to watch the plays put on for the occasion by Lord Oxford's troupe of actors. There were parties every night for a series of guests. These festivities lasted until after the Twelfth Night of January 1552, when the Dorsets moved on to stay with Lady Audley, Dorset's sister, at Saffron Walden.[8] Meanwhile two deaths had prepared the way for the Dorsets' rise in status and wealth. In the summer of 1551 both of Frances Dorset's half-brothers had died of the sweating sickness, and in 1552 she and her husband succeeded, jointly, as Duke and Duchess of Suffolk. Then a conspiracy and an execution revolutionized their circumstances, and with them, Katherine's destiny. By the time Katherine was thirteen the dynastic situation had changed again, suddenly, dramatically, and her life moved into the pattern that was to bring about her destruction.

NOTES TO CHAPTER ONE

[1] John Throsby, *Select Views in Leicestershire*, vol. I, pp. 118-19.
[2] Calendar of Letters between England and Spain, vol. X, p. 229.
[3] Brewer, *Letters and Papers of Henry VIII*, vol. XIII, pt. 1, No. 236, and vol. IX, No. 153.
[4] Roger Ascham, *Works*, vol. III, pp. 115-16.
[5] Watson, *Vives and the Renaissance Education of Women*, pp. 56, 59, 71-5, 103, 141-6.
[6] Parker Society, *Original Letters*, vol. I, pp. 3-7, 275, 279, 281-2.
[7] Harleian MSS, 6286.
[8] H.M.C.: Middleton MSS, pp. 520-1.

CHAPTER TWO

THE story of Katherine Grey is in no sense a sequel to Surrey's. Yet their lives are linked by the recurrence of two persons — the Duke of Somerset and his ultimately triumphant enemy, John Dudley Viscount Lisle, who had helped Somerset to bring about Surrey's death and Norfolk's disgrace. The alliance between Lisle and Somerest was still unbroken in 1547, the year of Edward VI's accession, when Lisle became Earl of Warwick and at once embarked on his elaborately planned scheme of destroying, in order to supplant, his former comrade in arms and fellow Councillor. In the autumn of 1549 Warwick had undermined the Council's allegiance to Somerset, with the result that in the following year the Duke was imprisoned, fined, and deprived of the Protectorship. In November 1551, while the Dorsets were amusing themselves at Tylsey and Saffron Waldon, Warwick and his faction manufactured enough evidence for a charge of high treason and conspiracy of murder to be brought against Somerset, who was executed in January 1552. This judicial slaughter was preceded by Warwick's being raised to the dukedom of Northumberland; with the support of the Suffolks, the indispensable Paget (whom he afterwards discarded), the Earl of Pembroke and the fourteen-year-old King, the new Duke obtained absolute control of the government. Northumberland was an able administrator; he might have succeeded in pulling the country out of economic, agricultural and religious chaos, if Edward, his key supporter, had lived to grow up; but by the beginning of 1553 it had become clear that the King was consumptive and would not survive more than a few months.

It is at this point in Katherine's life — she was in her fourteenth year — that Northumberland emerges as her first enemy. He was a typical sixteenth-century politician — cruel, unscrupulous and fast-working. His career is highly characteristic of the age, and perfectly illustrates the background of her tragedy.

By this time both Katherine and Jane were of marriageable age. Jane's intellectual powers and her correspondence (in Latin and Greek) with a number of Protestant divines had given her a reputation for learning and piety equalled only by that of the Princess Elizabeth, and in this respect Katherine was completely outshone. But Katherine was prettier than Jane. Jane had red hair, freckles, and a plump, short build, though these did not detract from her charm of manner when she chose to exercise it; whereas Katherine was small, slight, and delicately made, with a fine, straight profile, red-gold wavy hair, and deep-set eyes — she rather resembled her cousin Elizabeth than the Greys. Her interests were still childish. It may have been during this year that she began to surround herself with the collection of birds, monkeys and dogs that accompanied her in later life. She appears to have struck the few who remembered seeing her, as quiet and retiring: a background figure. So she was treated, and so she remained, till the spring of 1553.

When early in 1553 Northumberland realized that the King was going to die, he had to change the tactics that he had perfected over a period of twenty years. His talents lay in the subtle and devious manipulation of events rather than in *coups d'état*, and the rapidity with which he now acted was to prove disastrous both to himself and to most of those he had chosen to operate with him. On Edward's death, the Princess Mary, who was very popular, must succeed. Northumberland decided, not only to destroy her claim, but also that of the Princess Elizabeth by invalidating Henry VIII's will and persuading the moribund Edward VI to make another, in which he transferred his half-sisters' rights to Lady Jane Grey. Meanwhile Northumberland arranged for Jane to marry his favourite son, Lord Guilford Dudley.

It was not impossibly difficult to induce the King to cut out the Princess Mary, on the grounds of her Catholicism. Under her rule

England, it was believed, would lose her newly established Church. To eliminate Elizabeth was harder, for she was a firm, not to say an ostentatious member of the reformed faith. Northumberland managed to discredit her claim by pointing out that her legitimacy was doubtful, and that if she married a foreign (and presumably Catholic) prince, the country was even more likely to be forced back into Popery than under Mary, who at that time had shown no signs of bigotry. Edward, after a short and agonizing hesitation, during which Northumberland warned him of eternal punishment if he failed in his duty,[1] made his famous 'Devise for the Succession'. This was signed by the Council and most of the heads of Church and State a fortnight before he died. Some months earlier Northumberland had strengthened his connection with the Suffolks by a series of what were then called cross-marriages, of which the thirteen-year-old Katherine was one of the victims.

The three weddings and one betrothal arranged by Northumberland were celebrated on May 25th, 1553. The most important was the marriage of Lady Jane Grey to Lord Guilford Dudley, for which the contract had been signed against the will of the bride; she disliked the twenty-year-old Dudley (he was a foolish, handsome mother's darling) and had put forward her engagement to Lord Hertford as a reason for disobeying her parents' commands. The Suffolks brushed her protests aside. Hertford, although still a friend of the family, was under the cloud of his father's attainder and execution, and not to be compared, as a match, with the petted son of the great Northumberland. Jane's obstinate spirit was subdued by a whipping,[2] and the preparations for her and her sisters' alliances continued. Mary Grey, considered too young at eight years old to be a wife even in name, was betrothed to her cousin, Lord Arthur Grey, whose father was another ally of Northumberland. Katherine's husband was the nineteen-year-old Lord Herbert, Pembroke's heir. At the same time Northumberland's fourth daughter, Katherine Dudley, became the wife of Lord Hastings, the Earl of Huntingdon's eldest son; he was a descendant of the Plantagenets, and thus himself in the line of succession.

It now only remained for Northumberland to ensure the crown

for his grandchildren by Jane and Guilford through the elimination of the Duchess of Suffolk. She and Suffolk were persuaded (perhaps also bribed: Northumberland's negotiations with them were never disclosed) that it would be more profitable to relinquish her personal claim; she did so in a last interview with the dying King before the marriages took place.[3]

The weddings and the betrothal were magnificently celebrated at Northumberland's palace of Ely Place in Holborn. The King sent presents of jewels — it was announced that he would be there himself, but he was too ill to be moved — and his Master of the Wardrobe was commanded to supply all the young people with more jewellery, gold and silver tissues and 'rich clothes' from Somerset's confiscated property.[4] The festivities were held in private; no foreign envoy was invited. The party consisted of the Grey, Dudley, Pembroke and Huntingdon connections, several of whom succumbed to food poisoning from a salad. Rumours of this disaster reached the Spanish Ambassador in a sinister and exaggerated form; then he wrote to Charles V to explain that 'the mistake was made by a cook, who plucked one leaf for another.'[5]

Northumberland did not attend any of these feasts; he hurried back to the King's bedside at Greenwich, where he remained until Edward's death in the early afternoon of July 6th.

Meanwhile Katherine and her husband had gone to live at her father-in-law's mansion of Baynard's Castle near the Temple Gardens. Apart from her waiting-women, she was without any companion of her own sex, for Pembroke was a widower and his daughters were married. There is no record of how she and young Herbert spent their time, nor of what her feelings towards him were. Pembroke and the Suffolks had agreed that the marriage should not be consummated as yet. During the seven weeks that passed between the weddings and Edward's death, when it seemed that Northumberland's conspiracy must be successful, Pembroke (if a contemporary, writing some years later, is to be believed) began to consider making his son's union binding in every sense.[6] Still he hesitated, and the young people continued to sleep in separate bedrooms. On July 8th, when the Lord Mayor and the City fathers were told that the

King was dead, Pembroke joined Northumberland and the Council at Greenwich, while Katherine and her husband remained in Baynard's Castle. On the 9th, Pembroke, the Suffolks and the Duke and Duchess of Northumberland went to Syon House to wait for Jane, who was brought up the river in a barge with another of Northumberland's married daughters, Lady Mary Sidney, in attendance. To Jane, who had been told nothing of the part she was to play, Northumberland broke the news of Edward's death and of her accession by his will, adding that if she and Guilford had no legitimate heirs, *they* (the use of the plural is significant), would be succeeded by the Lady Katherine. The whole company — her parents, the Northumberlands, Pembroke and the other Councillors — knelt and acknowledged her as their lawful sovereign. Jane burst into tears: then she fainted.[7]

Next day Jane, Guilford, the Suffolks, the Northumberlands and the Council proceeded in state to the Tower, where she was publicly proclaimed and greeted by a salute of guns. Here Lord Herbert and Katherine had been summoned to await her coming. As soon as they all reached the state apartments the Marquis of Winchester, Lord High Treasurer, sent for the crown imperial from the Jewel House and attempted to place it on Jane's head, 'to see how it fitted her'. According to her own account, Jane, who was already wearing the royal robes, refused; then she allowed Winchester to proceed, and told him that the crown required no alteration. She seems to have been on the point of fainting again, for Winchester said, 'Your Grace may take it boldly, for I will have another made to crown your husband withal.' The whole company then withdrew, and Jane was left alone to realize that she was merely the adjunct to Northumberland's ambitions for his youngest son.[8]

This scene took place on the evening of July 11th. Between then and July 19th, Pembroke, Lord Herbert and Katherine remained in the Tower. During those eight days the Princess Mary's following rose in strength; Northumberland, setting off to join battle with them in Norfolk, was arrested, and Jane's reign came to an end.

Pembroke, now clamouring to make public his allegiance to Mary, was allowed to return to Baynard's Castle with Lord Herbert and Katherine. There, 'throwing away his cap full of angels' to the crowd outside the gates, he acknowledged Mary as the rightful Queen. His next action was to announce that his son's marriage would be dissolved; then he turned Katherine out of the house. She was sent to Sheen, a palace the Suffolks had acquired from Northumberland after Somerset's fall, and remained there alone, for her parents, and Jane and Guilford Dudley, were still in the Tower. She never saw Jane again.[9]

During this short, bloodless yet violent interregnum, all attention had been centred, once more, on Jane, while Katherine remained, as always, in the shadow. It is in view of this situation, and of Jane's nine days' reign, that Katherine's subsequent behaviour must to some extent be judged. Only so can her wild folly, her almost insane presumption, be understood. The brilliant elder sister, who had eclipsed her in the schoolroom and at the altar, had now, finally, in the ancient fortress of the monarchy, been proclaimed (and passively acknowledged by the sullen and disapproving people) as Queen of England, Scotland, Ireland and France, by the Grace of God Defender of the Faith and Head of the Church; her Tudor cousins were declared illegitimate. Northumberland's brief triumph was to have grisly repercussions: not least on the feather-headed, thirteen-year-old Katherine. She had seen her mother, the mother she feared and shrank from, carrying her sister's train as they proceeded into the Tower: she had seen the arrogant Guilford Dudley, walking beside her, bow almost to the ground whenever Jane spoke to him; she had seen the bullying Suffolk and the all-powerful Northumberland fall on their knees before Jane when she addressed them from beneath her canopy of state. It was this phantasmagoria of greatness, not the picture of the masked executioners, the block, the sawdust soaked in blood from a headless corpse, that was to remain with Katherine Grey. Queen of England – the words that, even now, have a strangely thrilling reverberation, were then a trumpet-call, irresistible, intoxicating, as impossible to forget as to disregard. Jane, who was experienced and intelligent enough to realize what they could portend, might tremble and plead and swoon at the feet of the evil men who were exploiting her. Katherine, surely, must have envied and desired and longed, with the corrosive and agonizing jealousy that is the peculiar curse of the unsuccessful and ignored. Nothing else can account for her actions during the years that followed.

From July 19th to 31st Katherine had time to reflect on her humiliations and the dangers ahead. 'She languished long', according to a Protestant historian, 'under the disgrace of this rejection, none daring to make any particular addresses to her, for fear of being involved in the like calamities as had befallen her father and the rest of that family.'[10] In fact, Suffolk had already slipped out of the net by leaving the Tower to proclaim Mary before Northumberland was arrested in Cambridge. On July 31st, accompanied by several officials who could be relied on to bear witness for him, he entered Jane's presence-chamber, and with his own hands tore down her canopy of state, telling her that she was no longer Queen. She expressed relief with her usual volubility, and asked if she might go home. Suffolk made no answer; he would not take the risk of releasing the daughter who had now become a state prisoner. With the Duchess, he left for Sheen, while Jane and Guilford remained in the Tower.[11] Suffolk then annulled Mary Grey's betrothal to Lord Arthur Grey.

On August 3rd Queen Mary, accompanied by the Princess Elizabeth and a great train of ladies and gentlemen, entered London in triumph and proceeded to the Tower. Her intention was to release Jane and Guilford at once, as the innocent victims of Northumberland's conspiracy. In a conversation with the man who was to be her evil genius, Simon Renard, the Spanish Ambassador, she said there could be no question of her punishing either of them. Renard, with some of her English advisers, among whom Bishop Gardiner was the most influential, reminded her that Jane had signed a paper declaring that both Mary and Elizabeth were bastards, with the words 'Jane the Queen'. Mary therefore agreed that Jane and Guilford must remain prisoners until with Northumberland and his coadjutors they stood upon their trial. She was resolved that in Jane's case this would be a formality, followed by a free pardon. Meanwhile she ordered her Catholic and Protestant subjects 'not to revile one another',[12] and received Pembroke, who fell at her feet, acknowledged his presumption with tears, and told her that Katherine and Herbert were already divorced; he added that he was making arrangements for his son to marry someone else.[13]

While the preparations for Mary's coronation were going forward the French and Spanish Ambassadors began the struggle about the succession that was to involve Katherine in life-long misery. Naturally, Mary would marry; but if she died childless, who should succeed her? Elizabeth was a heretic, and her legitimacy had never been acknowledged by the Catholic powers. Lady Jane was imprisoned on a charge of treason, and might end her days in the Tower. The choice therefore lay primarily between Katherine (of whose existence the Spanish Ambassador had only just heard) and Mary Stuart, now Dauphiness of France. The French were of course backing Mary Stuart; so the Spanish, concerned chiefly with defeating them, decided to place Katherine next in the succession; in this they were supported by the Venetian Ambassador, and by the Queen herself, whose hostility to Elizabeth was beginning to emerge. It was assumed by all these persons that Katherine was sufficiently young and biddable to be converted to the old faith.

When the Duke of Northumberland stood upon his trial in Westminster Hall, he told the peers who judged him (many, according to an eye-witness, wept at his 'miserable state')[14] that Pembroke had forced on Katherine's marriage to Lord Herbert against his advice. Neither this nor his other defences, nor his confessions of past villainies, nor his last-minute reconciliation with the Catholic Church, could save him; with two of his collaborators, he was executed at the end of August 1553. Jane and Guilford Dudley, although condemned with him, remained in the Tower and were leniently treated, being allowed to walk on the leads and to correspond with one another and with their families. Meanwhile the Queen made it clear that her attitude towards the Suffolks was not only kindly but protective; it seems as if her intention at this time was to release Jane and Guilford as soon as she herself had married, produced an heir and set England on the road back to Catholicism. She received the Suffolks, and installed Katherine as lady of the Privy Chamber. At the coronation Katherine took precedence of her companions as princess of the blood, riding immediately behind her mistress and the Lady Elizabeth in a gown of red velvet on a horse trapped with the same material.[15]

In November the Spanish Ambassador was told that the Grey sisters might be relegated as bastards, on the supposition that Suffolk's first marriage was valid. When this scheme for eliminating them fell through, his interest in Katherine was renewed, and he again began to assess the chances of her conversion. At first, the Protestantism of the whole family appeared unshakeable; then in the second week in November Suffolk was converted, and Spanish hopes rose; a few days later the Duke recanted, and the whole question had to be reconsidered. Suffolk was irremediably unstable; but for Katherine something might be achieved; and the influence of the Catholic Lady Jane Dormer, who afterwards married Feria, one of the Spanish envoys, was brought to bear. Jane Dormer, pious, cultivated, charming, and one of the Queen's closest friends, was a few years older than Katherine. It seems, although the information on this point is uncertain, that she began to proselytize her fellow maid-of-honour with some success.

So the year 1553 came peacefully to an end. In the last week of January 1554 the rising on behalf of the Princess Elizabeth and the Protestant cause, engineered by Sir Thomas Wyatt the Younger, drew Suffolk into its toils, with the result that he, Wyatt, Jane and Guilford Dudley, and Suffolk's brother Lord Thomas Grey, were condemned to die.

Jane declared herself relieved. At sixteen she was weary of a world in which she had found nothing but brutality, treachery and horror. During her preparations for death she composed a series of farewell letters and messages, of which the most often quoted is that to Katherine. It was written on the blank pages of a Greek Testament, her last present to the sister she had outshone and dominated, and loved best.

This celebrated discourse – which does not, even in the sixteenth-century sense, read like a personal communication – is concise, loaded with biblical slogans, and dictatorially pious; a stern directive from a strong-minded guide to a backward pupil, and thus one of

the most bewildering documents of an age that in this particular
context is so spiritually remote as sometimes to appear incom-
prehensible. Naturally Jane's thoughts were set on her immediate,
and Katherine's future, union with God and His Protestant elect; it
therefore only remained for her to forgive her enemies (of whom
her father was the principal) and set her sister in the way of righteousness. Yet what she wrote during the hours that preceded a hideous
death sets an insoluble problem for those who would explore the
past. Understanding — save in a literal sense, for this strange composition is clearly and forcibly expressed — breaks down. What sort
of heroine, martyr, prototype, example, was this girl? And what
could the effect of her letter on the thirteen-year-old Katherine have
been? Imagination is struck dumb: conjecture withers up, as Jane's
phrases — marmoreal, icy, facile — seal, apparently for ever, the
barrier between her age and our own.

Lady Jane begins by explaining to her 'good sister Katherine' that
the Testament, 'although not outwardly trimmed with gold ...
inwardly is of more worth than precious stones', and goes on, 'It
will win you more than you would have gained by possession of
your woeful father's lands.' After urging Katherine to abide by its
precepts, she reminds her to 'live still to die ... deny the world, deny
the devil and despise the flesh ... Take up your cross ... As touching
my death, rejoice, as I do, and adsist [consider] that I shall be delivered
from corruption and put on incorruption.' After another scriptural
passage she concludes, 'Farewell, dear sister; put your only trust in
God, Who only must uphold you. Your loving sister, Jane Dudley.'[16]

Katherine may have wished and intended to follow this advice,
but in fact she was not capable of doing so. How deeply she felt
Jane's death must remain a matter of dispute; in any case, it was not
her feelings but her situation that concerned those who were to
influence her destiny. In the event of the Queen dying without
leaving an heir, Katherine would be nearer the succession than
before — preferred by some to the Princess Elizabeth, on a level
with her in the view of others. The Protestant section was in her
favour because her family belonged to it; many of the Catholics
were backing her because they feared the Franco-Scottish influence

and believed that the Lady Katherine was about to be, or had already been, converted.

Youth, volatility, pride of birth, the favour of Queen Mary, and the sudden removal of the sister who had been in more than one sense her superior, now began to work upon Katherine, with results that were to end in ruin, heartbreak and a miserable death.

NOTES TO CHAPTER TWO

[1] Godwin, *Annals of England*, p. 225.
[2] Strickland, *Lives of the Tudor and Stuart Princesses*, p. 85.
[3] Heylyn, *History of the Reformation*, p. 11.
[4] Strype, *Ecclesiastical Memorials*, vol. II, pt. II, pp. 111-12.
[5] Calendar of Spanish State Papers, June 13th, 1553, p. 53.
[6] Naunton, *Fragmenta Regalia*, pp. 25-6.
[7] Strickland, *Tudor and Stuart Princesses*, p. 91.
[8] Ibid.
[9] Nichols (ed.), *Queen Jane and Queen Mary*, pp. 9, 11, 15.
[10] Heylyn, vol. II, p. 383.
[11] Froude, *History of England*, vol. V, p. 207. Strickland, *Tudor and Stuart Princesses*, p. 103.
[12] de Guaras, *Accession of Queen Mary*, p. 110.
[13] Naunton, pp. 25-6.
[14] de Guaras, p. 102.
[15] Nichols, p. 21.
[16] Strickland, *Tudor and Stuart Princesses*, pp. 118-19.

AFTER the Wyatt rebellion Katherine's life became easier and pleasanter, partly because she was removed from her mother's household by Queen Mary, who gave her an allowance of £80 a year. The Queen treated Katherine rather as a younger sister than as a dependant, thus again making it clear that she had no personal animosity against the Greys. In the opinion of Mary's advisers, the rising had made Jane's death a necessity; as long as she remained alive, similar outbreaks might have continued, ending in civil war and possibly the defeat of the Catholic cause. Now that danger was removed, Mary could indulge her family feeling, and make a *protégée* of the lonely thirteen-year-old cousin of whom she had always been fond.

The ruler into whose hands Katherine's fortunes thus fell was a delicate, obsessively conscientious, rather commonplace woman of thirty-eight. Mary Tudor had known very little happiness and much misery and disappointment. Her personal tastes were domestic rather than intellectual, turning towards small talk, dress and the care of children and servants; although she could rise to an occasion, and had shown great courage in the face of many dangers, she preferred, in her public capacity, to lean on the hard-bitten and unscrupulous politicians whom she had entrusted with the government of her realm. Her dedication to her faith was not, at this time, so belligerent or so fanatical as it became after the disaster of her marriage to Philip of Spain and the gradual and disintegrating realization that she was to be childless. Her attitude towards Katherine, and towards the nine-year-old Mary Grey, for whom also she made herself responsible, was therefore considerate and kind.

Queen Mary's pity for the widowed Duchess of Suffolk was shown to have been wasted, when less than a month after the Duke's execution the Duchess married her equerry, Adrian Stokes, a penni-less, low-born, flashily handsome youth of twenty-one. The Queen received Stokes and his elderly bride; but she placed Mary and Katherine Grey in the charge of the Duchess of Somerset, one of her closest friends, who with her only unmarried daughter, Lady Jane Seymour, and Hertford, her favourite son, was living at Hanworth Palace, a property bestowed on her by the Queen. Jane Seymour, then nineteen or twenty years old, was frail, dominating and romantic. She took charge of Katherine, who became devoted to her – so much so, indeed, that when Lady Jane had to retire to Hanworth to recover from an illness, Queen Mary allowed Katherine to go too, and to stay with her during the greater part of the summer of 1554. So once more Katherine and Hertford were thrown together, this time in an atmosphere of quiet and informal domesticity.

The Duchess of Somerset, although haughty, grasping and bad-tempered, treated Katherine well. When she became aware that Hertford was falling in love with her, she questioned him as to his intentions, and seems to have given him some sort of warning about displeasing the Queen. His reply shows that he and Katherine had already reached an understanding. 'Mother,' he said, 'young folks meaning well may well accompany.' In fact Hertford planned, with the Queen's permission, to marry Katherine, for he went on, 'Both in this house and in Queen Mary's Court, I trust I may have Lady Katherine's company, not having been forbidden by the Queen's commandment.' The Duchess and Lady Jane were a little disturbed by this, to them, sudden attachment, for Hertford, questioned again, reassured his sister. 'Lady Katherine hath been sent by the Queen to live with my mother at Hanworth knowing I was there,' he said. 'Therefore her feelings in this matter cannot be doubted.'[1]

This is the optimism of the accepted suitor; and it was as a triumphant hero of romance that the seventeen-year-old Edward

Hertford, whom Katherine later learnt to call 'Ned', 'my good Ned' and 'my sweet lord',[2] caught and held her fancy: the fancy of a girl whom none but an exacting tutor and a masterful elder sister had loved, and who had been deserted by her first husband and her parents at the outbreak of danger. Hertford was slender, dark, and not very tall, with the aquiline profile and large, deepset eyes that he inherited from his magnificent father. Both the Duke and Duchess of Somerset had spoilt and indulged him; educated by Protestant intellectuals with Edward VI, he had been brought up to think of himself as a privileged person; and this treatment had continued, in some degree, after Somerset's execution. Although relegated politically, Hertford had been protected by his cunning and formidable mother during the progress and collapse of the Northumberland conspiracy, and owing to her friendship with Queen Mary he was allowed to practise his religion openly throughout the five years of her reign. While Latimer, Hooper, Ridley and a host of humble men and women went to the stake — when Cheke, who had tutored him and the boy King, recanted, dying of a broken heart because he could not face an agonizing death — Hertford was able to behave as if religious persecution did not exist. In Katherine's eyes he became, as her few surviving letters to him show, perfection: an Adonis who could do no wrong; and the fact that he had been betrothed to Jane may have enhanced his attractions. To such a young man, ambitious, self-confident and enforcedly idle, Katherine's gentle femininity, her delicate prettiness and adoring, uncritical compliance must have been irresistible.

So the idyll began in an adolescent yet passionate devotion that strengthened and deepened with the anxieties and troubles of the reign. Marriage, although discussed and hoped for, had to be postponed as the Queen's personal life darkened and the tortured, maniacal side of her temperament prevailed. From 1554 till 1558 times were hard for Protestants, however favoured. Thus it came about that Katherine, when she was in attendance on her cousin, conformed, outwardly at least, with the result that she gave the Catholic envoys the impression that she had experienced, and was acting upon, a genuine change of heart.

By the end of 1557 it had become obvious that the Queen had no hope of bearing a child and that she was not likely to last much longer. Katherine and Mary Grey were not in attendance at Court, not because they had fallen from favour, but because their mistress was living in seclusion. The sisters were staying with their mother and stepfather in Southwark when fresh rumours of Queen Mary's plans for the succession began to circulate. The Venetian Ambassador was told that the Lady Katherine would claim the crown as her sister had, but that she would not be similarly opposed, in spite of the provisions laid down in Henry VIII's will, for the Queen, distrusting and hating the Princess Elizabeth, favoured Katherine's succession. After much talk of Katherine's becoming Queen (with an effect on her that may be imagined) it was objected that both she and Lady Mary Grey were 'reproached' by Lady Jane's treason, and were therefore to be excluded.[3] Katherine herself, now just seventeen, seems to have believed that she might be preferred to Elizabeth, and not without reason; for both her temperament and her circumstances barred her from sharing or even understanding public opinion, or grasping the popularity of the Princess. She and Elizabeth had seen almost nothing of one another; and Katherine had no notion, either then or later, what sort of rival she was facing.

In the early hours of November 17th, 1558, Queen Mary died, and Elizabeth was rapturously proclaimed and acknowledged. On December 13th Katherine and Mary Grey attended the funeral, riding horses whose black trappings reached the ground; they sat down to a funeral banquet in the Abbey.[4] By that time Katherine had been relegated. She still had her place at Court, but as Lady of the Bed-Chamber instead of Lady of the Privy Chamber.[5] In the eyes of the world, the difference was negligible. To Katherine it meant that she was removed to a lower sphere, no longer ranking, as in Queen Mary's reign, as Princess of the blood, when she had often taken precedence of the daughter of Anne Boleyn.

It is at this point that Katherine's character begins to emerge from the chrysalis of obscurity, neglect, misfortune and detrimental influences that her upbringing and circumstances had combined to create. She has been dismissed as a girl whose intellectual limitations were such as to make her uninteresting: contemptibly so. This is partly because, with the accession of Queen Elizabeth, she was fated to stand for ever in the shadow of an extraordinary and baffling genius, whose many-faceted brilliance has dazzled memoirists, historians and biographers for four hundred years. It is not possible — it may never be possible — to recreate Elizabeth in her habit as she lived. She defies the acutest and most careful analysis; her image bursts out of the moulds and canvases that her detractors and admirers have set up, destroying and transcending personal recollection, perceptive learning and meticulous scholarship in turn. In order to visualize Katherine Grey's development and behaviour during the first years of this cousin's reign, it is necessary to presuppose her total collapse and defeat, not only as an aspirant and a rival, but as an individual. If this hypothesis is accepted, it becomes easier to guess, however dimly, at the impact made by Elizabeth upon Katherine; to picture the process as rather like that of a tigress brushing aside and then swallowing a gadfly, and so to perceive Katherine at first unaware, afterwards bewildered, and finally eliminated. Meanwhile, a few facts may be disinterred from the political and dynastic imbroglio as it appeared to Katherine and her supporters during the first months of the reign.

At the age of twenty-five Elizabeth Tudor gave the impression of being a vigorous and reasonably healthy young woman, perfectly fitted for marriage and motherhood. Yet in this respect her family record was not good; and she became Queen of an England in which plague, assassination, revolution, or invasion by a foreign power might at any moment destroy her before she had a chance to produce an heir and re-establish the national stability. Furthermore, Elizabeth's own conduct was, from the outset, so daunting, capricious and enigmatic as to force those concerned with the welfare of the kingdom to settle on an heir-presumptive for themselves; for Her Majesty's equivocal statements and rapid *volte-face* intensified the prevailing conditions of suspense, cross-purposes and intrigue. Out of a group of claimants and counter-claimants Katherine Grey seemed to rise to the top as next in the succession under Henry VIII's will and as the candidate favoured by Spain, then England's most powerful ally, thus representing both the Protestant and the Catholic interests.

One of the first results of this situation was the reappearance in her life of Lord Pembroke. Not having arranged another alliance for his son, he began to speak of remarrying Lord Herbert to Katherine. Katherine mentioned this plan to Feria, the Spanish Ambassador, who was then courting her friend Lady Jane Dormer; through Jane Dormer, Feria insinuated himself into Katherine's confidence. Katherine was cautious, even disingenuous; she gave Feria the impression that she was not averse to remarrying Herbert, perhaps because she was beginning to realize that her wish to marry Hertford must for the present remain a secret.

Feria did not give Philip II a full report on this aspect of English affairs till March 1559, three months after the accession.[6] During that time Katherine had been flattered, cajoled and deluded by a number of politicians, and snubbed by the Queen, whose capacities she was utterly unable then or later to assess.

Feria's conversations with Katherine were conducted in French, a language which both spoke fluently. It is possible that Katherine was at times confused, not only by the marked attentions the Spanish envoy was paying her, but also by his accent; this would account for her demure, non-committal attitude, which later became plaintively confidential. Her first appearance as a leading figure at Court and on the political scene gives the impression of a gentle but by no means characterless femininity. She was neither pert nor verbose, like her elder sister, nor graciously genial, like her cousin Elizabeth; her way of listening and agreeing to what was said, combined with her frail, fair beauty and her apparent unwillingness to assert herself, made an immediate appeal to the middle-aged Spaniard, whose views on women's place in public affairs were old-fashioned and conventional. It was not in Katherine's nature to behave as the Tudors did. All her life she had been so dominated and surpassed, that to swear, to laugh loudly, to gesticulate, to introduce a dogmatic or unusual strain in her conversation, was beyond her. She waited till the other person had finished speaking, and then replied as became a modest and strictly brought up girl. This correctness misled Feria; he believed that Katherine was meekly waiting, as a young princess in his own country would have waited, until her chosen husband's name had been announced to her, and her future settled. In fact, Katherine's submissiveness concealed a fiery determination, at present known only to Hertford and his sister; for Lady Jane Seymour had now become the lovers' confidante and go-between. Feria of course knew nothing at all of the schemes that were being formed by the three young people, nor that they were considering a concerted approach to Queen Elizabeth in which the Duchesses of Suffolk and Somerset would be persuaded to share. He therefore encouraged Katherine to speak of her altered circumstances on the assumption that she would tell him about all her most private hopes and fears.

Katherine began by saying that the Queen did not wish her to succeed in the event of her own death without heirs. ('She is dissatisfied and offended at this', Feria told his master.) 'The late Queen,' Katherine went on, 'showed me much favour. The present Queen beareth me no good will – ' and she gave her relegation from the Privy Chamber to the Bed-Chamber as a proof of Elizabeth's unkindness.[7]

It was one of her greatest misfortunes that nobody whose opinion she valued came forward to point out to Katherine that she was lucky to remain at Court in any capacity, and that her talks with Feria were observed by, and displeasing to, the Queen. Hertford might have warned her: but he also was young, hopeful, ambitious, and deluded.

Feria then explained to Philip that, for reasons he did not define, Lady Katherine, who had been talking of marrying Lord Herbert (the envoy seems to have been unaware of their original marriage and divorce) had now ceased to do so. Feria asked Katherine not to marry without consulting him. She agreed, and he turned to the most important aspect of her position. 'Do not change your religion without my consent,' he urged.[8] To this also Katherine agreed, though with mental reservations which, while necessarily conjectural, are sufficiently characteristic of the age and of her situation to be outlined. She had conformed, merely, under the late Queen, by attending Mass as part of her official duties. If Feria, or any of the other Catholic envoys, had been deceived by the gesture, that was not her business. She was and always would be, a Protestant, and when she married, would marry in that faith.

At about the same time that Katherine was encouraging Feria's assumptions, she and Hertford made the first advances towards arranging their betrothal. The Duchess of Somerset approved, on condition that Her Grace of Suffolk gave her consent and took the responsibility of obtaining that of the Queen. It therefore only remained for Hertford to approach the Duchess of Suffolk. He did so with justifiable confidence, for she had long been in the habit of calling him 'son', and had never made any objection to his frequenting the daughter whose marriage was now her chief concern.[9] The Duchess of Suffolk was optimistic about Queen Elizabeth's response, for she had great belief in her own influence and her powers of persuasion. To Adrian Stokes she said that there was 'goodwill' between Katherine and Hertford, adding, 'In my opinion, he is a very fit husband for her.'[10] At the end of 1558 Queen Elizabeth went on progress with an entourage that, besides Katherine and Lady Jane Seymour, included the thirteen-year-old 'crouchback Mary', as the courtiers called her.[11] Hertford and Katherine made their farewells, and, as she afterwards stated, 'love did again renew' between them.[12] When the Queen returned to Hampton Court Katherine went to stay with her mother. Hertford then called on the Duchess of Suffolk and formally asked for her hand. The Duchess gave her consent, and summoned Katherine, to whom she said, indicating the handsome, dark-eyed suitor. 'I have provided a husband for you, if you can like well of it, and if you are willing to frame your fancy and goodwill that way.' Katherine replied in the terms required by the occasion. 'I am very willing,' she said, 'to love my lord of Hertford.' The Duchess then sent for Adrian Stokes, and they conferred as to the best way of approaching Her Majesty — should a letter be composed, or should the Duchess obtain a private audience? Stokes, delighted to play his part in a matter of such moment, was full of advice and suggestions. 'If it so please the Queen's Highness and the Council,' he said pompously, 'it were a fit match.' Hertford agreed. Lady Katherine remained modestly silent, and Stokes went on, 'Her Grace will write for your lordship to the Queen's Majesty.' Here the Duchess interposed, and it was decided that she and Stokes should together concoct a letter to the Queen. Then the Duchess, who had not been well, said to Stokes, 'Devise a letter, and rough draw it for me to copy, so that I may write to the Queen's Majesty for her goodwill and consent to the marriage.' The rough draft, presumably addressed to the Council, ran as follows — 'The Earl of Hertford doth bear goodwill to my daughter the Lady Katherine, and I do humbly require the Queen's Highness to be a good and gracious lady unto her, and that it may please Her Majesty to assent to her marriage to the said Earl.'[13]

This conversation took place in March 1559. It was agreed to post-pone sending the Duchess's letter to the Council until she was well enough to follow it up by coming to Court and personally obtaining the Queen's favour; but this step was delayed throughout the spring and early summer. Hertford and Katherine submitted, continuing to meet whenever it was possible, either at the Suffolk residences, or at Court, where Lady Jane Seymour arranged more than one private interview for them, or at Hanworth. 'Love continued,' Katherine said afterwards, 'with sundry meetings and talks, without making any creature privy of our council, saving the Lady Jane.'[14] Both Hertford and Katherine knew that these rendezvous would not be approved of by their mothers; but suspense and delay had their inevitable effect; life was unendurable without those stolen and ecstatic hours in which they renewed their vows.

In July 1559, Henri II was killed in a tournament; Francis II and Mary Stuart became King and Queen of France, and were persuaded by their Guise uncles to usurp the royal arms of England. Immed-iately the Spanish Court retaliated by setting in hand a plot to kidnap Katherine, in order to marry her to Philip's son, the imbecile Don Carlos, and proclaim her heiress-presumptive to the English throne. Knowing nothing of Katherine's private affairs, their agents took her co-operation for granted — had she not complained of the Queen's treatment on several occasions? 'They take her to be of a discontented mind,' said the English envoy to whom these plans were revealed, '*as not regarded by the Queen or her friends,*' underlining the last sentence in his report to Queen Elizabeth, as if in warning. He added that if Katherine's marriage to Don Carlos fell through, the Spaniards would make an alliance for her with 'some other person of less degree.'[15]

By the beginning of October the Courts of Europe were full of rumours of the plot to seize Lady Katherine Grey. The Catholic Duke of Saxony wrote to Cecil that the King of Spain would be certain to defeat the French interest and the Guise contingent thereby, and commented on Queen Elizabeth's dislike of Katherine and all her family. He said that his ambassador had informed him that Her Majesty 'could not well abide' Lady Katherine. Nor did her mother and stepfather love her: and her uncle, Lord John Grey, 'would in no wise abide to hear of her. She lives', he concluded, 'in great despair.'[16]

It was at this point that Katherine, beset on every side, distracted, it would seem, with alternating fears of being kidnapped by the Spaniards, parted from Hertford and permanently ignored by her mother, who alone could help her to achieve the marriage on which her heart was set, lost her head completely. 'In the presence of the Queen and of others standing by, she spoke very arrogant and unseemly words.' So the Duke of Saxony was told by his envoy, who gave no details of the scene.[17]

Queen Elizabeth made no official gesture of displeasure towards Katherine: an ominous sign, unheeded by the newly appointed Spanish Ambassador, Bishop de Quadra, who told Philip II that this young lady would make 'a much more desirable queen' than Elizabeth. 'If any disaster', he went on hopefully, 'were to befall Queen Elizabeth, such as may be feared from her bad [i.e. heretically inclined] government, the Archduke [Ferdinand, Philip's nephew] might be summoned to marry Lady Katherine, *to whom the kingdom falls if this woman dies.* If the Archduke sees Lady Katherine, he should so bear himself that she should understand this design, which ... may be beneficial, and even necessary.' In other words, de Quadra advised the forwarding of Katherine's claim by force of arms, if the circumstances called for strong action.[18]

So the web was spun, while Hertford and Katherine remained dependent on the Duchess of Suffolk's approaching the enigmatic ruler of their destinies. If the Duchess had chosen this moment to ask permission for their marriage, Elizabeth might possibly have given it, as the best means of removing her tiresome cousin from both French and Spanish intriguers; on the other hand, Elizabeth knew Hertford to be ambitious, to the point, indeed, of lending himself and Katherine to foreign rivalry; she trusted neither of the two young people, nor their families. So she kept the threads of the situation in her hands, and took no action. Meanwhile, her dislike or Katherine, as of all the Greys, crystallized into a watchful and merciless anger.

The most inexplicable aspect of the situation is Katherine's crazy outburst in the presence of the Queen. How it was phrased and of what it consisted will never be known, and in fairness to her and in view of the fact that it was reported by a foreigner, it should not be conjectured. From that moment the wretched fool was doomed; if she felt or knew that she had finally destroyed her credit with the Queen, then her subsequent desperate action may be accounted for and understood. If 'All for Love' had now become her and Hertford's password, she might take on the stature of a tragic figure. She cannot, as the evidence stands, be so visualized. Her behaviour was presumptuous and rash to the point of lunacy. What conflicting influences drove her to it may be guessed at, but, unfortunately for her and her story, not categorically defined.

So Katherine remained helpless, and in great danger from both her supporters and her enemies. Her mother was the only person who could have improved her situation by obtaining leave for her to marry Hertford, while guaranteeing that she would publicly renounce all claim to the throne. It is unlikely that the Duchess of Suffolk would have consented to remove Katherine from the succession; whatever plans she had, came to an end with her death on November 20th, 1559.

While she lay in state, the Duchess's letter remained as she had copied it, with the additional plea of her dying request that Katherine and Hertford should be allowed to marry.[19] Yet who could now take the responsibility of putting it before the Privy Council? The Duchess of Somerset held back; the dead Duchess's brother-in-law, Lord John Grey, seems not to have known of its existence, and would not in any case do anything for the niece he disliked; the widowed Adrian Stokes, formerly so eager in his step-daughter's cause, would make no move without Hertford's support.

And Hertford had lost his nerve. When Stokes asked him what he wanted done, he said, 'I will meddle no further in the matter.' Stokes thereupon destroyed the document that, if it had been discovered, might have got them both into trouble.[20]

On December 5th the Duchess of Suffolk was buried in Westminster Abbey with royal honours. At the Queen's command, her daughters were restored to their position as Princesses of the blood by privileges reserved for that rank; they had cushions to kneel on before the altar, and their mourning trains were carried by Ladies of the Bed-Chamber. After the funeral service they took Communion and then returned to the Suffolk palace at Sheen 'in their chariot'.[21]

Hertford's terror of the Queen's displeasure and his refusal to approach her were understood and shared by Katherine. Although their loves were now further darkened and their prospects almost hopeless, their devotion was undiminished. There was however an essential difference between them. Katherine's passion for Hertford did not waver: it governed her life. His feelings towards her sometimes fluctuated, and were influenced by other emotions — his instinct for self-preservation, and the desire to make his way in the world and restore the greatness of his family. Katherine seems to have sympathized with this ambivalence; nothing that her dear lord did or inflicted upon her was censurable in her eyes.

So it was that in the months following the Duchess of Suffolk's death Hertford began to look round for support for himself, and for Katherine, if it could be managed, among the most influential of the English statesmen. It is at this point that William Cecil, Queen Elizabeth's Secretary of State, and Robert Dudley, afterwards Earl of Leicester, then Cecil's enemy and rival, appeared as it were from the wings, and joined the circle of Katherine's destroyers.

LADY KATHERINE GREY

NOTES TO CHAPTER THREE

[1] Harleian MSS, 6286.
[2] H.M.C.: Northumberland MSS, vol. III, p. 47.
[3] Calendar of Venetian State Papers, vol. VI, No. 1077.
[4] Machyn, *Diary*, p. 182.
[5] Calendar of Letters Relating to English Affairs, vol. I, No. 21.
[6] Cal. English Affairs, vol. I, No. 21.
[7] Ibid.
[8] Ibid.
[9] Harleian MSS, 6286.
[10] Ibid.
[11] Godwin, p. 255.
[12] Harleian MSS, 6286.
[13] Ibid.
[14] Ibid.
[15] Calendar of Foreign State Papers, 1559, No. 1116.
[16] Ibid.
[17] Ibid.
[18] Cal. English Affairs, vol. I, No. 74.
[19] Harleian MSS, 6286.
[20] Ibid.
[21] Nichols, *Progresses of Queen Elizabeth*, vol. I, p. 53.

LORD ROBERT DUDLEY, now in his twenty-seventh year, was the best-looking and most attractive of Northumberland's sons. His father's tendency to spoil him had been shown eight years before Elizabeth's accession by his allowing Robert to marry Amy Robsart for love, instead of arranging a great match for him. That youthful passion had long since withered, on Dudley's side, at least; now, handsomer than ever, he was enthroned in the Queen's favour, believed by many to be her paramour and by some to have her leave to claim her in marriage, if he became a widower.

In September 1560 Amy Dudley fell downstairs and broke her neck. For the rest of his life, and long after it, Dudley was thought to have planned her murder. (The collated evidence points to suicide, and it is possible that he had hoped for and encouraged this form of release.) The Queen's attitude towards him appeared in no way affected by this hideous scandal, with the result that their marriage was talked of as imminent and anticipated by Cecil and other members of the Council, who saw in it the downfall and expulsion of their mistress. Shortly after Amy Dudley's death it became known that Philip II was supporting Elizabeth's marriage to Dudley in order to discredit her and place Lady Katherine on the throne. Thereupon Cecil, who was determined to prevent the Elizabeth-Dudley marriage, and who had observed that Hertford was apt to seek out Katherine when he came to Whitehall, began to consider arranging an alliance between them in order to frustrate the Spanish plan of marrying her to Don Carlos or the Archduke Ferdinand. When he asked Hertford if there was 'goodwill' between him and Lady Katherine, the young man replied sharply, 'No such thing.' Cecil abandoned the idea of marrying Katherine to Hertford when the Queen assured him that she did not intend to marry Dudley; but his temporary encouragement of Hertford's suit must have had some effect on both Katherine and her lover.

At about the same time the Queen was warned again, not only of the Spanish plots centring on Katherine, but of the Scots Council's scheme of marrying her to Lord Arran, Katherine's and Elizabeth's semi-imbecile second cousin, who was heir-apparent of Scotland. Randolph, the English envoy at Holyrood, wrote to Cecil that 'as [Lady Katherine] is heir-apparent to England, so shall she be matched with an heir-apparent to Scotland, so that if both those [Elizabeth and Mary Stuart] who are in possession of the crowns die without succession, the right shall come to them.'[1] Nothing came of this plan; then fresh rumours reached Cecil of Katherine's being 'enticed away' to Spain by some Catholic Englishman (Lord Arundel was suggested) in Spanish pay. In this way Philip would be able to disclaim all responsibility for kidnapping her, for 'it would be suspected that some within the realm had done it, thinking to marry her.'[2]

Elizabeth's response to these threats was highly characteristic of the Tudors. She restored Katherine to her position as Lady of the Privy Chamber, and told Bishop de Quadra that she looked on her as a daughter. The bishop could not quite swallow this. After much thought, he came to the conclusion that the feeling between Her Majesty and the Lady Katherine 'can hardly be that of mother and child'. 'The Queen', he went on, 'makes much of her in order to keep her quiet. She even talks about formally adopting her.' But it was puzzling; what did Her Majesty really mean? Finally de Quadra appealed to Cecil. The Secretary said that Lord Huntingdon, as a descendant of the Plantagenets, was a more likely candidate for the throne than Lady Katherine, and blandly asked the bishop whether his master was thinking of marrying her himself. 'Would Her Majesty consider Lady Katherine as her successor?' de Quadra inquired. 'By no means,' the Secretary replied, 'because, as the saying is, the English run after the heir to the crown rather than after the wearer of it.'[3]

Meanwhile Elizabeth's tactics had had their effect. Katherine and Hertford — weaned children playing in the cockatrice's den — began to hope once more and, urged on by Lady Jane Seymour, to consider marrying out of hand, thereafter throwing themselves on the Queen's mercy. If the thing were done, she must eventually relent. While she might never allow a public marriage, she would perhaps forgive a secret love-match. The all-powerful Cecil seemed to be on their side; and Dudley, the brother-in-law of Lady Jane Grey, also might help them. (The fact that he was the most hated man in England seems not to have concerned them.) Yet Hertford could not quite make up his mind to take the final step, and between August and November 1560 continued to play for time, covering up his tracks by paying attentions to other Court ladies. And then, suddenly, the gentle and acquiescent Katherine gave way to an outburst of jealous rage. The scene took place at Hampton Court, in Lady Jane Seymour's closet, in her presence. Katherine accused Hertford of having made advances to a daughter of Sir Peter Mewtas. 'You bear her goodwill,' she exclaimed.[4]

It was the first time she had ever spoken harshly to him, and Hertford, unaccustomed to being found fault with by anyone, seems to have been shocked into a passionate declaration. He had never thought of Mewtas's daughter, or of anyone but Katherine. 'I will marry you out of hand,' he went on, 'if convenient time be found, when the Queen's Majesty shall come to London.'[5]

Eventually this first and only quarrel was made up, and the decision reached that resulted in years of misery for both Katherine and Hertford. It is at this juncture that Lady Jane Seymour takes her stand beside the lovers. Without her help and encouragement — without her plotting and scheming — Katherine's and Hertford's devotion might have yielded to adversity and died a natural death.

Almost nothing is known of this Lady Jane Seymour, except that when her father was made Duke of Somerset and Lord Protector she had been led to believe that she might become Queen of England by marrying Edward VI. He was her first cousin, for his mother, another Jane Seymour, who died twelve days after he was born, was Somerset's sister. In fact, Somerset had planned a continental alliance for his nephew; but there was enough talk about the young King being betrothed to Jane to make her feel that her father's attainder and execution had deprived her of a great position. This resentment may have been intensified by the fact that thereafter no other marriage was arranged for her; and by the time Elizabeth succeeded, Jane had probably given up all hope of a life of her own. In the autumn of 1560 she had only three months to live, and may have realized that she was very ill. In any case, she put all her energy, the desperate, fanatical energy of the dying, into her schemes for her brother's future. His marriage to Katherine became a cause: one that must triumph, no matter what the result. In the weeks that passed between the beginning of October and the middle of November Lady Jane watched and waited. Then her plans were held up by Hertford's falling ill. Once more, he seemed to waver.

The story of the steps taken by Jane Seymour to bind Hertford to his promise, and the consequences of that promise, is preserved in a manuscript in the Harleian Collection (No. 6286) now in the British Museum. This is a long report to the Privy Council of the courtship and wedding of Katherine and Hertford, as described by themselves and by others concerned. It is one of the most detailed and intimate documents of the period. A number of historians and biographers seem to have glanced through it; it has never been printed, nor used in full; yet it provides a picture that is unique in the annals of the sixteenth century.

The setting for that picture was Hertford's house in Cannon Row, a comparatively small establishment in which there was accommodation for some ten or twelve servants. It had two entrances, one on the river and one leading into a courtyard. Hertford's bedroom overlooked the water-gate. Shortly after his return from the country, where he, Jane and Katherine had spent the day with Sir Thomas Hoby at Bisham Abbey,[6] he was lying there when he came to his final decision. He wrote to his sister, asking her to 'further his suit' to Lady Katherine. Although their wedding must be secret, his intention was formally to propose, to be betrothed and then to marry according to the accepted customs, so that there should be no doubt about the legitimacy of their children. Lady Jane had a talk with

Katherine, and then visited her brother. She told him that Katherine was 'well inclined' to any arrangement he might make, and would give him her 'resolute answer' in person when the Court moved from Greenwich to Westminster. As soon as he was well enough, Hertford met her in Lady Jane's closet at Whitehall, a small room leading out of the 'Maidens' Chamber', where, at certain times of the day, privacy was ensured. He said, 'I have borne you goodwill of long time, and because you should not think I intend to mock you, I am content, if you will, to marry you.' Katherine replied with the same solemnity, 'I like both you and your offer, and am content to marry with you.' 'When?' Hertford asked. 'Next time the Queen's Majesty shall leave the Palace.'

Then came the ceremony of betrothal. Nothing was written down; calling his sister to witness, Hertford took Katherine's hands in his, kissed her and put a ring on her finger. It was agreed that when the Queen went to Greenwich or to Eltham to hunt, which she was likely to do at any time during the next few days, Jane and Katherine should send word to Hertford, and come to Cannon Row. Jane engaged to find a minister of the reformed faith to marry them there, and herself to stand witness. Of Katherine's two personal maids, Mrs Coffin and Mrs Leigh, Mrs Leigh was selected as the second witness; she was to be told nothing till the day of the wedding, when Hertford would send all his upper servants out of the house, as soon as word came from the Palace that the Queen had left for the country.

In the first week of December 1560 — the exact date is not recorded — the Queen's departure for Eltham was announced and her entourage told to be prepared to leave with her. Jane and Katherine were ready with the excuse on which they had agreed some time before. Lady Jane was, as so often, ailing, and Lady Katherine had toothache and a swelled face; could they be excused attendance on Her Majesty? The Queen gave her permission, and that night Hertford was told to expect the two girls early the next morning. He then desired Penne and Fortescue, his gentleman-ushers, Barnaby and Jenkins, his body-servants and Cripps, his groom of the chambers, to take that day off, returning in the afternoon. He told Barnaby, whom he did not quite trust, to go to a goldsmith's in

Fleet Street, with a letter of great importance; he was not to return until this had been delivered. Hertford, knowing that this tradesman had left the City, thus planned to keep Barnaby out of the way till the wedding was over.

When Hertford's men told the other servants of these orders, there was much talk and conjecture. Their master's 'goodwill' towards the Lady Katherine had been noted during her and Lady Jane's visits to Cannon Row. Then orders came from my lord that a cold meal — comfits, meat, bread, ale and wine — was to be prepared and placed in his bedroom early in the morning, and that the rest of the staff was to remain below stairs until after their dinner hour, that is, till about eleven o'clock. The cook, William Powell, decided to keep a lookout from the window overlooking the water-gate. Barnaby also made up his mind to disobey orders and remain in the house till he knew what was going forward; they do not seem to have confided in one another.

About an hour after the Queen departed for Eltham — between seven and eight in the morning — it was possible for Jane and Katherine to leave the Palace unobserved. As the tide was out they decided to go on foot along the river-bank. It was probably the first time in their lives that they had walked so far unattended; but they were in too much of a hurry to think of danger, or of anything but secrecy; if they were not back at the Palace for dinner with the Lord Controller they would be missed, and their activities discovered. At the last moment it had been decided that Lady Jane should be the only witness, and that Mrs Leigh might be told that her mistress was a wife later on, when Hertford visited her at Whitehall.

So Katherine had neither time nor help to make any change in her dress on her wedding day. She was wearing the ring set with a pointed diamond that Hertford had given her at their betrothal; and in the pocket of her dress she had hidden the official insignia of the married woman — the white, three-cornered 'cover-chief' that she was determined to tie over her caul as soon as the ceremony was over, although she would have to take it off before she left Cannon Row. She was deeply agitated, so much so that she observed no one and nothing as she and Lady Jane hurried along in the cold December dawn.

Meanwhile Hertford, who had got up at six, waited in an agony of suspense. The preparations were complete. The sideboard in his bedroom was heaped with food and drink: the house seemed empty and quiet: the bed was made, and the covers had been thrown back. He could settle to nothing. He tried to read a book, and, finding that impossible, walked up and down, pausing to look out over the water-gate every now and then. At last he saw the two cloaked and hooded figures in the distance, and hurried down to the 'withdrawing chamber' to let them in himself.

Lady Jane had remained calm and resolute during the walk, and was on the watch for witnesses of their arrival. As they came up to the water-gate Barnaby passed them, and tried to slip by. 'Barnaby, whither go you?' Lady Jane asked sharply. 'On business of my lord's,' he replied. The two girls entered the house, and Hertford took them upstairs.

The priest engaged by Lady Jane had not appeared. Waiting was out of the question; so the indomitable bridesmaid decided to go out and find another. She was away half an hour.

When questioned about the time alone with her lover, Katherine, who could recall nearly all the details of that morning, had no idea what they had said to one another. Mercilessly pressed, she answered, between her sobs, that their talk had been 'such as passeth between them that intended as they did'.

When the minister and Lady Jane appeared, Hertford and Katherine said little or nothing, leaving her to make the arrangements for the ceremony. They remembered afterwards that he was high-coloured, red-bearded, rather short, dressed in black, like a Genevan, and that his gown was furred. Neither then nor later did they hear his name.

Katherine and Hertford then took up their positions facing the window with their backs to the bed. Lady Jane stood at the side. The service began. Hertford produced the wedding ring that he had had made with a spring that opened into five gold links, on which was engraved his 'posy':

As circles five by art compact show but one ring in sight,
So trust united faithful minds with knot of secret might,
Whose force to break (but greedy death) no wight possesseth
power,
As time and sequels well shall prove; my ring can say no more.

Lady Jane and the clergyman seem to have agreed on a shortened
version of the ceremony, for it was soon over. She then gave him ten
pounds and showed him the way out. When she came back Hertford
and Lady Katherine were standing by the sideboard. In what appears
to have been an attempt to create a festive atmosphere, Lady Jane
drank their health and offered her sister-in-law wine, beer and
sweetmeats in turn. Katherine was unable to swallow anything.
Lady Jane looked at them, and, according to Katherine, 'perceiving
them ready to go to bed, withdrew herself'.

Two hours passed while she waited downstairs. It is at this point
in the report that Hertford takes over from his wife. She had no
night-gear with her, and his was not laid out. They therefore, he
explained, 'went into our naked bed, in a manner both together.'
Further pressed, he recollected that he had taken less time than she
to undress, and that she was in his arms a few minutes later. Spared
nothing, he took refuge in what now reads like police-court phraseology. 'We had carnal copulation,' he said. 'I lay sometimes on one
side of the bed, and sometimes on the other.'

Returning from that brief and terrible ecstasy to the world of
every day, they were flung into a panic of haste. They got up at the
same time, and dressed in five minutes, in spite of the fact that neither
had ever done so before without help. Then they went downstairs
to where Lady Jane was waiting. The tide had risen by this time,
and a wherry was hailed. At the water-gate Hertford kissed his wife,
'and told her farewell'. Within half an hour she and Lady Jane were
again at Whitehall; ten minutes after that, they sat down to dinner
with the Lord Controller.

In the winter dusk Hertford's servants returned to Cannon Row.
They did not see their master. When Barnaby and Jenkins went up
to prepare his room for the night, they found the food untouched on

the sideboard and the bed in disarray. They remade the bed, and hurried below to inform the rest of the staff. William Powell said he had seen two gentlewomen arrive. 'There is goodwill between my lord and Lady Katherine,' he added. 'I did hear that the Queen's Majesty hath gone to hunt at Eltham,' put in another significantly. 'I have seen the Lady Katherine visit my lord once or twice with the Lady Jane,' Powell rejoined. So their talk continued, on a basis of scandalous conjecture. None of them seems to have guessed what had really happened.

NOTES TO CHAPTER FOUR

[1] Cal. Foreign S.P., September 23rd, 1560, No. 556.
[2] Ibid.
[3] Cal. English Affairs, vol. I, Nos. 60, 84.
[4] Harleian MSS, 6286.
[5] Ibid.
[6] Hoby, *Diary*, p. 128.

CHAPTER FIVE

LADY KATHERINE'S folly in marrying without Queen Elizabeth's consent has been justly condemned by those historians and biographers who can take a bird's-eye view of her situation. At first glance, it seems incredible that this young woman, however deeply in love she may have been, should not have taken warning by her sister's and her father's fate (for in marrying Hertford Katherine played the part of a rebel, if not of a traitor) and taken to heart the latent peril that was the concomitant of her Tudor blood. Why did she not understand that to be in the line of succession set her apart, and that, from the moment of Lady Jane Grey's execution, complete subservience to the monarchy was her only hope? Part of the answer to these questions is to be found in the comments of Katherine's contemporaries. They also censured her, not for what now seems an idiotic rashness, but for her unmaidenly concupiscence, as shown by her falling in love before marriage, and that with a man of her own choice, instead of waiting for a husband to be selected for her. (Not even her forceful and audacious elder sister had dared to go so far.) For a well born, let alone a royal, personage to put emotion before custom, was then considered disgusting; and this, coupled with her lending her name to the Spanish intrigues against the Queen, made her virtually, if not technically, a criminal. As a correspondent later pointed out to Cecil, by yielding to her 'lewd affections', Lady Katherine had defiled the blood royal through an unlawful connection — unlawful, because it was not arranged by the state or approved of by the sovereign.[1] In fact, she was considered to have behaved immorally, not stupidly.

The supplementary answer to those who demand some further explanation of Katherine's disregard of her sister's misfortune is more disputable. It may however be put forward as a suggestion, that in the sixteenth century the death of great personages on the scaffold was so frequent as to be accepted almost as part of daily life: at least, as a danger that, avoided by the majority, was always in the background. It could not have brought with it the feeling of horror and loathing that comes to those who read about such events from behind the barriers of the twentieth century. It is possible that execution was, to the great-niece of Henry VIII, neither shameful, nor shocking, but merely unfortunate; so a young person today might contemplate death from poliomyelitis or cancer: as an accepted scourge, a risk that all dread, but cannot count on avoiding.

Katherine's personal problems at the time of her marriage provide another reason, if not an excuse, for her temerity. Apart from any temptation that the crown may have held out to her, she was in hourly danger of being kidnapped by one of two warring factions; both were ready for her with semi-degenerate husbands, one of whom she would be forced to marry, once she was captured. To be subjected to the legalized embraces of either Don Carlos or the Earl of Arran was a disaster that any girl of spirit would have tried to escape, even if she were not passionately in love with someone else. Katherine's break-away is therefore to some degree comprehensible. Its results on her hopes of happiness were as destructive as the most censorious could have anticipated or desired. By her marriage she conjured up a destiny that to many seemed more wretched than a bloody death on Tower Green. And at the end of her life she herself seems to have realized and admitted that that destiny was achieved through her own fault, bought in frenzy, and paid for with tears.

Hertford's attitude is harder to assess; how much he was influenced by ambition and how much by love, cannot now, or ever, be determined. His sister's purposes are darker still. She may have been divided between a romantic impulse, a proclivity for intrigue and the desire to see her brother, the head of her house, married to the heiress-presumptive, no matter what the danger. She was perhaps a political gambler, as many of the Seymours were. Both she and Hertford carried the secret of their motives with them to the grave.

The last months of Jane Seymour's life were divided between her duties as Lady of the Bed-Chamber and her arrangements for the Hertfords; for the first week after the wedding she and Mrs Leigh were the only persons who knew their secret. Hertford's visits to his sister were the pretext for the hours he spent alone with Katherine, when he 'used her as his wife'. Lady Jane sometimes took her to Cannon Row, where, according to Hertford, he and Katherine 'had company' together, while she waited in another room.[2]

Six days after their marriage Hertford gave Katherine a deed of gift, in which he named her as his wife, to the value of £1,000 in land. Katherine put this, the sole written proof of her status, in a coffer in her room. Such a settlement of property could not be concealed from Hertford's next brother, Lord Henry Seymour; he was told of the marriage, and when he came to Court, consented to carry messages and presents from Hertford to Katherine. Sometimes Hertford sent her sums of money, sometimes jewellery; it was at about this time that he gave her one of his greatest treasures: a little book, three inches square, that had belonged to his father, containing calendars and tables in the Duke's writing; it was bound in red velvet and inscribed by him to his son, 'The day before my death, from the Tower.' Katherine added her signature to this rather ominous present, in a minute and delicate hand.[3]

So her situation remained unchanged, until the beginning of March 1561, when, she, Lady Jane and Hertford being alone together, Katherine suddenly announced that she thought she might be going to have a baby; she was not sure. 'Then,' said Lady Jane, 'there is no remedy but it be known how the matter stands.' Hertford agreed, adding, 'We must abide by it, and trust to the Queen's mercy.'[4] Katherine's agitation and his sister's failing health combined to prevent his breaking to them another piece of news: he had been commanded to go to France, partly on a diplomatic mission, and partly as the companion of Sir William Cecil's son Thomas, who was to complete his education in Paris. A few days later Katherine saw Hertford's passport lying on a table in Cannon Row, and burst into a passion of tears; he soothed her by telling her that the date of his departure had not been fixed, and that he might not go at all.[5]

On March 23rd Lady Jane Seymour died, and three days later was buried with great state beside Katherine's mother in Westminster Abbey. Thenceforth Katherine had to arrange her rendezvous with Hertford through Mrs Leigh who, when he visited her mistress at Whitehall, would slip out of the room as soon as she saw them whispering together. A week after Lady Jane's death Mrs Leigh, alarmed by her undesired and dangerous responsibilities, asked leave to visit her dying mother in the country — and disappeared. Katherine never saw her again.[6]

The result of Lady Jane's death and of Mrs Leigh's departure was that Katherine and Hertford found it more difficult to meet regularly, or for so long at a time; and Katherine's uncertainty as to whether she was pregnant or not added to their anxiety when they did manage to be alone together. At the beginning of April Hertford, realizing that he would soon have to leave, asked Katherine whether she was going to have a baby. She replied that she did not know. 'If you are with child,' he said, 'I will not leave you.'[7] A few days later he received his orders, and went to Whitehall to tell Katherine. It seems that he was not able to go to her room, for he broke the news in the orchard at Westminster: presumably this was one of the few places where they could talk without being overheard. There he showed her his passport, told her that he would write 'by the common packet', as well as sending letters and messages by a new servant, Glynne, who would bring him hers. He gave her a further sum of money, and said that if he heard her pregnancy was certain, he would not 'tarry from her'.[8]

Within a very short time of Hertford's departure Katherine realized, not only that she was pregnant, but that both her state and her meetings with him had become the subject of Court gossip. She was in attendance at Greenwich when she had to speak to Cecil about her allowance, which had not been paid. He took the opportunity to warn her about her 'familiarity' with Hertford. He seems to have been trying to sound her, while hinting that she would do well to confess everything to Elizabeth, and throw herself on the royal clemency. The miserable girl, now more than ever aware of her terrifying cousin's dislike, could not bring herself to follow this advice, in spite of the fact that, apparently at Cecil's suggestion, it was repeated to her, more openly, by Lady Northampton and Lady Clinton.[9] By the end of June her pregnancy was still sufficiently unknown for the question of her remarriage to Lord Herbert to arise again. 'The Earl of Pembroke cannot yet bring his purpose to pass,' wrote one courtier to another, 'for the Lady Katherine will not have his son. And whatsoever is the cause, I know not — but the Queen has entered into a great misliking with her.'[10]

By the end of July Katherine felt herself trapped. She wrote to Hertford, 'I am quick with child, I pray you therefore to return, and declare how the matter standeth between us.'[11] This letter was delayed, presumably through Glynne, who may have been bribed by Cecil to spy on his master. While Katherine waited for a reply, or for news of Hertford's return, she received a present of bracelets from Paris — but no letter. Then she became aware that her husband was sending similar 'tokens' to other Court ladies.[12]

In fact, Hertford had been writing to her regularly, from Rouen at first, and then from Paris; that his letters had miscarried was probably due to Glynne, who at this point disappeared, and was never heard of again. Meanwhile, Thomas Cecil's tutor, Mr Windebank, who had been instructed by his employer to report on Hertford as well as on his pupil, was complaining that Hertford was responsible for young Cecil's idleness and dissipation; Windebank gave the impression that both Hertford and Thomas Cecil were absorbed in undesirable pleasures, adding that Hertford had said he might travel in Italy as soon as he tired of Paris.[13] No doubt Katherine heard these rumours, and connected them with her husband's silence.

At the end of July Katherine, with the rest of the Court, was commanded to accompany the Queen on progress in Suffolk. At Ipswich, where they stayed for a night, her courage left her; resolution and self-control crumbled away. She looked round for someone to advise and plead for her with the Queen. Her choice fell on

Robert Dudley. In the middle of the night she crept into his room, and, falling on her knees by the bed, poured out her story.[14]

The elegant and accomplished Lord Robert was, like his father, calculating, ambitious and stony-hearted. His first thought appears to have been that Lady Katherine's sobs and adjurations might be overheard by, or reported to, the Queen: for his room adjoined hers and those of her ladies. Somehow, he got rid of Katherine, whether with promises he had no intention of keeping, is not clear, and she then went in her despair to Mrs Saintlow, another Lady of the Bed-Chamber, to one of whose children she had been godmother. The tortured creature could hardly have selected a more deadly confidante. Before her marriage Mrs Saintlow had been Bess Hardwick; many years later, when she became the wife of the Earl of Shrewsbury, she was known throughout the country for her ruthlessness, her avarice and her wicked tongue. Shrewder, harder, more stubbornly self-regarding even than Dudley, Mrs Saintlow listened in cold silence; then she burst into tears and vituperations, accused Katherine of immorality and deceit, and asseverated her own unshakeable devotion to her mistress.[15]

So the night passed. Next morning the conscientious Dudley obtained a private audience with the Queen, and told her everything. Characteristically, Elizabeth took no action until her splendid and triumphant progress, unmarred by disagreeable scenes, came to an end, and the Court returned to Westminster. Then she gave orders for Lady Katherine to be arrested and sent to the Tower, for Hertford to come back without delay, and for the Privy Council at once to examine, 'very straightly', Katherine, Hertford's servants, Lord Henry Seymour and Mrs Saintlow. By this time, Hertford had received Katherine's letter about her pregnancy, and had begun, in rather a leisurely fashion, to prepare for his return. In a letter to the Earl of Sussex Cecil grimly and succinctly summed up the situation. 'At Ipswich', he wrote, 'was a great mishap discovered. The Lady Katherine is certainly known to be big with child, as she saith, by the Earl of Hertford, who is in France. She is committed to the Tower. He is sent for. She saith that she was married to him secretly before Christmas last. Thus is God displeased with us.'[16]

The Almighty's displeasure may be visualized as more objective than the Queen's; and indeed from Elizabeth's point of view, Katherine's behaviour since the beginning of her reign had been ungrateful, disloyal and insolent, culminating in senseless deceit and crowned with unseemly hysteria. If Katherine's child lived and was a son, Elizabeth's position would become infinitely more complicated in respect of the succession, as long as she herself remained unmarried; and she had many good political reasons, apart from any personal predilection, for avoiding a husband. Single life enabled her to play off one European power against another, while they competed for her hand, and her own people clung to her as their only safeguard against invasion, imploring her to establish the dynasty; she must try none too high, while pleasing and encouraging all. Elizabeth was therefore in the situation of an acrobat poised over a great height who suddenly feels the tight-rope twitched from below — and that by the hand of a relation whom, in spite of her dislike, she had always treated well. In fact, Katherine, having been a nuisance since Elizabeth's accession, had now become a danger: one that was extraordinarily difficult to cope with, for by Henry VIII's will her claim to the throne preceded Mary Stuart's, although genealogically the Scots Queen was the heiress-presumptive; and Henry's will was indisputably valid, according to contemporary and later authorities.[17] Furthermore, Elizabeth was now beginning to suspect that some within her own circle, Cecil perhaps among them, not only had been privy to Katherine's marriage but were supporting her claim to the succession; she might be the centre of a plot engineered and financed by Spain, or Scotland.

Having locked up Katherine, the next thing to do was to trace any connection that might exist between her and her husband and intriguers at home and abroad. Elizabeth therefore wrote to the Lieutenant of the Tower, Sir Edward Warner, that he must find out, before the official examination by the Privy Council, 'how many hath been privy to the love between her and the Earl of Hertford from the beginning; and let her certainly understand that she shall have no manner of favour, except she will show the truth, not only of what ladies or gentlewomen of the Court were thereto privy, but

also what lords and gentlemen; for it doth now appear that sundry
personages have dealt herein; and when it shall appear more mani-
festly, it shall increase our indignation against her, if she will forbear
to utter it ... Ye shall also send ... secretly, for Saintlow, and shall
put her in awe of divers matters confessed by the Lady Katherine;
and also deal with her that she may confess to you all her knowledge
in the same matters. It is certain that there hath been great practices
[plots] and purposes; and since the death of the Lady Jane — '
Katherine's sister-in-law, not Lady Jane Grey, seems here indicated
— 'she hath been most privy ... ' In fact, Lady Katherine had shown
herself to be both sly and ambitious.[18]

Elizabeth's greatest difficulty remained unstated; it was this.
Between 1536 and 1553 the marriage of persons to royalty without
consent of the sovereign had been illegal; now that law was rescinded, and so it was impossible either to attaint Lady Katherine
(thus eliminating her from the succession) or to behead her for high
treason. It was equally impossible, in view of Katherine's flouting of
the Queen's authority with regard to her marriage and her suspected
flirting with the Spanish interest, to forgive her and recognize her as
heiress-presumptive; that would antagonize the Scots and the
French, and foster a centre of rebellion and disloyalty within the
Court. It now seems strange that no one thought of suggesting that
Katherine should publicly renounce her claim; but even if she had
been forced, or had agreed, to do so, she would not have been
trusted to keep her word, and her assurance would in any case have
been worthless, as long as she had a following within and without
the realm. The problem was insoluble, while Katherine survived
and Elizabeth did not marry.

At least, it seemed so — until Sir William Cecil's ingenuity was
brought to bear on this agitating and intolerable situation. Within
a few hours of Katherine's incarceration, he directed that the Privy
Council, in conjunction with Sir Edward Warner, should so conduct
their examinations of Lady Katherine and her husband as to find their
marriage invalid and their child, if it survived, illegitimate. If this
could be proved, and there were strong hopes that it might be, then
it only remained to punish the offenders, while Lady Katherine

would be automatically discredited and her claim would cease to exist. On these lines the state prepared to destroy first Katherine's defence and then Hertford's.

NOTES TO CHAPTER FIVE

[1] Wright, *Queen Elizabeth and her Times*, vol. I, p. 129.
[2] Harleian MSS, 6286.
[3] H.M.C.: Ashburnham MSS, p. 301.
[4] Harleian MSS, 6286.
[5] Ibid.
[6] Ibid.
[7] Ibid.
[8] Ibid.
[9] Ibid.
[10] Cal. Foreign S.P., June 28th, 1561, No. 272.
[11] Harleian MSS, 6286.
[12] Ibid.
[13] Cal. Foreign S.P., June 28th, 1561, No. 272.
[14] Harleian MSS, 6286.
[15] Ibid.
[16] Wright, vol. I, p. 69.
[17] Nicholas, *Life and Times of Lady Jane Grey*, p. 49.
[18] Haynes (ed.), *Burleigh MSS*, p. 378.

CHAPTER SIX

THE picture of a twenty-one-year-old girl, near her time, alone, friendless, unadvised, and separated from her husband, under merciless cross-examination by a gaoler instructed to trap her into admissions fatal to her interests and her good name, is not a pleasant one. In the sixteenth century such situations were taken for granted; and in the glittering Court of Queen Elizabeth no one, except perhaps her little hunchbacked sister, pitied Katherine. Certainly none came forward to speak for her.

Of the witnesses to her marriage one was dead, and the other, the clergyman, whose name neither Katherine nor Hertford knew, had disappeared; it was impossible to find him: perhaps Cecil did not try very hard. Nor could Mrs Leigh be traced. The only proof of Katherine's status as a wife was Hertford's deed of gift. When Katherine was arrested, on the charge of carnal copulation within the precincts of the palace, her first impulse had been to produce this document. She could not find it. Like Mrs Leigh and the parson, it had vanished. Her statement about this, the most crucial point in her defence, gives the impression that she did not realize its value to herself, and that her carelessness in such matters was habitual. (Nor did it occur to her that the deed might have been stolen.) 'The Earl of Hertford delivered to me such a deed,' she said, 'being written in a parchment, which I put into a coffer – and with removing from place to place, it is lost, and I cannot tell where it is become.'[1]

Having disposed of what she seems to have thought of as a triviality, Katherine poured out the story of her courtship and marriage in a flood of reminiscent detail. Between her sobs – she

cried during most of this and the subsequent cross-questionings[2] —
she recreated the relationship that had begun nearly eight years
earlier in the Duchess of Somerset's household, when, divorced and
deserted at thirteen, she had begun to love her dear lord, and to see
and feel in him her only hope of happiness. Everything was recalled;
the loving words: the quarrel about Sir Peter Mewtas's daughter:
her dead mother's sanction of the betrothal, and her promise to
speak to the Queen: the presents, the messages, the stolen hours of
rapture, the watchfulness and efficiency of Lady Jane, the final
decision, the wedding day, the entry of the parson in his gown and
bands — till she was faced with the second most important question.
'Of what like was the minister?' asked Sir Edward Warner.

Katherine's answering description came without hesitation — red
beard, medium height, and so on. 'He was a well-complexioned
man, in a long gown faced with budge [lambskin] the collar thereof
turned down — he wore no surplice.' Then she rushed on to the
climax of her story. The Earl her husband had given her a ring; it
was her wedding ring: she had worn it ever since; and she took it
from her finger, pressed the spring and revealed the 'five links of
gold'.[3]

Warner returned to the clergyman. 'What was his name?' 'I did
never hear it.' 'Would you know him if you saw him again?' Lady
Katherine hesitated; then she said that she thought so: she was not
sure.[4]

The Lieutenant reverted to Mrs Leigh. She, at least, knew of the
marriage, and perhaps the whereabouts of the deed of gift — where
was she? 'She departed from my service before the Queen left
Greenwich for Westminster, after my marriage,' Lady Katherine
replied, 'her mother's death being the excuse. And where she is now
become, I know not.'

Warner then asked her to recall the morning of the wedding.
Katherine told him how after it she and Lady Jane got back to
Whitehall in time for dinner. 'Thereafter I used the Earl of Hertford
as his wife in my own heart,' was all she would say; and with this
confused avowal the Lieutenant had to be contented. 'It was no small
grief and trouble to me when I saw his passport into France,'

Katherine continued. 'I saw it by chance.' She added that shortly after Hertford's departure she had known herself watched and her pregnancy suspected by the courtiers. So ended the unofficial examination.[5]

From the point of view of Cecil's plan to discredit the legality of the marriage, this preliminary interview could not have been more promising. It was decided, nevertheless, to proceed cautiously, and to take down no further statements until Hertford arrived. Then his evidence could be collated with that of Lady Katherine, whom, naturally, he would not be allowed to see. Cecil's comment shows his satisfaction, and the trend of the conclusion on which he had already made up his mind. 'Lady Katherine is in the Tower, and near the time of her delivery,' he wrote, 'yet no one appears privy to her marriage, nor to the love, but maids — or women going for maidens. The Queen thinks, and others with her, that some greater drift was in this, but I can find none such.'[6] In fact, Cecil's plan was to play down the supposed plot for the succession, and concentrate on pillorying Lady Katherine for immorality.

This scheme received immediate support from the Duchess of Somerset, who when she heard of her daughter-in-law's arrest wrote to Cecil disclaiming all responsibility for, or knowledge of, the marriage. She begged the Secretary not to believe what she described as Lady Katherine's 'tales' before Hertford had the chance to refute them, and added that if he could not do so, she herself must not be blamed, for she had often 'schooled and persuaded him' not to think of allying himself with Katherine. 'And to conserve my credit with Her Majesty, good Master Secretary, stand now my friend,' she concluded, 'that the wildness of mine unruly child do not minish Her Majesty's favour towards me.'[7]

When Hertford received orders through his Ambassador to return at once, he was advised by his French friends to disobey them. At that moment it would have been diplomatically inadvisable for the English government to extradite or kidnap him: he must be lured back into England. So the Ambassador told him that Her Majesty did not intend to punish him, but required his presence merely in order to 'decide by law' whether he and Lady Katherine had been properly married. Again Hertford hesitated, and said something about going on into Italy; he added that he had not been feeling very well. (He did not know that Katherine was in the Tower, and may have thought that he would best help her by remaining abroad until the sensation caused by the discovery of their marriage had died down.) When one of his Parisian acquaintances, the Vicomte de Gonz, said to him, 'You have married the Lady Katherine for your pleasure – now your Queen may marry the Lord Robert for hers,'[8] he acted on this optimistic view of the situation and departed, arriving at Dover on September 3rd, 1561. Here he was arrested by Mr Crisp, the Captain of the Castle, and locked up for the night. Next morning, while he and Crisp were at breakfast, Hertford caught sight of his body-servant, Goddard. 'What news?' he asked. Before Goddard could answer, Crisp sent him out of the room, and told Hertford he must speak to no one. Next day, escorted by Crisp and a strong guard, he arrived at the Tower.[9]

On September 12th the official examination by the Privy Council of the Hertfords, their servants, Mrs Saintlow and Lord Henry Seymour began. The examiners were Grindal, Bishop of London, Sir Edward Warner, the Marquis of Winchester (who in that very place had crowned Lady Jane Grey eight years before), Sir Edward Turner and Sir William Petre.[10]

Within a few hours of Hertford's first interview it became clear to Cecil that to prove the marriage invalid was going to be more difficult than had been hoped. Hertford's and Katherine's evidence agreed on every point except one, even to the lines he had composed for the wedding ring. The author knew these by heart and, not without complacency, recited them to his five judges, who solemnly incorporated his verse in their report to the Queen.[11]

After Hertford had described what happened when the priest and Lady Jane Seymour left him and Katherine alone together, he was dismissed, Katherine summoned again and asked why she had not told Sir Edward Warner everything. She then confirmed all that Hertford had said, even to the details of their getting up and dressing themselves without help. The Councillors repeated their question –

why had she not given all the information in her first interview? 'I had trouble of mind,' Katherine faltered, 'for fear of the Queen's Majesty's displeasure.' Again pressed, she sobbed out incoherently, 'My husband's absence — being great with child — ' and the broken phrases were written down.[12]

When the statements of the servants, Mrs Saintlow and Lord Henry Seymour confirmed those of the Hertfords, the witnesses were all released, and no further announcement was made about the lawfulness or otherwise of the marriage; for Cecil had decided to wait until Katherine was delivered, presumably in the hope that both she and her child would die, thus solving the whole problem. Katherine was in the Bell Tower and Hertford in the White Tower, and they were not, of course, allowed to meet. Hertford managed to bribe his gaolers to send messages and little presents to his wife.[13]

At half past two in the afternoon of September 24th their child, a healthy boy, was born. Katherine's labour was short, and she began to regain strength within a few days. Hertford recorded the news in the only book he had with him, a French Bible, in which he wrote his and Katherine's names, his family motto, *Foy pour Devoir* and, in Greek, a single comment, 'In human affairs nothing is certain.'[14] Cecil's report shows some discouragement; his resolve to find the marriage illegal was not abandoned. 'This day Lady Katherine gives birth to a son in the Tower. Lord Hertford and she agree upon the place, time and company [sexual intercourse] of their marriage, but cannot bring either minister or witness. They must either find out the minister, or determine what the law will say, whether it be a marriage or no. The matter lies ... in the Queen's mercy.'[15]

At the request of the Lieutenant of the Tower, Elizabeth's mercy extended to the loan of some furniture for a suite of rooms for Lady Katherine and her attendants from the Palace stores. This was so worn and old as to be almost unusable; what we should now call the soft furnishings dated from the middle years of Henry VIII, and were in such a state that Sir Edward Warner felt obliged to make a descriptive inventory, for his own protection. His comments on Her Majesty's 'parcels' make curious reading. He noted that the tapestries were 'very old and coarse', the damask bed-coverlet 'all to-broken and not worth tenpence', the quilt 'stark naught', the Turkey carpets rubbed, the single chair 'nothing worth', its cushion 'an old, cast thing', and the bed 'mean'. The footstools displeased him most, for he recognized them from the days when he had been in attendance at Court as those used 'for King Henry's feet'. On that faded and stained green velvet the old King had been wont to rest his suppurating leg.[16]

Sir Edward, a kindly and, for that age, rather a sentimental man, was so moved by compassion for his prisoner, and perhaps so shamed by the Queen's economies, that he allowed Lady Katherine's women to bring with them her monkeys and dogs. These undisciplined and incontinent animals may have cheered up their mistress; their depredations of the furniture were sustained and disastrous. When the Lieutenant of the Tower saw what was going on, he became very uneasy, for he knew that he might have to pay for the damage out of his own pocket; but he was too tender-hearted to deprive Katherine of her pets.[17]

As soon as the news of the Hertfords' marriage and the birth of their son became known, public opinion showed that the common people were on their side. Affectionate memories of Somerset — 'the good Duke' — inclined them to his son, that gallant gentleman, who had dared the Queen's anger in marrying the woman he loved; and the recollection of Lady Jane Grey's magnificent courage and her adherence to her faith in the hour of death, shed an aura of martyrdom over her sister. Regardless of the report that Lady Katherine might be the centre of a Spanish plot, 'with the connivance and countenance of some of the nobles',[18] it was asked 'why should man and wife be let from coming together?' A number of rumours began to circulate. Hertford and Katherine were to be attainted and beheaded: Cecil had been privy to their marriage: the Queen was going to pronounce their child a bastard by Act of Parliament: the Lady Katherine, as Her Majesty's nearest kinswoman, was to be acknowledged heiress-presumptive.

Elizabeth's patience may not quietly have endured this gossip; she told Cecil she was very anxious; but she continued her policy of tolerance by allowing the Hertford baby to be christened. The ceremony took place in the chapel of St Peter-ad-Vincula on Tower Green, where Hertford's son received the name and title of Edward Seymour, Viscount Beauchamp. He was enrolled as the soldier and servant of Christ over the headless bodies of seven relatives; Somerset, his paternal grandfather: Admiral Seymour of Sudeley, his paternal great-uncle: Lord Thomas Grey, his mother's uncle: the Duke of Suffolk, his maternal grandfather: his uncle by marriage, Lord Guilford Dudley: that uncle's father, the Duke of Northumberland: and his aunt, Lady Jane Grey.

NOTES TO CHAPTER SIX

[1] Harleian MSS, 6286.
[2] Fuller, *Worthies of England*, vol. II, p. 227.
[3] Harleian MSS, 6286.
[4] Ibid.
[5] Ibid.
[6] Cal. Foreign S.P., August 26th, 1561, No. 455.
[7] Strickland, *Tudor and Stuart Princesses*, p. 139.
[8] Cal. Foreign S.P., September 24th, 1561, No. 533.
[9] Harleian MSS, 6286.
[10] Ibid.
[11] Ibid.
[12] Ibid.
[13] Ibid.
[14] *Wiltshire Archaeological Magazine*, vol. XV, p. 154.
[15] Cal. Foreign S.P., September 24th, 1561, No. 534.
[16] Wright, vol. I, pp. 140-1.
[17] Ibid.
[18] Cal. English Affairs, vol. I, No. 59.

THE quantity of information, trivial and otherwise, contained in the Privy Council's report on the courtship and marriage of Katherine and Hertford provides no clue to the most interesting aspect of their relationship – the difference between his love and hers. On this point, guesswork further confuses the issue; it is safer to draw conclusions from the discrepancies in Hertford's attitude and also from Katherine's actions.

Her behaviour, however besotted, was, on the whole, that of a person in whom affection outweighs self-interest. She had much to lose and nothing to gain by marrying Hertford with or without the Queen's permission. To remain unmarried and in touch with Spain and Scotland would have enabled her to play off one set of diplomats against another, thus eventually forcing Elizabeth to arrange a marriage for her in which she would have found a home and a life of her own. If Elizabeth had died, as she very nearly did, the year after Katherine married, Katherine might have succeeded instead of the recently widowed Mary Stuart, who left France to govern Scotland in the summer of 1561. But Katherine's chances of succeeding would have been lessened by her being the wife of a man whose father had been executed for high treason; and she must have realized this when she joined her fortunes with Hertford's.

While Hertford does not emerge as completely disinterested or grandly heroic, he was faithful to Katherine during her lifetime; and when they were both in the Tower he risked such privileges as he still retained in order to keep in touch with her. The furious and spiteful censure of Sir John Mason, a correspondent of Cecil, who described Hertford's behaviour as 'presumptuous, contemptuous and outrageous', shows that this young man, however much he may have erred, was looked on as recklessly bold in regard to his marriage; that he stuck to Katherine during the eight years that preceded it indicates a devotion that must, in some respects, have been genuine. 'There is not,' Mason goes on, 'a more *oultreayd* [*outré?*] youth – I speak French for lack of apt English – neither one that better liketh himself, neither that promiseth himself greater things.'[1] Yet in marrying Katherine secretly, Hertford, who, although arrogant and self-willed, was certainly no fool, knew, as he afterwards admitted, that he had destroyed his credit with the Queen while greatly reducing his wife's chances of the succession in the event of Elizabeth's death without children. Setting aside his occasional lapses, he did not, in the long run, fail Katherine. He might have re-established himself in the Queen's favour by denying the legality of their marriage, or by applying for its annulment: he did neither. (The contemporary view was that he would have been right in adopting one of these courses.) And the fact that Katherine remained selflessly devoted to him during the years of their separation and imprisonment, although not exactly a proof of his moral worth, at least argues a deep reciprocity, if not an equality, of feeling. In fact, while Hertford and Katherine cannot be seen as a dramatically star-crossed couple, of the kind (if such exists) who rate love higher than death, dishonour or financial loss, they may be said to have shown steadfastness in the face of ruin and shared trust throughout all their misfortunes. Few husbands and wives can claim as much: none should expect more of one another. In contemplating the Hertfords, we should forget Romeo and Juliet, and remember Rachel and Laban.

In the deliberations of the Privy Council, the emotional aspect had of course no place; and their difficulties were enhanced by the sustained claims of the Scots Queen and the intrigues of her cousin, Margaret Countess of Lennox, the mother of Lord Darnley. This lady was the daughter of Henry VIII's elder sister Margaret Tudor Queen of Scotland, by her second husband, the Earl of Angus. Lady Lennox considered that she had a better claim to the English throne than Mary Stuart, or Katherine, or any of the Plantagenet descendants. She was now plotting against Elizabeth, with the result that plans were being made to arrest her and her husband as soon as the necessary evidence could be collected. The Council had to proceed with more than usual care, partly because they did not know which claimant Her Majesty disliked least. (It was conjectured then, as it is now believed, that she hated them all.) Nor could they disregard the fact that the infant Viscount Beauchamp had been added to the list of possible successors by those who preferred a Protestant Regency to the rule of a Catholic or a Protestant female.

Another, less innocent, conspirator against the régime was Arthur Pole, the great-great-nephew of Edward IV, who at about this time prepared to leave for France in order to raise an army for invading the realm in Mary Stuart's cause. He was captured, arraigned of high treason, and sentenced to death; the sentence was later commuted to imprisonment. The alarm caused by such poorly supported plotters as Pole and the Countess of Lennox soon died down (Lady Lennox was released after a year's captivity), but its effect was detrimental to the hopes of Katherine and Hertford, who were seen as more dangerous, potentially at least, and were more than ever in the public eye. At the same time, the story of their secret wedding and the baby born in the Tower struck the popular fancy. The Hertfords were young, in love, of high lineage, and persecuted; of such stuff heroes and heroines of romance have always been made.

In the face of the Hertfords' combined declarations that they had been legally married and that as soon as the mysterious clergyman was found they would be able to prove it, the Privy Council withheld their verdict for four months, hoping that the Queen would come to a decision. In a conversation with the Scottish Ambassador Elizabeth assumed an indifference she did not feel. She told him that the Lady Katherine's rights had been invalidated by her father's attainder and execution, and that, although she had received secret support from some of the nobles, the majority favoured Mary Stuart's claim.[2] Meanwhile the rumour spread that there were witnesses to the marriage who were being kept out of the way in order to blacken the Hertfords and bastardize their child. 'This affair', wrote Bishop Jewel to a foreign correspondent, 'hath much disturbed the minds of many persons; for if this marriage be a legal one, the son now born will be brought up with the hope of succeeding to the crown.'[3]

In the first week of February 1562 the findings of the Privy Council were placed before Parker, Archbishop of Canterbury, who was instructed by the Queen to re-examine the prisoners at Lambeth and 'judge of their infamous conversation [sexual intercourse] and *pretended* marriage'. Her Majesty added to this strong hint her command that the Hertfords were to be conducted to Lambeth under guard and not allowed to speak to anyone, or to one another.[4] Once more, every detail of their relationship was recapitulated, some additions being provided by themselves. Hertford admitted and Katherine confirmed that he had sent 'to know how she did' as soon as he realized that she was in the Tower, and that his gaolers had brought her rhymed messages and presents of money. 'What was the content of the posies?' Parker asked. Lady Katherine could not repeat them, and this line of inquiry was dropped. Hertford further weakened his case by confessing that he had not made a will in Katherine's favour, only the deed of gift; Katherine's other maid, Mrs Coffin, examined on this point, declared that she had never seen it.[5]

On May 12th, 1562, the Archbishop's commission pronounced sentence. In the absence of witnesses and documents the marriage could not be proved, and was therefore declared to be illegal. Parker added that the Earl of Hertford's 'carnal copulation' with the Lady Katherine was 'unlawful and illegitimate' and censured them both for fornication.[6] The commission recommended a heavy fine and imprisonment for life. The Queen herself informed Sir Edward Warner of their decision, and he broke the news to his prisoners.

Public sympathy with the young couple intensified; it was said that they had been 'sharply handled',[7] and the general view seems to have been that their inability to produce proofs of the marriage was rather a misfortune than a sign of guilt. Why should they not be believed? And even if they had committed fornication, why should they be indefinitely imprisoned? To those who could only guess at the hidden difficulties of the situation, the government's procedure appeared monstrously unfair; for it was assumed that the Queen would soon marry and have a child, thus setting aside all danger from presumptive heirs.

This seems to have been Sir Edward Warner's point of view. His pity for the Hertfords had been shown before the Archbishop's pronouncement in a number of little ways; now that they were found not to have been married at all, he felt himself free to exercise his benevolence in a more practical manner. His line of reasoning, as afterwards reported by himself, was that since the Hertfords were not husband and wife, but lovers who had already produced one bastard, then their behaviour was no longer dangerous to the state, or even important; as long as they did not escape, it did not really matter what they did; and there was no reason why they should not console one another.

So it was that a few days after the Archbishop's decision Hertford became aware that if he were discreet, he and Katherine would be able to meet and every now and then to spend the night together, as long as they did so without drawing attention to themselves and took care to fee their gaolers; and thus, for the first time since their wedding day, they achieved the nearest approach to a regular married life that they were ever to enjoy. During the summer of 1562 they were forgotten, undisturbed, not uncomfortable in their respective suites of rooms, and from time to time reunited, while the health of their son gave them no anxiety. The sudden calm and relief that was a new experience for both is shown in a letter of Katherine's, no doubt one of many; for when they could not meet, they corresponded.

She begins by describing her joy that her dear lord is well, and her thankfulness to God that 'in this most lamentable time' they are able to communicate. 'Though of late I have not been well,' she goes on, 'yet now, I thank God, pretty well, and long to be merry with you, as you do to be with me.' Then comes a passage that shows the uncertainties of their arrangements. 'I say no more, but be you merry, as I was heavy when you, the third time, came to the door, and it was locked. Do you think I forget old forepast matters? No, surely I cannot, but bear in memory far more than you think for. I have good cause so to do when I call to mind what a husband I have of you, and my great hard fate to miss the having of so good a one.' She then acknowledges the receipt of some money, and a book — 'which is no small jewel to me. I can very well read it, for as soon as I had it, I read it over with my heart, as well as with my eyes.' Having signed herself as the most loving and faithful wife of her 'good Ned', Katherine adds an intimate and allusive postscript, in which her locked door becomes at once a symbol and a private joke. The 'poet' who sent her the book is to be given a message by Hertford; he must not be jealous of this *alter ego*, for 'he [the poet] should have come to me — but when he wished, he groaned.' There follows a sentence that has been obliterated, perhaps by a later and more prudish hand. 'Well,' Katherine concludes, 'yet though he would not come to me, I would have been glad to have seen him; but belike he [will] make no more account of me as his mistress, which I cannot but take unkindly at his hands.'[8]

The activities indicated in this letter resulted in another pregnancy; by July 1562, at latest, Katherine and Hertford must have realized that they had again, and more seriously, offended, and prepared to accept their punishment. It was to be heavier than anything they had anticipated; from Katherine's point of view, death would have been preferable.

The dynastic situation was further complicated, in October of this year, by the Queen's succumbing to smallpox. She became very ill indeed, and for several days was not expected to live. In this appalling crisis, while Elizabeth herself was in no state to name a successor, the Privy Council was divided between the two principal Protestant claimants, Lord Huntingdon and Lady Katherine.[9] The Archbishop's verdict had placed the Councillors in a very difficult position. If Katherine's marriage was unlawful, then she was not fit to succeed; if the Queen died, and she and Hertford proved its legality, what would his position be? No one wanted him as king, and the question of a prince consort had never been visualized. These problems were resolved, if only for a time, by Elizabeth's rapid recovery; the result of her illness was a frenzied onslaught by Parliament and Council urging her to marry at once, and to name her successor; she dealt with both requests in her usual elusive manner. Robert Dudley, now Earl of Leicester, was no longer in favour of Katherine's claim, and at his suggestion Lady Lennox was set free in order to lower Katherine's chances by providing a competitor.[10]

These wranglings and intrigues continued till February 7th, 1563, when at a Council meeting the majority of the ministers, still unaware of Katherine's pregnancy, declared in her favour. The reason for this was the renewed alarm of Leicester's marrying the Queen. (Huntingdon was now backing this marriage as the price of being elected successor.) The minority voted for Mary Stuart, who had indicated her willingness to marry Don Carlos and so re-establish the Catholic régime.[11]

Three days later news came that Katherine had given birth to another son. The Queen's wrath resulted in Sir Edward Warner's being imprisoned — in one of his own dungeons — and deprived of his place. Hertford was ordered to appear before the Court of the Star Chamber on the triple charge that he had, two years before, 'deflowered a virgin of the blood royal in the Queen's house: that he had broken prison [in visiting Katherine] and that he had ravished her a second time.' Hertford boldly replied, 'I have lawfully con-tracted marriage with the Lady Katherine. I deny not but that I have passed through the doors of the prison standing open, to comfort her who mourned for the sentence pronounced, and have paid my marriage debt.'[12] He was sentenced to a fine of £15,000 (it was afterwards reduced to £3,000) and to be imprisoned during Her Majesty's pleasure.[13] After this, there was of course no question of Katherine and Hertford being able to meet again. In his prayer-book Hertford noted the birth and baptism of the infant Thomas Seymour, and added, in French, a few lines of gratitude for his wife's safe delivery. He subjoined some references to Queen Elizabeth's '*mau-vaise grâce*', God's displeasure, and his and Katherine's '*longs maux, et estant encore battus de plusieurs de Tes verges*' with the hope that he might profit by these punishments in the end.[14]

The indignation of the people was renewed by the Hertfords' sufferings, and the Council was warned that the City fathers might

protest, or even organize a rising on their behalf.[15] Cecil's comment
on this further complication was one of resigned despair. 'The
matter is so deep I cannot reach it', he wrote. 'God send it a good
issue.'[16]

Cecil's prayer was answered before Hertford's. From February to
August 1563, he and Katherine were under the same roof, and
might have caught a glimpse of each other from time to time. Then
an outbreak of the plague made it necessary to remove them from
the Tower, and they were placed in charge of different custodians.
Hertford's farewell present to Katherine was a mourning ring
engraved with a death's head, and the words 'While I live, Yours.'[17]
They never saw each other again.

NOTES TO CHAPTER SEVEN

[1] Wright, vol. I, p. 129.
[2] Read, *Mr Secretary Cecil and Queen Elizabeth*, p. 230.
[3] Zurich Letters, vol. I, p. 126.
[4] Strype, *Life of Archbishop Parker*, vol. I, p. 214.
[5] Harleian MSS, 6286.
[6] Strype, *Parker*, vol. I, p. 235.
[7] Camden, *Queen Elizabeth*, p. 84.
[8] H.M.C.: Northumberland MSS, vol. III, p. 147.
[9] Cal. English Affairs, vol. I, No. 191.
[10] Ibid., No. 198.
[11] Ibid.
[12] Camden, *Queen Elizabeth*, p. 85.
[13] Wright, vol. I, p. 130.
[14] *Wiltshire Archaeological Magazine*, vol. XV, p. 154.
[15] Cal. English Affairs, vol. I, No. 221.
[16] Read, p. 267.
[17] Ellis, *Original Letters*, Series 2, vol. II, pp. 272-87.

THOSE Catholics who supported Mary Queen of Scots and the French interest were in theory Katherine's enemies. They did her no harm, and if they had prevailed, might have relegated her to a peaceful obscurity, had she so desired it. Her friends and supporters — Lady Jane Seymour, the Spanish Ambassadors and Sir Edward Warner — descending upon her in turn, put an end to any chance of happiness she may have had before they abandoned or were removed from, her interests. Between February 1563 and April 1564 two still more dangerous allies took up her cause; both were of the middle class, and both were prepared to risk the consequences of the Queen's displeasure in Katherine's name. Neither of them troubled to consult Katherine herself; they had no personal feeling for her, nor any concern for what would happen to her if their schemes failed. One of these was Francis Newdigate, the Duchess of Somerset's second husband; the other, 'Club-foot' John Hales, was Clerk of the Hanaper to Queen Elizabeth. Newdigate was pushing and ambitious; Hales was fanatical, conceited and aggressive. If their energies had not combined in an attempt to prove the legality of Katherine's marriage, as well as her right to the succession, she might, in course of time, have been allowed to rejoin Hertford, if only to live with him in retirement and disgrace; for Elizabeth was generally ready to show kindness and tolerance to her relatives, even when she disliked them. Hales and Newdigate made that impossible, from the moment that they began to occupy themselves with Katherine's future.

While removing Katherine and Hertford from the Tower the

Queen made it clear that they were still prisoners. Cecil's directions indicate that his mistress had not forgotten Katherine's arrogance, nor her folly. Her change of residence would in fact ensure a stricter supervision, for she, her servants and her younger son were placed in charge of Lord John Grey, the uncle who had always disliked her, in his country house at Pirgo in Essex. Hertford and the elder boy were sent to live with the Duchess of Somerset at Hanworth. In his letter to Lord John, Cecil emphasized that his niece was to be treated 'as in custody, not to depart from you till Her Majesty's pleasure be further known, neither to have any conference with any person not of your household ... which Her Majesty meaneth she should understand ... as part of her punishment.' A faint hope for the future is hinted at in the concluding sentence. 'And therein Her Majesty meaneth to try her disposition, how she will obey ... till she may obtain more favour of Her Majesty.'[1]

Newdigate was empowered to escort Lady Katherine to Pirgo. For nearly five months after her arrival and installation Queen and Council were able to dismiss her from their minds. Then Sir Edward Warner, who had been released and had now retired to his property in Norfolk, sent the Secretary a piteous appeal ('from my poor house') about his expenses over Lady Katherine's imprisonment. Having supplemented Her Majesty's loan of furniture and hangings with some of his own, he felt it most unfair that the ruin effected by Lady Katherine's 'monks' — who had behaved worse than the dogs — should not be made good. His 'stuff', he explained, was 'almost all marred ... and so torn and tattered it will serve to small purpose'. He subjoined his list, with 'some notes in the margent, truly written',[2] to which no answer survives; perhaps he never got one: for by this time Cecil was in unwilling correspondence with Lord John Grey, who begged for release from his responsibilities. Lord John began by writing in Katherine's favour, in the hope of getting rid of her. Having reminded Cecil of their relationship through Lady John Grey, who was his cousin, Lord John described his charge's 'miserable and comfortless estate'. It was now Lent; and he felt that 'this time of all others may be accounted a time of mercy and forgiveness

... In faith, I would I were the Queen's confessor,' he went on, 'that I might enjoin her in penance to forgive and forget, or otherwise able to step into the pulpit to tell Her Highness that God will not forgive her unless she freely forgive all the world.'[3] To this flight of fancy Lord John received no reply. Nor did his next letter, in which he dwelt on Katherine's 'penitent and sorrowful condition'. When he heard that the Queen had complained of the cost of the new arrangements for her, he sent Cecil an account of his niece's weekly expenditure. It amounted to £4. 12s. 8d. a week, and consisted of the following items:

Lady Katherine herself	16s. 8d.
Child	18s. 4d.
Nurse	6s. 8d.
Mrs Isham	6s. 8d.
Mrs Woodford	6s. 8d.
Mrs Page	6s. 8d.
Nowell	5s.
Robert	5s.
William Hampton	6s.
Lackey	5s.
Launder	5s.
Widow that washeth the child's clothes ...	5s.[4]

The modern equivalent of this budget is difficult to assess; compared with that of other state prisoners — Mary Stuart's, for instance — it is extremely moderate, not to say parsimonious, judged by sixteenth-century standards of catering for royalty.

This aspect of Lady Katherine's treatment was not used by Hales and Newdigate in the attack on the government which they were now preparing. Hales began by interviewing Lord John Grey as to Lady Katherine's antecedents. Was her Tudor grandmother's marriage to Charles Brandon Duke of Suffolk valid? Was her mother legitimate? Lord John laughed and said, 'That is a thing very strange to be asked,' adding that the late Duchess's legitimacy had been proved in the reign of Edward VI.[5] Hales then took expert legal advice as to the validity of the Hertfords' marriage from both

English and continental sources, and having obtained confirmation
on this point, settled down to writing his pamphlet, *Declaration of
the Succession*, with the approval of Hertford and his mother, who
were primarily interested in proving the legitimacy of Hertford's
sons.[6]

Meanwhile Lord John Grey, unaware that he was going to be
involved in what came to be known as the *tempestas Halisiana*,[7]
continued to bombard Cecil on his own and Lady Katherine's
behalf. After seven months of misery Katherine wrote to the
Secretary in the hope that he would pass on her letter to the Queen,
as showing a development of the better disposition which might
result in her being allowed to rejoin her husband and her elder son.
Having expressed her gratitude for her release from the Tower, she
begged Cecil to intercede for her with Elizabeth, 'for the obtaining
of the Queen's Majesty's most gracious pardon and favour towards
me, which with upstretched hands and down bent knees from the
bottom of my heart most humbly I crave.'

When no answer was vouchsafed Lord John wrote again, to
Cecil, and to Leicester. He was beginning to worry about his niece's
health. She wept continually, and could eat almost nothing — what
if she were to become very ill, or to die? Would he be held responsible? He pointed out that if Katherine were not given some hope,
'thought and care' would 'pine her away'. 'She will not long live
thus', he declared. 'Before God I speak it ... She eateth not above
six morsels in the meal.' He then described a scene that was often
repeated. Seeing Katherine unable to touch anything, he said, 'Good
madam, eat somewhat to comfort yourself.' The utter lack of com-
prehension in the words broke down Katherine's control. She burst
into tears, left the dining-chamber and went up to her own room.
Lord John followed her and asked her why she wept. She could not
answer at once. Then she said, 'Alas! uncle, what a life is this to me,
to live in the Queen's displeasure! But for my lord and my children,
I would to God I were dead and buried.' Pity was beginning to
make headway against Lord John's dislike of his niece; genuinely
moved, he reiterated his plea to his 'good cousin Cecil' to ease
Katherine 'of this woeful grief and sorrow [and] rid me of this life,

which I assure you, grieveth me, even at the heart roots'. Neither he nor his niece received any reply to these appeals, and after a fortnight both wrote again, Katherine this time to the Queen herself. 'I dare not presume,' she began, 'most gracious sovereign, to crave pardon for my disobedient and most rash matching of myself without Your Highness's consent ... I acknowledge myself a most unworthy creature to fail so much of your gracious favour as I have done. My just felt misery and continual grief doth teach me daily, more and more, the greatness of my fault, and your princely pity increaseth my sorrow, that I have so forgotten my duty to Your Majesty. This is my great torment of mind. May it therefore please Your excellent Majesty to license me to be a most lowly suitor unto Your Highness ... which upon my knees in all humble wise I crave ... '⁸ Abasement could not go further; nor tact, in the writer's care not to mention the real cause of her grief. But there was no result, save for Cecil's methodical filing of these cries for mercy.

A month later Lord John reported that Lady Katherine was seriously ill; he thought that her sickness came from exhaustion caused by continual weeping. She had been in bed some four days, and looked ghastly. Would not Cecil send one of the Queen's physicians to visit her? Her chest, he was sure, was affected; for when her maids came to call her in the morning, they found her 'so fraughted with phlegm' that she was speechless and unable to move. He feared that she was consumptive and likely to die. 'If she had not painful [conscientious] women about her,' he concluded, 'I tell you, Cousin Cecil, I could not live in quiet.'⁹

It must have been at about this time that the last portrait of Katherine was painted, that in which her likeness to Queen Elizabeth is so pronounced. It is a study of sorrow, of beauty worn and ravaged by confinement and mourning. The face is that of a thoughtful, highly sensitive woman, neither foolish nor arrogant, but proudly withdrawn into the hollow-eyed, sleepless endurance of grief. From the depths of her despair, Katherine wrote again to Leicester, and then to Cecil, describing the effect of the Queen's disfavour — she did not question its justice — on 'this my miserable and wretched body ... to the torment and wasting thereof ...

which, if it do any long time thus continue, I rather wish of God shortly to be buried in the faith and fear of Him, than in this continual agony to live.'[10]

Such letters as these might, eventually, have had their effect on Elizabeth, if not on her advisers. It was not to be. In the spring of 1564 Hales's book came out, and caused an uproar in the House of Commons. Once more, Lady Katherine was in the limelight, whether as a martyr, or as a nuisance, or as a plotter, mattered little, least of all to Hales and Newdigate. Attention was refracted on them, and on their propaganda for the Protestant succession. They rightly guessed that anti-Catholic feeling in the country would prevent the Queen from punishing them with mutilation, or even with crippling fines.

When summoned before the Privy Council, Hales, Newdigate and Lord John Grey went through the usual process of contradicting one another and asseverating their loyalty to the Queen. Hales swore, 'by Christ's Passion', that he had never dreamed of substituting Lady Katherine for Her Majesty, for whom he desired a long and happy reign; his aim was to prevent the succession of Mary Queen of Scots. His declaration that the English people were 'bound, both by our laws, and also by our oaths to take [Lady Katherine]', presupposed Queen Elizabeth dying without children; he added that 'there is great cause of thanks that [the succession] lighteth upon such a poor woman, which hath no friend liable to do ... hurt to the Queen's Majesty.'[11] Hales then tried, rather belatedly, to exonerate Lord John (whom he described to the Queen as 'the faithfullest man in England') and Hertford, as being free from all suspicion of employing him to plead his cause; but he stuck to his opinion about the marriage being legal; according to the experts he had consulted, to pronounce it otherwise was 'unjust, unreasonable and null', and he thought Hertford should be released.[12]

Meanwhile, Hertford's lawyers, acting independently, were preparing to appeal against the verdict on his marriage, also using the opinion of continental experts. Cecil dismissed their campaign as a 'troublesome, fond matter', and sent Hales to the Fleet for six months. His difficulties were increased by the Queen's suspicions;

she and Leicester accused him of writing Hales's book himself, in order to force her to marry.[13] By the summer of 1564 the sensation caused by the case was beginning to die down; but the Queen's rage against the whole Hertford faction still simmered. There could now be no question of Lady Katherine's being allowed to join her husband, with the result that the Franco-Scottish Catholic party began to hope that Mary Stuart would be proclaimed heiress-presumptive. When Cecil suggested to Elizabeth that she should 'remit her displeasure' to Hertford and Katherine in order to puzzle and curb Mary, she refused to consider such a notion, although she remembered to use it a few months later. She was further embittered against Katherine by Parliament's partial support of her claim.[14] Yet her sense of justice prevented her punishing Hertford for continuing to try and prove his sons' legitimacy, perhaps because, however deeply their parents had offended her, the children were, after all, her cousins. The three-year-old Viscount Beauchamp and the baby Lord Thomas Seymour were one-eighth Tudor. On these grounds Elizabeth was prepared to treat them fairly, although their mother's chance of being forgiven had become more than ever remote.

In the autumn of 1564 Lord John Grey died, and Katherine and her younger son were removed to the care of Sir William Petre at Ingatestone in Essex. Here the prisoner sank into the silence of despair. She made no attempt to communicate with her husband or with the Queen. Her health improved, in spite of the fact that she was weary of life – or so she afterwards declared.[15]

Yet even now, once the agitation caused by Hales's book had ceased, Elizabeth, so strangely, capriciously tolerant, might have relented. In the spring of 1565 it was believed that she was going to take Katherine's side against Mary Stuart, whose marriage with Lord Darnley had so displeased her. The newly appointed Spanish envoy, de Silva, told his master that Her Majesty had promised to lend him her copy of Hales's book; he eventually borrowed Leicester's: but as he could not read it, he decided to ask the Scottish Ambassador to translate the key passages for him. King Philip, who was now backing Mary Stuart, wrote to de Silva that Queen

Elizabeth must at all costs be prevented from supporting Katherine's claim in the coming Parliament; even Huntingdon would be more acceptable than the 'other heretics'.[16] Then, in August of that year, Katherine's hopes of better treatment were irreparably destroyed by the sudden, dramatic and slightly absurd appearance of her sister Mary on the political scene.

Mary Grey was just nineteen. No marriage had been arranged for her, partly because she was almost penniless, and partly because none of her few remaining relatives was sufficiently interested to approach the Queen or the Privy Council on this dangerous and controversial matter. After Katherine's disgrace and imprisonment she retained her position at Court — an example of Elizabeth's fairness of mind — and, although she was probably cold-shouldered, suffered in no other way from the cloud that had fallen on her family. Mary had her full share of Grey independence and determination. She was neither humble nor retiring (nor particularly grateful to the Queen), and her spirit had been in no way crushed by her sisters' misfortunes; indeed, her deformity may have engendered what would now be recognized as a compensatory boldness of action that, combined with an instinct to follow and imitate both Katherine and Jane, resulted in her reproducing, with variations, their pattern of behaviour. Her tastes, like Jane's, were intellectual, with a strong turn for Calvinistic and Zwinglian theology. Like Katherine, she was affectionate and domestic, and, in spite of an upbringing that had alternated between strictness and neglect, had no notion of sacrificing inclination to expediency.

In the spring of 1564 a romance began between the dwarf princess and the tallest man in the Court — Thomas Keyes, Queen Elizabeth's Sergeant-porter, a middle-aged widower with several children. Keyes and Mary Grey were connections, for he was a distant cousin of the Queen through the Knollys, her mother's relations; otherwise he had nothing to recommend him as a husband but height, good looks and pleasant manners. He seems to have been rather a simple man: he was certainly a foolish one. For a year he and Mary concealed their attachment; in the summer of 1565 they decided to marry in secret and without permission, taking care, however, to provide enough witnesses to prove the marriage lawful; yet, as in Katherine's and Hertford's case, the priest's name and identity were never disclosed, because he disappeared immediately after the ceremony. The number of persons present and, presumably, the fear of being accused of collaboration in a conspiracy if Mary became pregnant, resulted in disclosure less than a month after the wedding. Keyes was imprisoned in the Fleet and Mary sent away from Court and put in the custody of a married couple in Buckinghamshire. The Star Chamber then declared their marriage a 'pretended wedlock', upon which Keyes offered to have it annulled in return for his liberty, a suggestion which was ignored. He remained in prison till his death in 1571.[17]

The rage of Queen Elizabeth may be imagined and understood. She expressed herself with some violence on the Greys in general and on Lady Mary in particular, to the Spanish Ambassador.[18] Her anger was further inflamed by a letter from the Duchess of Somerset, who was beginning to feel that her idolized boy had been punished enough, and was being too harshly treated. Through Cecil and Leicester, the doting mother blandly suggested that it was 'unmeet that this young couple should thus wax old in prison ... ' (Hertford was not in prison, but living under house arrest with Sir John Mason in London). 'Far better it were for them to be abroad and learn to serve ... ' Surely Her Majesty would relent? It was now Holy Week, a suitable time for a gracious gesture.[19] A little later Mary Stuart wrote asking Elizabeth to show kindness to Hertford and Katherine, a speech was made in Parliament on Katherine's undoubted right to the succession, and Sir William Petre declared that he could no longer afford to keep her. She was therefore moved to the custody of Sir John Wentworth at Halstead, and a year later both she and Mary were allowed to receive profits from Grey properties in Warwickshire.

NOTES TO CHAPTER EIGHT

[1] Haynes, p. 405.
[2] Wright, vol. I, pp. 140–1.
[3] Ellis, pp. 272–87.
[4] Ibid.

[5] Haynes, p. 416.
[6] Strype, *Life of Sir Thomas Smith*, pp. 92-3.
[7] Ibid.
[8] Ellis; Ibid.
[9] Ibid.
[10] Ibid.
[11] Haynes, p. 412.
[12] Camden, *Queen Elizabeth*, p. 84.
[13] Read, p. 277.
[14] Ibid., p. 279.
[15] Ellis; Ibid.
[16] Cal. English Affairs, vol. I, Nos. 296-7 and 300.
[17] Strickland, *Tudor and Stuart Princesses*, pp. 165-6.
[18] Cal. English Affairs, vol. I, No. 315.
[19] Ellis; Ibid.

CHAPTER NINE

IT is hard to understand the train of thought of those historians who have censured Queen Elizabeth for her harshness to Katherine and Mary Grey. In regard to them, her position might be compared to that of Gulliver, when the Lilliputians bound him with threads and pricked him with pin-points – except that Elizabeth was no wanderer in a strange land, but a great leader engaged in a stupendous and life-long struggle to keep England free and set her among the strong nations of the civilized world. To be dedicated to such a task and at the same time to endure the endless irritants caused by the mere existence, let alone the behaviour, of these two young women, was enough to bring out those traits in Elizabeth's character that her idolators do not care to recall: cruelty, petty malice, indifference to suffering. If the Queen had ever condescended to explain her point of view about her Grey cousins (and it is almost impossible to imagine her doing so), her defence would have been that she could not afford, and therefore did not entertain, any personal feelings on the matter. As long as they lived and had a following, however small, they were a source of peril, not only to her sovereignty, but to the peace of the nation. And when they broke, not the law, but the accepted, although unwritten, rules for the marriages of princesses, they and their husbands had to pay the penalty. The punishment and unhappiness of four persons weighed as nothing against the risk of a dynastic split that might have brought with it chaos and misery for thousands of people. The threat of civil war and invasion by Spain, Scotland or France hung over Elizabeth and her ministers during the whole of their working day, and beyond it. And within those thunder-clouds stood, among others, the small, helpless figures of Katherine and Mary Grey, victims of their Tudor blood and of their own simple-minded folly.

The most curious aspect of the situation is the attitude of the transgressors themselves. Quite apart from the pain they endured – and of which Katherine, in fact, died – through separation from those they loved, their sufferings were immeasurably enhanced by their awareness of the Queen's displeasure. Such, then, was the semi-divinity of the monarch, that to be disgraced as Katherine and Mary were disgraced, engendered a sense of personal degradation and deep despair. They could never forget or escape the anger of Elizabeth. They might dislike and resent her as an individual; they prostrated themselves before her as their ruler and mistress, and were utterly dependent, in some way that is now indefinable, because it was not material, on the magic of her favour. Their cries of anguish and remorse sprang, not only from expediency, sycophancy or terror, but from a genuine and awestruck sense of loss that had nothing to do with practical considerations, and that remained with them to the last hour of their lives.

Thus the burden of Elizabeth's wrath stimulated Katherine's capacity for suffering and further darkened her existence; for her temperament was of the kind that feeds on the extremity of grief or joy, and can never be bludgeoned into indifference. Rumours of what she was going through, of her health breaking down, of the longing for her husband and elder son that nothing, not even the care of her younger boy, could diminish, reached the outside world, and became a legend. The beauty that seems to have been refined and enhanced by illness and sorrow was celebrated, long after her death, in Fuller's elegiac description of this Elizabethan Niobe, 'this Heraclita, this lady of lamentation ... seldom seen with dry eyes ... so that though the roses in her cheeks looked very wan and pale, it was not for want of watering.'[1] The determination, the wild desire that had driven Katherine from the security of Court life to Hertford's arms, and so to the Tower, now plunged her into an abyss; she could neither adapt herself to her deprivations, nor accept them philosophically. She longed for death; yet for four years she fought the tuberculosis that was caused by her misery, and for which no remedies then existed. She was in fact the protagonist of those innumerable heroines wasting in a decline (so valuable to eighteenth- and nineteenth-century novelists), whom experts now accept as potentially genuine cases. Katherine's greatest disability was that she could not resign herself to the results of her own errors.

From 1563 till 1567 she may still have had some dim hopes of release: they could only have rested on the possibility of Elizabeth dying before her. In 1565 Hertford was imploring Leicester to 'gain unto us our Prince's over-long wanted favour',² with no result. De Silva reported 'the heretics furiously in favour' of Katherine's claim to the succession, and the Duke of Norfolk so far supported them as to propose a contract of marriage between his infant daughter and the little Viscount Beauchamp. So by the autumn of 1566 the Queen's anger against the Greys had been revived and hardened. It was expressed in a definite and apparently sincere statement to the Spanish Ambassador. When he spoke of Parliament's voting for Katherine's nomination, Elizabeth said that she was afraid they might choose her, if only for her Protestantism. She added that she would never allow this, but that her policy was to encourage a free debate, so as to know the members' wishes, and to discover how many opposed Katherine's claim with those of Huntingdon, Lady Margaret Lennox and Mary Stuart.³

It is unlikely that any word of these discussions reached Katherine, for in September 1567 Sir John Wentworth died, and she was removed to the care of Sir Owen Hopton at Cockfield Hall in Yoxford. The bleak remoteness of this Suffolk parish, with its single manor-house, cluster of cottages and half ruined church, produced complete isolation. She was allowed no letters, and was told nothing of what was going on in London or anywhere else. There were amenities, even luxuries, at the Hall; there may have been distractions: Katherine rejected them all, finding no comfort in needlework, music or reading, and very little in the company of the baby Thomas Seymour (what would become of him when she died?) as her physical resistance began at last to give way. By the end of 1567 she was in the final stages of consumption.

The care for Katherine's health that had resulted in her being permanently separated from her husband and child during the plague epidemic, now prolonged her miserable existence. One of the Queen's physicians, Dr Symonds, visited her at regular intervals, and another was with her when she died.⁴ That she should see Hertford, if only for an hour and for the last time, was not in question; nor did Katherine herself expect or ask for the one favour that would have brought her a little comfort, and soothed her anxiety about her children's future: for she had never been allowed even a censored correspondence with her husband about this or any other matter.

On January 8th, 1568, she was put to bed, and did not get up again. During the last three weeks she prepared for the end as for a public ceremony. She may even have chosen and given instructions to the anonymous witness who described it, and whose account exemplifies, with what may seem an insensitive and unctuous parade, the contemporary attitude towards death-bed scenes.

It is now rather difficult to accept, let alone sympathize with, the assumption that the dying were expected to pay their debt to nature as deliberately and as eloquently as their condition allowed. In the sixteenth century those last hours provided a unique opportunity for the rhetoric, the fluent piety and the prolonged moralizing that we associate with literature, or with the operatic stage. Persons of breeding and eminence died as if they were actors in a tragedy written for and played to a select audience; if they were unable to perform, they were doubly pitied; the longer they continued to gasp out farewells, reflections, messages and aphorisms, the more lovingly and admiringly they were remembered. Such customs, endemic, ingrained, may have relieved the distress of the bereaved, and deadened the fear and pain of the principal characters; indeed, one might perhaps look on them as the precursors of, and the substitutes for, the anaesthetics and anodynes now in common use. However regarded, their re-creation brings with it an impression of artificiality, of consciousness, and of a peculiarly glib self-assurance that results in bewilderment, if not in distaste.

As a princess of the blood and a person of international importance, it became Katherine Grey to show that she could die correctly and in the highest traditions of spiritual well-being. She was not tempted to instil remorse and guilt into the hearts of those who had misled or punished her. Such pettiness was not in her character, apart from the fact that it would have struck a jarring note in the smooth and mellifluous orchestration of her last public appearance in the world of the living.

Katherine inaugurated what was later described as 'the manner of her departing' on the night before her death.[5] 'She continued in prayer,' the record opens, 'saying of psalms, hearing them read of others, sometimes saying them after others, and as soon as one psalm was done, she would call for another to be said; divers times she would rehearse the prayers appointed for the visitation of the sick, and five or six times ... she said the prayers appointed to be said at the hours of death ... '

Katherine's attendants were Mrs Isham, Mrs Woodford, Mrs Page and Mrs Coffin, who had watched during the night and were joined by the doctor and her three menservants. Some knelt at the foot of the bed, of which the curtains had been drawn; two of the women stood at the side. It was now five o'clock. The energy that had enabled her to spend many hours in prayer deceived them, and they began to think that she was perhaps going through one of those bouts of illness from which she had so often rallied. One of them came up to the bed and said, 'Madam, be of good comfort – with God's help, you shall live and do well many years.' 'No, no,' Katherine replied calmly. 'No life in this world. But in the world to come I hope to live ever – for here is nothing but care and misery, and there, is life everlasting.'

A little later she gasped out, 'Lord, be merciful unto me, for now I begin to faint.' As she was very cold, the women began to massage her hands and feet. 'Father of Heaven,' she went on, 'for Thy Son Christ's sake, have mercy upon me!'

Lady Hopton then came in; after interchanging a word or two with the women, she bent over Katherine and said, 'Madam, be of good comfort, for with God His favour you shall live and escape this. For Mrs Coffin saith you have escaped many dangers, when you were as like to die as you be now.' Katherine replied, 'No, no, my lady, my time is come – and it is not God's will that I should live any longer – and His will be done, and not mine.' Looking round at the ring of faces, she added, 'As I am, so shall you be. Behold the picture of yourselves.' For a short time she said nothing more.

Daylight was now creeping into the room. Between six and seven o'clock Katherine asked for Sir Owen Hopton, who had been waiting for the summons. 'Good Madam, how do you?' he asked. 'Even now going to God, Sir Owen,' Katherine answered, 'even as fast as I can.' After giving herself time to collect her strength, she went on, 'And I pray you and the rest that be about me to bear witness with me that I die a true Christian, and that I believe to be saved by the death of Christ, and that I am one that He hath shed His most precious blood for. And I ask God and all the world forgiveness – and I forgive all the world.' They waited for her to continue; presently she was able to do so. 'I beseech you,' she said to Hopton, 'promise me one thing, that you yourself with your own mouth will make this request to the Queen's Majesty, which shall be the last suit and request that ever I shall make unto Her Highness – even from the mouth of a dead woman – that she would forgive her displeasure towards me, as my hope is she has done.' She added, 'I must needs confess I have greatly offended her, in that I made my choice without her knowledge – otherwise, I take God to witness I never had the heart to think any evil against Her Majesty.' Having thus absolved herself from any suspicion of treasonous plotting, she went on to the next point. 'And that she would be good to my children, and not to impute my fault unto them, whom I give wholly unto Her Majesty – for in my life they have had few friends, and fewer shall they have when I am dead, except Her Majesty be gracious unto them.' Sir Owen promised that he would do as she asked. Katherine was then able to give herself up to the dearest memory of all. 'And I desire Her Highness,' she went on, 'to be good unto my lord – for I know this my death will be heavy news to him – that Her Grace will be so good as to send liberty to glad his sorrowful heart withal.'

She said no more for a little while. Then, turning again to Hopton,

she began, 'I shall further desire you to deliver from me certain com-
mendations and tokens unto my lord.' To Mrs Coffin she said,
'Give me the box wherein my wedding ring is.' She managed to
open this, and drew out the ring with the pointed diamond. 'Here,
Sir Owen,' she went on, 'deliver this unto my lord. This is the ring
that I received of him when I gave myself unto him, and gave him
my faith.' Her voice had become very weak, and Sir Owen was not
sure that he had heard her correctly. 'What say you, madam?' he
asked. 'Was this your wedding ring?' The reply came distinctly.
'No, Sir Owen. This was the ring of my assurance to my lord' —
and she took out another. 'Deliver this also unto my lord, and pray
him, even as I have been unto him — as I take God to witness I have
been — a true and faithful wife, that he would be a loving and a
natural father unto my children, unto whom I give the same blessing
that God gave unto Isaac, Abraham and Jacob.' She then gave
Hopton the five-linked ring, with Hertford's posy; its associations
could not touch her now. Finally she gave him the third ring, that
engraved with the death's head and the motto, 'While I live, yours.'
'This shall be,' she said, 'the last token unto my lord that ever I shall
send him.' After a short silence, she added — and we may be sure
that the phrase, so strangely terrible now, was sorrowfully and
calmly accepted then — 'It is the picture of myself.'

As the last ring passed from Katherine's hand into Hopton's, she
glanced down at her fingers. The nails had turned purple. 'Lo! here
He is come,' she murmured, and they saw her smile. 'Welcome,
death!' She crossed her arms. A moment later she looked up and
stretched out her hands; then she beat them on her breast. 'O Lord!'
they heard her say, 'for Thy manifold mercies, blot out of Thy book
all mine offences.'

During the pause that followed, Sir Owen must have thought she
had fallen into a coma, for he said to the doctor, 'Were it not best to
send to the church that the [passing] bell may be rung?' Katherine's
answer came first. 'Good Sir Owen, let it be so.'

An hour passed. In the bedchamber there was silence, while from
across the park they heard the bell tolling a peal for each of the
twenty-eight years of Lady Katherine's life. Suddenly, she knew that

the moment of release had come. She said, 'O Lord! into Thy hands I commend my soul! Lord Jesus! Receive my spirit!'

Her eyes were fixed. She raised one hand and pressed down the lids. The hand fell to her side. Still she breathed. Nine o'clock struck. With the last stroke, she died.

Sir Owen Hopton took the responsibility of having Katherine embalmed, so that she might lie in state, as became the grand-daughter of a queen, and for three weeks she remained in the church at Yoxford, while the arrangements for her funeral were discussed by the Queen and the Privy Council. When Sir Owen received their instructions it became clear that his prisoner was to be magnificently honoured. The resultant account reads rather oddly, in view of the fact that neither Hertford nor his elder son was allowed to share in its splendours. Lady Katherine's last attendants were her servants, the Hoptons, their household and a few of their tenants, whose expenses were listed as follows:

Funeral charges	...	...	...	£56
Cering & Mourning		...	...	£140
Alms for the Poor	...	...	...	£5
Arms & Banners	...	...	...	£70
Singingmen & Watchers	...	...	£66
Hearse	...	...	...	...	£685

Total £1022[6]

So Queen Elizabeth paid her debt to the cousin her Protestant subjects continued to mourn. She told de Silva that she was sorry for Lady Katherine's death, but he reported, 'She does not feel it. She was afraid of her,' and he added complacently that the two Hertford boys were still considered illegitimate, and likely to remain so. Then de Silva received the surprise for which even his limited experience of Her Majesty should have prepared him. The six-year-old Viscount Beauchamp was considered as heir-presumptive by the Council, and there was talk of his being granted his grand-father's dukedom of Somerset. Meanwhile he and his brother were put in charge of their Somerset grandmother, and 'brought up in state', much to the envoy's disgust. Six years later the political pattern changed, and they were declared illegitimate, although the Protestant party still supported their claim.[7]

For twenty-eight years their father kept the promise engraved on the death's head ring. In 1596 he married Frances Howard, daughter of William Lord Howard of Effingham, and a great-niece of Surrey's. He had spent his widowerhood in the tireless and eventually successful pursuit of the Queen's favour, and in unobtrusive efforts to establish his sons' legitimacy. In 1600 his second wife died, and he married another Frances Howard, Surrey's granddaughter.

Three years later, as Queen Elizabeth lay dying, she was implored to choose her successor, and Beauchamp's name was mentioned. Immediately the old, fierce resentment surged up again. 'I will have no rascal's son to succeed me,' she said. They were the last coherent words she uttered.

In the following year Hertford won the battle for his sons' rights. Beauchamp was proclaimed his lawful heir by Parliamentary statute. In 1606 the clergyman who had married Hertford and Lady Katherine emerged from the obscurity of an unnamed parish, gave his account of the ceremony, and vouched for its legality. Forty-five years had robbed that strange episode of all interest, save for Hertford and his descendants; the evidence that resulted in the marriage being 'found good' caused no comment in Court circles.[8] And no Grey cousins of Katherine's generation were left to trouble King James, for Lady Mary had died, widowed, childless and penniless, nearly thirty years before.

Five years later, in 1611, Hertford's grandson, Lord William Seymour, re-enacted his story. He secretly married and attempted to elope with Lady Arabella Stuart; she was the great-granddaughter of Margaret Tudor Queen of Scotland, and the granddaughter of that Lady Margaret Lennox whom Henry VIII had imprisoned for marrying Surrey's uncle, Lord William Howard, and whom Queen Elizabeth had imprisoned for her claims to the succession. Arabella Stuart was sent to the Tower – where she died insane four years afterwards – and William Seymour escaped into France. The seventy-two-year-old Hertford was at his house in Cannon Row, in the very room where he had married Katherine half a century before, when news was brought to him of his grandson's crime against the state. Hertford himself survived another ten years, dying in 1621.

In the reign of Charles I, William Seymour, now third Earl of Hertford, was restored to favour, and in his turn set about re-establishing the family reputation. His monument to his grandparents sealed the triumph of his house. The Hertfords became respectable. Romantic folly, arrogant indiscretion, obstinacy, disobedience, disgrace, captivity — the memory of all these was buried with the bones of Katherine Grey, and obliterated by her grandson's long-winded euphemisms and solemn glorification of her royal lineage. That hers was a love-story, did not concern him; and that her Tudor blood had been her curse, was better forgotten. It was enough that under a towering weight of gilded marble and painted alabaster she and her husband were together again at last.

NOTES TO CHAPTER NINE

[1] Fuller, vol. II, p. 127.
[2] H.M.C.: Magdalen MSS, p. 204.
[3] Cal. English Affairs, vol. I, Nos. 385, 387, 390.
[4] Cal. Domestic State Papers, January 11th, 1568, pp. 304-6.
[5] Ellis, pp. 272-87.
[6] Cal. D.S.P., January 27th, 1568, pp. 304-6.
[7] Cal. English Affairs, vol. II, No. 403.
[8] Collins, *Peerage of England*, vol. I, p. 166.

EPILOGUE

IN a mystery play, Surrey and Katherine might stand respectively for the knave and the fool, minor attendants on the Muse of History, who interrupt her discourses with odd irrelevancies and unexpected gestures. Yet from the contemplation of such apparently trivial and worthless creatures, some sympathy with and understanding of the past may be obtained. Their function is to hold up the panorama of great deeds, dramatic incident and thrilling tragedy, giving the reader time to reflect, to observe, to reassess, to leave the auditorium for the wings, and to eavesdrop and linger in the *coulisses* of the sixteenth century. As characters in their own right, Surrey and Katherine are neither heroic, nor admirable, nor agreeable: perhaps not even particularly interesting. As guides, they have a certain value, because the study of their lives throws a peculiar light on the huge, dominating, striding figures of their time. To see Henry VIII as Surrey saw him, to feel Queen Elizabeth's power as Katherine felt it, is to break off a fragment of the shell that encloses the microcosm in which they dwelt. So perceived, the world of the Tudors emerges, momentarily, out of chaos; its values become dimly comprehensible, its standards are vaguely realized, before it disappears, and the vision sinks and fades. 'The earth hath bubbles as the water has, And these are of them. Whither are they vanished?'

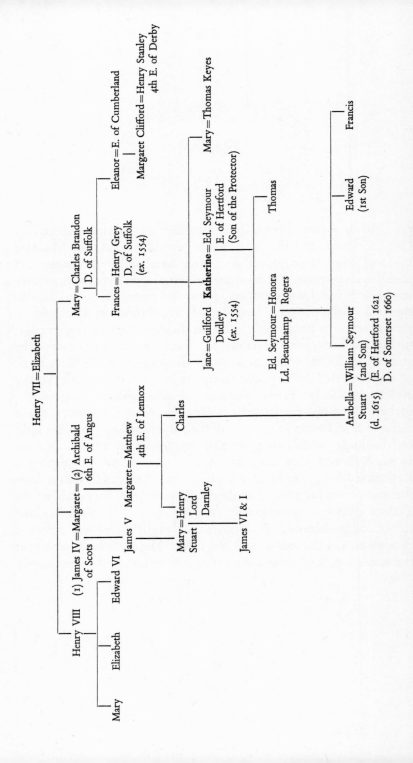

Henry VII = Elizabeth

Henry VIII

Mary   Elizabeth   Edward VI

(1) James IV = Margaret = (2) Archibald
     of Scots   6th E. of Angus

James V   Margaret = Matthew
                      4th E. of Lennox

Mary = Henry   Charles
Stuart   Lord
        Darnley

James VI & I

Mary = Charles Brandon
         D. of Suffolk

Frances = Henry Grey
          D. of Suffolk
          (ex. 1554)

Eleanor = E. of Cumberland

Margaret Clifford = Henry Stanley
                    4th E. of Derby

Jane = Guilford   **Katherine** = Ed. Seymour   Mary = Thomas Keyes
     Dudley   E. of Hertford
      (ex. 1554)   (Son of the Protector)

Ed. Seymour = Honora   Thomas
Ld. Beauchamp | Rogers

Arabella = William Seymour   Edward   Francis
Stuart   (2nd Son)   (1st Son)
(d. 1615)   (E. of Hertford 1621
          D. of Somerset 1660)

BIBLIOGRAPHY

Archaeologia, vols. XXIII and XXV

ASCHAM, ROGER: *Works*

AYLMER, JOHN: *Harbour for the Faithful Subject*

BAPST, EDMOND: *Deux Gentilhommes-poètes de la Cour d'Henri VIII*

BELLAY, MARTIN DU: *Mémoires* (ed. Michaud and Poujoulat)

BINDOFF, S. T.: *Tudor England*

BLACK, J. B.: *The Reign of Elizabeth*

BLOMEFIELD, R.: *History of Norfolk*

BRENAN, G. and STATHAM, E. P.: *The House of Howard* (2 vols.)

BREWER, J. S.: *Letters and Papers of Henry VIII* (1517-47)

BURNET, GILBERT: *History of the Reformation*

Calendar of Domestic State Papers

Calendar of Foreign State Papers

Calendar of Letters between England and Spain

Calendar of Letters Relating to English Affairs

Calendar of Spanish State Papers

Calendar of Venetian State Papers

CAMDEN, WILLIAM: *Queen Elizabeth*
                    Remains

CASADY, E.: *Henry Howard, Earl of Surrey*

CASTIGLIONE, B.: *The Courtier*

CAVENDISH, WILLIAM: *Life of Cardinal Wolsey*

CHAPMAN, HESTER W.: *The Last Tudor King*

COLLINS, A.: *Peerage of England*

COURTHOPE, W. J.: *History of English Poetry* (vol. II)

DODDS, M. H. and R.: *The Pilgrimage of Grace*

ELLIS, SIR HENRY (ed.): *Original Letters*

ELTON, G.: *England under the Tudors*

ELYOT, T.: *The Book of the Governor*

EVERETT-GREEN, M. A.: *Letters of Royal and Illustrious Ladies* (vol. II)

FISHER, H. A. L.: *History of England* (1475-1547)

FLORIO, M. A.: *Life of Lady Jane Grey*

FORTESCUE, J. W.: *History of the British Army* (vol. I)

FOX, JOHN: *Acts and Monuments*

FRIEDMANN, P.: *Anne Boleyn*

FROUDE, J. A.: *History of England*

FULLER, T.: *Worthies of England*

FURNIVALL, F. J.: *Early English Poems and Treatises on Manners*

GIUSTINIANO, S.: *Four Years at the Court of Henry VIII*

GODWIN, F.: *Annals of England*

BIBLIOGRAPHY

GRAFTON, R.: *Chronicle*
Greyfriars' *Chronicle*
GUARAS, A. DE: *Accession of Queen Mary*
HALES, JOHN: *Declaration of the Succession*
HALL, E.: *Chronicle*
Harleian MSS, 6286
HAYNES, S. (ed.) *Burleigh MSS*
HERBERT OF CHERBURY, LORD: *Henry VIII*
HEYLYN, PETER: *History of the Reformation*
Historical MSS Commission: *Ashburnham MSS*
          Hardwick MSS
          Magdalen MSS
          Middleton MSS
          Northumberland MSS

HOBY, SIR THOMAS: *Diary*
HOLINSHED, R.: *Chronicle*
HOWARD, GEORGE: *Life of Lady Jane Grey*
HOWARD, HENRY: *Memorials of the Howards*
HOWELL, T. B.: *Collection of State Trials* (vol. I)
HUGHES, P.: *The Reformation in England* (vol. I)
HUME, M. (ed.): *Chronicle of Henry VIII*
JENKINS, ELIZABETH: *Elizabeth the Great*
KAULEK, J.: *Correspondance de MM. de Castillon et de Marillac*
LEVER, J. W.: *The Elizabethan Love Sonnet*
LEWIS, C. S.: *English Literature in the Sixteenth Century*
     The Allegory of Love
MACHYN, L.: *Diary*
MACKIE, J.: *The Earlier Tudors*
MALORY, SIR THOMAS: *The Morte d'Arthur*
MAYNARD SMITH, H.: *The Reformation and Henry VIII*
MERRIMAN, J. W.: *Life and Letters of Thomas Cromwell*
MORRIS, CHRISTOPHER: *The Tudors*
NASH, JOSEPH: *Mansions of England in the Olden Time*
NAUNTON, SIR ROBERT: *Fragmenta Regalia*
NICHOLS, JOHN: *Progresses of Queen Elizabeth*
NICHOLS, J. G.: *Literary Remains of Edward VI* (2 vols.)
     The Duke of Richmond
     Narratives of the Reformation
NICHOLS, J. G. (ed.): *Queen Jane and Queen Mary*
NICOLAS, SIR HARRIS: *Life and Times of Lady Jane Grey*
NORTHUMBERLAND, EARL OF: *Household Book*
NOTT, F.: *Works of Surrey* (2 vols.)

NUGENT, E. M.: *Thought and Culture of the English Renaissance*
PADELFORD, F. M.: *Works of Surrey*
Parker Society: *Original Letters*
     Zurich Letters
POLLARD, A. F.: *Henry VIII*
    History of England
    Thomas Cranmer and the English Reformation
POLLARD, A. F. (ed.): *Tudor Tracts*
POLLINI, G.: *Historia Ecclesiastica*
PRESCOTT, H. F. M.: *Mary Tudor*
PUTTENHAM, G.: *Art of English Poesy*
READ, CONYERS: *Mr Secretary Cecil and Queen Elizabeth*
RICHARDSON, E. M.: *The Lion and the Rose*
ST MAUR, H.: *Annals of the Seymours*
SALZMANN, L. F.: *England in Tudor Times*
SELLS, LYTTON: *The Italian Influence in English Poetry*
SELVE, O. DE: *Correspondance Politique*
SPEED, JOHN: *History of Great Britain*
State Papers of Henry VIII
STOW, JOHN: *Annals of England*
    Survey of London
STRICKLAND, AGNES: *Lives of the Tudor and Stuart Princesses*
      Lives of the Queens of England (vol. II)
STRYPE, JOHN: *Annals of the Reformation*
    Ecclesiastical Memorials
    Life of Archbishop Cranmer
    Life of Archbishop Parker
    Life of Bishop Aylmer
    Life of Sir Thomas Smith
THOYRAS, RAPIN DE: *History of England* (vol. VII)
THROSBY, JOHN: *Select Views in Leicestershire* (vol. I)
TIPPING, AVRAY: *English Homes* (vol. I)
TROYES, CHRETIEN DE: *Works*
TURNER, SHARON: *History of England*
TYTLER, P. F.: *Reigns of Edward VI and Mary I*
WATSON, F.: *Vives and the Renaissance Education of Women*
WEEVER, J.: *Ancient Funeral Monuments*
WILLIAMSON, J. A.: *The Tudor Age*
Wiltshire Archaeological Magazine (vol. XV)
WRIGHT, THOMAS: *Queen Elizabeth and Her Times*
WRIOTHESLEY, C.: *Journal*
WYATT, SIR THOMAS: *Works*

INDEX

INDEX

INDEX

Francis I (France), 30, 36, 38, 39, 40, 61, 63, 86, 91, 94, 112, 113, 135
Francis, Dauphin of France (later Francis II), 40, 181

GARDINER, Bishop, 31, 65, 69, 125, 168
Granvela, Cardinal, 82
Grey, Lord, 93, 95, 105, 109
Grey, Lord Arthur, 164, 168
Grey, Henry, Marquis of Dorset, 104, 152, 154, 156, 159-60, then Duke of Suffolk, 161, 165, 166, 167, 168, 170, 210
Grey, Lady Jane, 145, 153, 154, 155, 156, 157, 158, 159, 160, 163, 166, 167, 168, 169, 170, 171, 175, 176, 188, 195, 207, 209, 210
Grey, Lord John, 182, 184, 220, 221, 222, 223, 224, 225
Grey, Lady Katherine
  the monument to her and her husband, and an outline of the story it commemorates, 151-3
  her descent and birth, 153-4
  effect on her of Lady Jane Grey's character and martyrdom, 154-5
  education, 155, 157-9
  how Henry VII's will affected the Grey sisters, 156
  a round of visits, 160
  outshone by her sister, Lady Jane, 163
  married to Lord Herbert, 164, 165
  becomes heir to the throne on proclamation of Lady Jane Grey, 166
  turned out of Pembroke's house, 167
  ambitions, 167-8
  divorced from Lord Herbert, 169
  involved in the struggle for the succession, 169-72
  made Lady of the Privy Chamber, 169-70
  Lady Jane Grey's farewell message to her, 170-1
  becomes member of the Queen's household, 173
  placed in charge of the Duchess of Somerset and falls in love with Edward Seymour, second Earl of Hertford, 174-5
  her succession favoured by Queen Mary, 176
  becomes Lady of the Bed-chamber at Elizabeth's court, 176
  her sense of defeat, 177
  Pembroke suggests her remarrying Lord Herbert, 178
  favoured as claimant to the succession by Spain, 177-80
  her Protestantism, 180
  plans for marriage with Hertford, 180-1, 183-4

Spanish plot to kidnap her, 181-2
  her outburst in the presence of the Queen, 182-3
  Cecil favours her marriage with Hertford, 186-7
  scheme to marry her to the Scottish heir-apparent, 187
  restored to position as Lady of the Privy Chamber, 187
  scheme for secret marriage with Hertford, 188-9
  betrothal and wedding with Hertford, 189-94
  censured for her act, 195
  suggested explanations, 196
  receives deed of gift from Hertford, 197
  her suspected pregnancy and decision to make the marriage public, 197
  difficulties of meeting Hertford, 198
  her pregnancy, 197, 198, 199
  no letters from Hertford, who is in France, 199
  accompanies the Queen on a progress in Suffolk, 199-200
  seeks help from Robert Dudley and Mrs Saintlow, 200
  imprisoned in the Tower, 201
  her conduct examined, 201-6
  Cecil directs the Privy Council to find the marriage invalid, 202
  official examination by the Privy Council, 207-8
  her child born in the Tower and christened, 208-10
  her love for Hertford discussed, 211-12
  deliberations of the Privy Council, 212-14
  her marriage declared illegal, 214
  meetings between her and Hertford in the Tower allowed by Sir Edward Warner, 215-16
  again pregnant, 216
  claimant to the succession again, 216-17
  gives birth to another son, 217
  Hales and Newdigate attempt to prove the legality of her marriage, 219-22
  she is placed in charge of Lord John Grey, 220-3
  her last portrait, 223
  her marriage asserted to be legal by the Hertford faction, 224-5
  she is removed to the care of Sir William Petre, 225
  her hopes for better treatment destroyed by Lady Mary Grey's secret marriage, 226-7
  moved to the custody of Sir John Wentworth, 227

INDEX

INDEX

Northampton, Earl of, *see* Howard, Henry

Northumberland, Duke of, *see* Dudley, John

ORLEANS, Duke of, *see* Henry

Oxford, Earl of, 36, 160

PAGET, Sir William, 93, 99, 100, 102, 103, 106, 107-8, 109, 116, 118, 120, 121, 125, 138, 139, 144, 146, 162

Papalist party, 31

Parker, Archbishop of Canterbury, 214

Parr, Katherine (Queen), 83

Pembroke, Earl of, 162, 165, 166, 168-9, 178, 199

Petrarch, 41

Petre, Sir William, 207, 225, 227

Philip II (Spain), 173, 178, 179, 182, 186, 187, 225

Pilgrimage of Grace, 50-5, 119

Plantagenet, Lady Anne (first wife of third Duke of Norfolk), 15

Pole, Cardinal, 53, 75, 119, 128

Pole, Arthur, 213

Pollard, Sir George, 102

Poynings, Sir Edward, 91, 92, 93, 95, 97

Protestant party, 57, 69, 83

QUADRA, de, Bishop, 182, 187

REEVE, Abbot John, 37

Renard, Simon, 168

Richmond, Duchess of, *see* Howard, Lady Mary

Richmond, Duke of, 30, 31, 32-4, 35, 36, 38, 39, 40, 42, 46, 84, 140, 144

Robsart, Amy, 186

Rochford, Lady, 71, 72

Rochford, Lord, 45

Roos, Lord, 46

Roos, Lady Anne, 46

Russell, Lord, 94

SAINTLOW, Mrs (Bess Hardwick), 200, 202, 207, 208

Seymour, Edward, first Earl of Hertford, 31, 46, 55, 57, 58, 69, 74, 79, 80-1, 87, 89, 92, 93, 94, 100, 103, 104, 105, 106, 107, 108, 109, 111, 114, 116, 118, 121, 125, 137, 143, 144, then Duke of Somerset, 145, 151, 152, 156, 160, 162, 188-9, 209, 210

Seymour, Edward, second Earl of Hertford
the monument to him and his wife, and an outline of the story it commemorates, 151-3

his marriage with Lady Jane Grey planned, 160

he is set aside in favour of Lord Guilford Dudley, 164

falls in love with Lady Katherine Grey, 174-5

schemes for their marriage, 179, 180-1, 183-4

Cecil encourages his suit, 186-7

a secret marriage with Lady Katherine planned, 188-9

their betrothal and wedding, 189-94

his attitude to it not known, 196

gives Katherine a deed of gift, 197

decision to make the marriage public on account of her pregnancy, 197

he is commanded to go to France, 197, 198

difficulties of meeting Katherine, 198

prepares to return from France, 200, 206

imprisoned in the Tower on return from France, 207-8

his love for Katherine discussed, 211-12

their marriage declared illegal, 214

they are allowed to meet in the Tower, 215-16

he is sentenced to fine and imprisonment, 217

he is sent to live with his mother, the Duchess of Somerset, 220

his lawyers prepare appeal against the verdict on his marriage, 224

the Queen angry with his faction, but prepared to treat his children fairly, 225

he implores Leicester to gain him the Queen's favour, 231

Katherine's dying wish that the Queen should grant him his liberty, 234

she requests that the rings he had given her be returned to him, 235

he is not allowed to attend her funeral, 236

he remarries twenty-eight years after her death, 237

marries again after the death of his second wife, 237

wins the battle for his sons' rights, 237

hears of his grandson's crime against the state, 238

dies, 238

Seymour, Edward, Viscount Beauchamp (son of above), 152, 210, 213, 225, 231, 236, 237

Seymour, Lord Henry, 197, 200, 207, 208

Seymour, Jane (Queen), 46, 57, 58, 188

Seymour, Lady Jane (daughter of the Duke of Somerset), 174, 179, 181, 188-93, 196-7, 198, 202, 205, 219

Seymour, Sir Thomas (later Lord Seymour of Sudely, High Admiral of England; younger brother of the first Earl of Hertford), 58, 70, 74, 111, 112, 120, 128

251

INDEX